T0351336

THE QUEER UNCANNY

SERIES PREFACE

Gothic Literary Studies is dedicated to publishing groundbreaking scholarship on Gothic in literature and film.The Gothic,which has been subjected to a variety of critical and theoretical approaches, is a form which plays an important role in our understanding of literary, intellectual and cultural histories. The series seeks to promote challenging and innovative approaches to Gothic which question any aspect of the Gothic tradition or perceived critical orthodoxy. Volumes in the series explore how issues such as gender, religion, nation and sexuality have shaped our view of the Gothic tradition . Both academically rigorous and informed by the latest developments in critical theory, the series provides an important focus for scholastic developments in Gothic studies, literary studies, cultural studies and critical theory.The series will be of interest to students of all levels and to scholars and teachers of the Gothic and literary and cultural histories.

SERIES EDITORS

Andrew Smith, University of Glamorgan
Benjamin F. Fisher, University of Mississippi

EDITORIAL BOARD

Kent Ljungquist,Worcester Polytechnic Institute Massachusetts
Richard Fusco, St Joseph's University, Philadelphia
David Punter, University of Bristol
Chris Baldick, University of London
Angela Wright, University of Sheffield
Jerrold E. Hogle, University of Arizona

The Queer Uncanny
New Perspectives on the Gothic

Paulina Palmer

UNIVERSITY OF WALES PRESS
CARDIFF
2012

www.uwp.co.uk

British Library CIP Data
A catalogue record for this book is available from the British Library.

ISBN   978-0-7083-2458-5 (hardback)
          978-0-7083-2459-2 (paperback)
e-ISBN 978-0-7083-2460-8

Typeset in Wales by Eira Fenn Gaunt, Cardiff
Printed by CPI Antony Rowe, Chippenham, Wiltshire

Contents

PREFACE

I first became interested in writing *The Queer Uncanny* from noticing the number of works of contemporary fiction that use motifs and imagery relating to the uncanny and Gothic to explore and represent different aspects of lesbian, male gay and transgender sexuality and experience.

Since I published *Lesbian Gothic: Trangressive Fictions* in 1999 the interest in the interrelation between 'Gothic' and 'queer' in both popular culture and academia has increased considerably, and numerous new critical and theoretical texts relating to the topic have appeared in print. In locating the fictional and theoretical texts that I have needed to write the book, I have been fortunate to have access to Gay's The Word bookshop in London, one of the few remaining queer bookshops in the UK and an invaluable source of material, both new and old. I have also utilized the resources of the Cambridge University Library, and very much appreciate the help provided by the staff.

My work as a sessional lecturer for the MA in Gender and Sexuality at Birkbeck College, University of London, and conversations that I have held with students and members of staff have been intellectually stimulating and influenced my writing, as have the workshops on Gothic and queer writing that I have taught at City Lit College. In addition, I am indebted to Professor Andrew Smith for encouraging my work on the Gothic, to Dr Emma Parker for recommending fiction relevant to the book and to Dr Ana Cecília Acioli Lima for sharing with me her readings of Jeanette Winterson's novels. I am grateful to Terry Ryman for reading sections of my work in progress, sharing his ideas with me and and talking over my readings of texts. I am also greatly indebted to Dr Les Brookes, the author of *Gay Male Fiction Since Stonewall*, for sparing time from his own writing to read and comment on my typescript and discuss my ideas.

For the queer community in Cambridge

1

Introduction: Queering the Uncanny

The uncanny *is* queer. And the queer is uncanny.[1]

Fiction, queer perspectives and the uncanny

Horace Cross, the sixteen-year-old African American protagonist of Randall Kenan's *A Visitation of Spirits* (1989), one of the novels discussed in this study, lives in the rural Christian Fundamentalist community of Tims Creek, North Carolina. Obsessed with guilt on account of his homosexuality and his inability to achieve the heterosexual masculinity that his family expects of him, he takes the risk of confiding the secret of his sexuality to his cousin Jimmy Greene, a minister at the local Baptist church. Jimmy advises him to pray in an effort to resist temptation, confirming Horace's role as sinner and outcast. When his attempts at prayer predictably fail, Horace rejects the rational approach to life that he learnt at school and from the books on science he borrowed from the library and turns, in desperation, to magic. However, instead of the transformation into a bird that he hoped to achieve when he recited the magic spell, he finds himself the victim of a monstrous demon that, erupting from his psyche, takes him on a tour of the neighbourhood. Scenes he is forced to witness include a sermon in the church denouncing the evils of homosexuality and a visit to a community theatre in the nearby town where he has had affairs with white male actors. Here he sees a black figure dressed as a clown in the act of putting on white makeup, and is horrified to recognize it as himself. He thinks, 'Of all the things he had seen this night, all the memories he had confronted, all the ghouls and ghosts and specters, this shook him the most'.[2] The novel concludes with him taking his grandfather's rifle and shooting himself in the head while his spectral double looks mockingly on.

Kenan's novel – as well as being of interest for its vivid representation of the conflict that Horace experiences, trapped as he is between the homophobia of the local community and his homosexuality, and its imaginative interweaving of fantasy and realism – is notable for its introduction of motifs and ideas relating to the uncanny, many of them recognizable from Sigmund Freud's essay on the topic and the work of theorists writing subsequently. There is, for instance, the idea that uncanny sensations, and the disturbing transformation of the familiar into the unfamiliar that they generate, reflect the projection of unconscious fears and desires originating in 'something repressed which *recurs*'.[3] This is illustrated by the way Horace's feelings of guilt about his homosexuality and his fear that he has betrayed his racial identity by engaging in affairs with whites return to haunt him, transforming his surroundings into the site of the supernatural. The novel also introduces other motifs with uncanny resonance. These include the secret of Horace's transgressive sexuality which, although the residents of Tims Creek would prefer it to remain hidden, nonetheless comes to light when he discloses it to Jimmy; his encounter with his double at the theatre; and his feelings of uncertainty about his identity – is he homosexual or heterosexual, black or white, a human being, a bird or a monster? In addition, central to the theme of the conflict between contrary value schemes that Kenan treats, there is the fatal shift that Horace undergoes from a rational approach to life to a reliance on superstition and 'old, discarded beliefs'[4] crediting magical transformation and demonic possession. And framing the narrative is the concept of taboo, another topic that Freud foregrounds. It is exemplified here by the Christian Fundamentalist prohibition of homosexuality. Jimmy endorses this by instructing Horace to pray to resist temptation, while the preacher vehemently hammers it home in the sermon he delivers.

Although Kenan's treatment of these themes is uniquely inventive, *A Visitation of Spirits* is not unusual in its use of concepts and motifs relating to the uncanny to represent facets of queer sexuality and experience and society's response to them. A number of other novels by contemporary writers, texts focusing on lesbian and transgender as well as male gay interests, employ them in a similar manner. Hélène Cixous describes the uncanny as appearing 'only on the fringe of something else',[5] while Rosemary Jackson, developing that thought, observes that it 'exists only in relation to the familiar and the normal. It is tangential, to one side.'[6] This tallies with the experience of the queer individual living in a minority subculture and existing, as Sara Ahmed remarks in her discussion of queer phenomenology, 'slant-wise'[7] and in oblique relation to heteronormative society. With this in mind, I aim in this study to investigate the roles that the uncanny plays in a selection of queer fictional texts and the different ways writers represent it. The project raises interesting questions. What roles does the uncanny play in fiction of this kind? Is reference to it introduced merely to arouse a frisson of excitement or unease in the reader or is it pertinent to the themes the writer treats? Which aspects of the uncanny do writers prioritize and which features of queer existence do they employ them to explore? What narrative strategies and structures do they utilize in depicting them? How, if at all, does the lesbian treatment of the uncanny differ from the male gay?

The works of fiction I have selected for discussion, while all published during the period 1980–2007, vary considerably in style and form. Some, such as Ali Smith's *Hotel World* (2001) and Christopher Bram's *Father of Frankenstein* (1995), are overtly Gothic, recasting from a queer perspective narratives and scenarios inscribing spectral visitation, the double and encounters with the monstrous. Others, such as Paul Magrs's *Could It Be Magic?* (1997) and Jeanette Winterson's *The Power Book* (2001), though lacking the dark, scary atmosphere that we associate with Gothic, interrelate fantasy and realism and introduce motifs and imagery with Gothic and uncanny connotations. There is also a third category of fiction on which I focus, exemplified by Emma Donoghue's *Stir-Fry* (1994), Alan Hollinghurst's *The Swimming-Pool Library* (1988) and Sarah Schulman's *People in Trouble* (1990), that is predominantly realist in style. However, it too employs Gothic imagery and structures. The texts in the latter two categories illustrate the tendency of motifs and imagery relating to the uncanny and Gothic to infiltrate different forms of fiction, demonstrating their versatility and the attraction they continue to hold for writers and readers.

Queer theory, as Annamarie Jagose explains, 'describes those gestures or analytical models which dramatise incoherences in the allegedly stable relations between chromosomal sex, gender and sexual desire'.[8] It encompasses a range of different sexualities and, since it is non-specific, has the potential to be utilized in different contexts. The novels that I discuss reflect this multifaceted focus. Some, such as David Leavitt's *While England Sleeps* (1998) and Ellen Galford's *The Dyke and the Dybbuk* (1993), operate primarily in terms of the identity categories 'gay' and 'lesbian'. Others, however, in keeping with the Foucauldian view of such categories as regulatory and oppressive, and influenced by the poststructuralist emphasis on the mobility of desire, seek to destabilize the notion of a stable sexual identification or gender. Accepting the view of identity as contingent and the product of fantasy, they interrogate and deconstruct the binary division of homosexual/heterosexual. Novels adopting this approach include James Purdy's *Mourners Below* (1981), Donna Tartt's *The Secret History* (1992) and Winterson's *The Power Book*. Fiction, however, unlike theory, frequently avoids defining its ideological perspective explicitly. It tends towards the dialogic, displaying tensions and ambiguities. As a result there is, as we shall see, a significant degree of interaction and overlap between these approaches, with texts combining and interrelating them. The usage of the term 'queer' is itself ambiguous. While employed in academia in relation to queer theory to challenge the concept of a stable sexual identification and problematize the binary division homosexual/heterosexual, it is alternatively used as a form of shorthand to encompass the categories of lesbian, gay and, on occasion, transgender. I use it in both ways, with the context indicating its meaning.

In addition to novels focusing on different sexualities, I discuss others, including Patrick McGrath's *Dr Haggard's Disease* (1993) and Stella Duffy's *Beneath the Blonde* (1997), that deal with transgender and transsexuality. These are topics that feature prominently on the queer agenda since the transgender and transsexual body, as well as being important in its own right, illustrates in a particularly readable form the constructedness of sex and gender in general.[9] And, taking account of Eve Kosofsky Sedgwick's observation that in queer discourse 'Race, ethnicity, postcolonial nationality crisscross with other identity-constituting, identity-fracturing discourses',[10] I also consider Kenan's *A Visitation of Spirits* (1989), Shani Mootoo's *Cereus Blooms at Night* (1996) and H. Nigel Thomas's *Spirits in the Dark* (1993) that represent African American and Caribbean constructs of queer sexuality and gender. In investigating the intersection between racial and sexual identifications and exploring different forms of hybridity, these works challenge and help rectify the Eurocentric bias that dominates queer writing.

The novels cited above form the focus of this study. They employ reference to the uncanny to explore, among other topics, what Ahmed describes in *Queer Phenomenology* as the 'dynamic negotiation between what is familiar and unfamiliar' (p. 7) that typifies queer existence in heteronormative society, and the efforts the queer individual makes to resist 'being kept in line, often by force' (p. 83) with its conventions and sexual mores. Some readers may assume that in the present era of civil partnerships and the improvements in the situation of queer people in the West that they reflect, negotiations of this kind are no longer necessary and their fictional representation is outdated. This, however, is not the case. As Jeffrey Weeks writes in his study of present-day lesbian and gay life in Western society aptly entitled *The World We Have Won*, 'Despite really significant transformations, in many quarters homophobia remains rampant, from vicious queer bashing to school bullying, from heterosexist jokes to the minstrelization of openly gay television personalities. A continuing undercurrent of unease remains pervasive.'[11] The increasing visibility of lesbians and gay men has, he observes, employing a phrase that itself has uncanny implications of ambiguity, 'a double edge' (p. 48). While bringing the queer subject a sense of freedom in certain areas of life, it simultaneously generates outbreaks of prejudice and hostility. These tensions and contradictions are registered in some of the novels by British and American writers discussed below. The texts by the Caribbean Thomas and the Trinidadian-Canadian writer Mootoo to which I refer also illustrate particularly vividly the struggles that queer sexuality and existence continue to involve for many people.

However, before turning to the discussion of fiction, I need to investigate a topic that is pertinent to it and furnishes a cultural and intellectual context for its analysis. This is the infiltration of motifs and images relating to the uncanny into queer theoretical discourse and the varied uses that theorists and critics make of them. As well as creating a frame for the discussion of the novels reviewed below, it sheds light on the interest that present-day writers display in the uncanny, illuminating their treatment of it as a vehicle for queer representation.

Theoretical approaches

The idea that the uncanny has sociopolitical significance and that reference to it can contribute to the perspectives and literature of emergent political movements occurs frequently in twentieth- and twenty-first-century writing. Motifs with uncanny connotations including the spectre and the vampire, the latter employed to represent the processes of modern capitalism, appear in the writing of Karl Marx,[12] while Saul Newman describes the concepts of the return of the repressed and the interplay between the familiar and unfamiliar associated with the uncanny as 'crucial for politics understood as the attempt to construct something new, coupled with something old'.[13] He observes that 'Radical politics is always haunted by the ghosts of the past – revolutionary traditions which are dead, yet remain unburied, which have been repressed, yet insist on returning in uncannily familiar forms' (p. 117). Andrew Bennett and Nicholas Royle, likewise developing the idea of the return of repressed emotions and desires, argue that the abilities of art and the written word to 'disturb, defamiliarize or shake our beliefs and assumptions are deeply bound up with the uncanny'.[14]

Pertinent to the role that the uncanny plays in queer theory and fiction is Rosemary Jackson's description of it as expressing 'drives which have to be *repressed* for the sake of cultural continuity'.[15] She explores the way in which the ghost story, the literary form that Freud cites as illustrating its operations, 'helps to make visible that which is culturally invisible' (p. 69), including topics that society regards as unspeakable and taboo. Topics of this kind include, of course, lesbian and male gay sexuality, and it comes as no surprise to find metaphors and motifs with uncanny connotations, spectral in particular, infiltrating queer theoretical discourse. Diana Fuss's essay collection *Inside/Out*, a publication that in the 1990s helped to promote an interest in homo-spectrality, illustrates some of their uses. Fuss comments on society's attempt to suppress homosexuality by relegating the lesbian and male gay subject to the role of 'phantom other'[16] and describes homosexual and heterosexual economies coexisting uneasily in a form of mutual haunting. She depicts the essays in the collection, though treating different facets of queer experience, as linked by a 'preoccupation with the figure of the homosexual as specter and phantom, as spirit and revenant, as abject and undead' (p. 3).

The spectre and phantom, key signifiers of the uncanny, carry connotations of 'excess' since their appearance exceeds the material, and this is another concept that connects the uncanny with 'queer'. The role of the uncanny as a signifier of excess is reflected in its ability, as Rosemary Jackson describes, to uncover the unfamiliar beneath the familiar and, by challenging the conventional view of reality as unitary, to prompt the subject to question mainstream, 'common-sense' versions of it. As James R. Kincaid remarks, the uncanny involves perceptions and phenomena that 'lie outside the realm of the explicable, outside of language',[17] such as fantasy and dreams which transcend rational explanation. Queer theorists too depict homosexuality, on account of its invisibility and transgressive dimension, as evoking (from a phallocentric viewpoint) connotations of excess. Lee Edelman argues that from a heteronormative viewpoint, the male homosexual – like the female – signifies both 'excess' and 'lack',[18] while Fuss represents homosexuality as occupying the role of 'supplement'[19] to heterosexuality, necessary to its self-definition though regarded by many as a threat. Lisabeth During and Terri Fealy portray gay culture itself as signifying 'a culture of excess'.[20] They investigate how 'the representations of the "respectable" world are turned upside down' in it, citing in illustration the different forms of role-play and innuendo that the gay individual employs in 'moving incognito through a heterosexual world'.[21] Bonnie Zimmerman also associates lesbianism with excess. Arguing that lesbian desire 'functions as excess within the heterosexual economy',[22] she illustrates how postmodern writers, in seeking to represent it, interrogate and critique accepted norms of both sexuality and textuality through their experimental use of narrative and the excessive proliferation of storytelling and fantasy it inscribes. This is the kind of narrative that, as we shall see, Smith's *Hotel World*, Waters's *Fingersmith* and Winterson's *The Stone Gods* create in interweaving multiple storylines and recasting from a lesbian viewpoint literary genres with hetero-normative associations.

Other motifs associated with the uncanny also infiltrate queer theory. They include doubling, a compulsion to repeat and different forms of mimicry and performance, such as that exemplified by the automaton Olympia in E. T. A. Hoffmann's 'The Sandman'. Whereas Freud tends to ignore Olympia in 'The uncanny', focusing his reading of Hoffmann's story on the male protagonist, Jane Marie Todd relates her to woman's oppressed social role and performance of femininity.[23] Mimicry and performance feature in queer theory with reference to the way in which gay and lesbian roles comment parodically on heterosexual roles; they reveal their constructedness, exposing them, to cite Butler, as 'a kind of naturalized gender mime'.[24]

Ideas of 'uncertainty' and 'ambivalence' also connect the uncanny with 'queer'. Freud describes how the word '*heimlich* . . . develops in the direction of ambivalence, until it finally coincides with its opposite, *unheimlich*',[25] while Royle, representing 'the emergence of "queer" . . . as a formidable example of the contemporary significance of the uncanny', cites 'generative, creative uncertainties about sexual identity'[26] as linking the two concepts. Reference to ambivalence and ambiguity features in addition in the discussion of queer existence and social life. Harold Beaver, commenting on the closeted lifestyle that many lesbians and gay men feel forced to lead, humorously observes that 'homosexuals, like Masons, live not in an alternative culture but in a duplicate culture of constantly interrupted and over-lapping roles. They must learn to live with ambiguity. Every sign becomes duplicitous, slipping back and forth across a wavering line.'[27] The term 'queer' itself hinges on ambiguity for, while employed colloquially as a tool of homophobic abuse, it also operates somewhat precariously in the manner of a reverse discourse, as a tool of gay resistance. Les Brookes in fact argues that 'Ambiguity is central to *queer*'s self-identity',[28] citing in evidence the equivocal approach that queer theorists adopt to identity categories. He refers, by way of illustration, to Butler's remark that though willing to appear under the sign 'lesbian' at political events, she would 'like to have it permanently unclear what precisely that sign signifies'.[29] While criticizing the regulatory, oppressive effect of identity categories, she nonetheless acknowledges their political usefulness and the need for us to resignify them positively.

A sense of ambivalence and uncertainty is also prominent, as numerous publications ranging from the 1990s to the present day illustrate, in the response that the queer movement has elicited from the Anglo-American lesbian and male gay community. Members of it, myself included, while welcoming certain features of the queer agenda such as its representation of sexuality as diverse and mobile and its deconstruction of the homosexual/heterosexual binary, regard others as problematic and retrograde. As well as criticizing the lack of specificity, excessive utopianism and resultant political ineffectiveness of 'queer', they alert attention to its narrowly American connotations and limited metropolitan associations.[30] They also complain of the elitist associations that queer perspectives have acquired in shifting from a grass-roots activist movement that came into being, as Iain Morland describes, 'through the turbulent conjunction of theory and politics'[31] to an academic discourse that shows signs of losing its political vigour. Another criticism directed at queer theory is that, though its advocates claim it to be gender-neutral, it nonetheless reflects an 'overwhelming maleness'.[32] As a result, its utilization frequently erases the specificity and importance of lesbian culture and history. It also fails to acknowledge the contribution that the lesbian feminist movement has made both to the struggle for sexual liberation and the formation of queer politics itself.[33]

It is interesting to note that reference to ideas and motifs relating to the uncanny, as well as infiltrating queer theory and the debates that it has provoked, also feature in the discourse of lesbian feminism that flourished in the 1970s and 1980s. A topic pivotal to the work of Adrienne Rich is 'the Great Silence'[34] to which lesbianism has been subjected as a result of being regarded as unmentionable. Elizabeth Meese, in addition, employs uncanny imagery to explore lesbian invisibility and the instability of the sign 'lesbian'. Commenting on the sign's slipperiness and the difficulty women experience in finding a language to articulate same-sex desire on account of it being pathologized, she writes eloquently: 'Lesbian is a word written in invisible ink, readable when held up to a flame and self-consuming, a disappearing trick before my eyes where the letters appear and fade into the paper in which they are written.'[35] Her evocation of the fluid, shifting nature of the sign looks forward to Butler's recommendation that its meaning should remain open and unfixed, furnishing an example of the way lesbian feminism has on occasion anticipated queer perspectives.

And while, as illustrated above, the discourses of queer, lesbian and male gay sexuality abound with references to concepts and metaphors with uncanny significance, so too does that of transgender and transsexuality. Significant in this respect is Freud's association of the uncanny with the psychological phenomenon of 'doubling, dividing and interchanging of the self' and the sense of 'doubt as to which his self is'[36] that this can generate in the individual. Jay Prosser remarks on the sense of doubling and 'gendered contradiction and ambiguity'[37] that the transsexual can experience in feeling trapped in the wrong body and experiencing a conflict existing between his 'real' inner body and his 'false' outer one. He employs spectral imagery to evoke the phantomic dimension of the body that the transsexual regards as signifying his 'real' embodiment and strives to 'liberate' (p. 163). Royle, developing Freudian thought, associates the uncanny with 'the experience of oneself as a foreign body'.[38] The transsexual's view of the body with which he is born as alien, conflicting with his 'real' embodiment and self, vividly exemplifies this uncanny sensation of 'foreign' embodiment.

Queering the Gothic

Accompanying the infiltration of motifs and ideas relating to the uncanny into queer, lesbian and transgender theoretical discourses, illustrated above, there is another form of infiltration and cross-fertilization pertinent to this study that is currently taking place – one that operates in reverse. This is the influx of queer interests and perspectives into Gothic critical studies. This too is relevant to the novels that I discuss, many of which appropriate and recast Gothic motifs, imagery and narrative structures.

Gothic is a highly mobile and fluid literary form. As Julian Wolfreys observes, 'Traces, remnants, ruins of the Gothic are found everywhere, in fiction and non-fiction alike, in realist and fantasy literature'.[39] He concludes his discussion of the mobility of its conventions and motifs with the observation that 'in short, Gothic transgresses the borders between the living and dead, between past and present literary formations, in resurgent spectral ways' (p. 97). The ability of Gothic to transgress, in both the 'itinerant' and 'unorthodox' senses of the term, is particularly apparent in its encounter with queer. For while theorists such as Edelman, Fuss and Rich utilize motifs and metaphors with uncanny connotations to investigate homosexual and lesbian desire and society's attempts to suppress it, critics working in the field of Gothic studies, influenced by the growth of queer theory and the development of gender studies in academia, investigate the queer dimension of the Gothic. Developing Rosemary Jackson's emphasis on the unorthodox nature of Gothic fantasy and its ability to articulate the individual's and society's repressed fears and desires, they uncover and bring to light reference to 'perverse' sexualities and genders in texts previously interpreted in a predominantly heteronormative context.

It is of course possible to claim, as William Hughes and Andrew Smith do, that 'Gothic has, in a sense, always been "queer"'[40] since it has traditionally focused on deviant forms of sexuality that mainstream society defines as taboo or transgressive. However, the critical discussion of Gothic texts with specific reference to queer theory and its interests, as is taking place in critical studies today, marks a relatively new intellectual departure. Here I have space to mention only a few of the critics who have contributed to this project, ones whose ideas are especially relevant to the novels discussed below. Eve Kosofsky Sedgwick, acclaimed for her pioneering work in queer theory, was one of the first critics to comment on the connections with male homosexuality apparent in eighteenth- and nineteenth-century Gothic fiction. In 1985 she coined the term 'paranoid Gothic',[41] using it to describe novels such as Mary Shelley's *Frankenstein* and James Hogg's *The Private Memoirs and Confessions of a Justified Sinner* that portray two male characters locked in an unstable relationship in which erotic attraction interacts with persecutory violence. William Veeder's discussion of homosexuality in Robert Louis

Stevenson's *The Strange Case of Dr Jekyll and Mr Hyde*, developed by Elaine Showalter and George Haggerty, also breaks new ground.[42] Significant too is Haggerty's perceptive thesis that certain eighteenth- and early nineteenth-century Gothic texts, in challenging, redefining and expanding the rigid classifications of sexuality proposed by the sexologists, are relevant to the history of ideas. He argues that they give a glimpse of 'behaviors otherwise invisible' in earlier culture, anticipating developments in the history of sexuality.[43]

Reference to Gothic motifs is also in evidence in lesbian history, as illustrated by Terry Castle's analysis of the spectralization of the lesbian in nineteenth- and twentieth-century fiction as reflecting an attempt on the part of hetero-patriarchal culture to banish and exorcize the perceived threat of female same-sex desire.[44] Among lesbian critical readings of particular fictional texts, Lucie Armitt's analysis of Charlotte Perkins Gilman's *The Yellow Wallpaper* merits comment. In illustrating that 'walled up . . . within the patriarchal text of the wallpaper is an alternative sexual identity' that the female protagonist seeks to liberate, Armitt demonstrates that Gilman's novella, as she wittily puts it, 'is concerned not just with "breaking out" but also, more significantly, with "coming out"'.[45]

Transgender, though it has until now generated less critical interest than lesbianism and male homosexuality in Gothic studies, is also starting to receive attention. This is illustrated by Kelly Hurley's analysis (1987) of Richard Marsh's *The Beetle* and the uncanny sex changes that the eponymous figure performs.[46]

In addition to investigating representations of queer sexuality and gender in Gothic texts produced in earlier periods, critics also discuss the queer recasting of Gothic motifs and narrative structures by present-day writers. Andrew Smith examines the parodic reworking of Oscar Wilde's *The Picture of Dorian Gray* in Will Self's *Dorian*,[47] while in *Lesbian Gothic: Transgressive Fictions* I discuss the utilization of Gothic conventions by contemporary women writers as a vehicle to represent lesbian sexuality and its sociopolitical import. I develop my interest in contemporary fiction here, extending it to encompass male gay and transgender as well as lesbian texts.

The interplay that, as illustrated above, is increasingly taking place between Gothic and 'queer' is particularly relevant to those novels reviewed in the following chapters that recast narratives appropriated from canonical Gothic works. Bram's *Father of Frankenstein* and Waters's *Fingersmith*, both discussed in chapter 2, exemplify this strategy. Bram constructs his fictionalized account of the final days in the life of James Whale, the homosexual director of the two acclaimed 1930s Frankenstein films, around intertextual references to Mary Shelley's novel, while Waters in *Fingersmith* develops from a lesbian viewpoint the representations of female romantic friendships and attachments in Wilkie Collins's *The Woman in White* and Dickens's *Bleak House*. Other writers, including Galford, Purdy and Smith, queer the figures of the ghost, the double and the witch, as well as reworking certain well-known Gothic tropes and motifs. These include, as we shall see, the family secret and curse, the repressed relationship between mother and daughter, the uncanny city, the breakdown of the family unit on account of paternal incest and the contrast between benevolent and tyrannical father figures.

Fiction and its queer phantoms

The infiltration of motifs and images with uncanny resonance into queer theory, combined with the inflow of queer perspectives into Gothic critical writing illustrated above, understandably create a fertile ground for the treatment of topics and ideas relating to the uncanny in contemporary fiction. As indicated by the roles that they play in Kenan's *A Visitation of Spirits*, discussed at the start of this chapter, references to the uncanny can take a variety of forms and perform different functions. They infiltrate the characters' trajectories and perceptions, inform the design of the narrative and furnish writers with a rich source of imagery to represent and explore queer subjectivity and experience. The disconcerting sense that the queer individual sometimes has of living in two interlinked but disparate worlds, the heteronormative and the less immediately visible one of the lesbian or gay subculture, lends itself particularly well to uncanny treatment. The synopsis of the chapters below indicates other facets of queer existence and their uncanny dimension that receive discussion in the pages that lie ahead.

Chapter 2, 'Secrets and their Disclosure', focuses on a motif that plays a pivotal role in contemporary queer studies. Schelling, as Freud writes, describes the *unheimlich* as 'the name for everything that ought to have remained . . . secret and hidden but has come to light',[48] while Sedgwick illustrates the relevance of this comment to queer existence by depicting homosexuality as signifying a key secret of phallocentric culture, marking the pairings of other binaries such as knowledge/ignorance and private/public.[49] I open the chapter by discussing Donoghue's and Hensher's treatment of the secrets and revelations that coming out and outing involve, along with the psychological strains and furtive pleasures attendant on the closet and the acts of passing that it promotes. I also examine the treatment of secrets relating to death and the fears they evoke in AIDS narratives by Tóibín and Schulman. The chapter concludes with reference to two novels by Waters and Leavitt. Set in the 1930s and 1940s, they investigate the secrets and revelations informing lesbian and male homosexual history.

Chapter 3, 'Queer Spectrality', opens with reference to the queering of the ghost story in two novels by Purdy and Smith. The 'phantom text', a term associated with Jacques Derrida registering the fact that no text is an independent entity since all are intertextually haunted by others,[50] also receives attention. I analyse novels by Bram and Waters, both of which recast from a queer perspective narratives from Victorian Gothic, in order to illustrate this concept. The double, a motif associated with the ghost and the role of uncanny double of the deceased that it performs, also receives attention. Duffy and McGrath, employing the popular genres of the thriller and the Gothic mystery, utilize the motif to investigate the sensation of gendered ambiguity and self-division that the transgender and transsexual subject can experience.

Different locations and spaces, psychological as well as domestic and geographical, traditionally feature in narrative as sites of uncanny sensations and perceptions. Chapter 4, 'Place and Space', investigates the role that they play in queer fiction. Jim Grimsley's *Dream Boy*, situated in North America, and Mootoo's *Cereus Blooms at Night*, set in the Caribbean, treat the motif of the haunted house. The two writers investigate male gay and lesbian rural existence, helping to remedy the neglect that, as Halberstam observes, the topic has received in fiction.[51] Winterson and Hollinghurst focus in contrast on urban locations, recasting the Gothic topos of the uncanny city.

They portray male gay and lesbian urban subcultures as exemplifying a culture of excess, their codes and fashions parodying or inverting the conventions of heteronormative society. Rituals and ceremonies with queer significance centring on different geographical and domestic locations depicted in Thomas's *Spirits in the Dark* and Tartt's *A Secret History* also receive discussion.

The figure of the monster, familiar from Victorian Gothic fiction and present-day horror film, frequently carries homophobic associations for, as Halberstam writes, 'Within contemporary horror, the monster tends to show clearly the markings of deviant sexualities and gendering'.[52] The stigmatization of lesbians and gay men as freakish and unnatural, along with texts by contemporary writers seeking to interrogate and challenge this bigoted view, receive attention in chapter 5 entitled 'Monstrous Others'. Novels considered here include Kenan's *A Visitation of Spirits* and Winterson's dystopian fantasy *The Stone Gods*. The concept of the comic uncanny,[53] a category associated with the Bakhtinian carnivalesque, is exemplified by Galford's *The Dyke and the Dybbuk* and Magrs's *Could It Be Magic?* As well as exposing the image of the homosexual and transgender individual as monstrous and unnatural as a construct created by homophobic society, the two writers exuberantly celebrate, in a series of carnivalesque episodes, instances of queer vitality and jouissance.

In addition to the themes and motifs referred to above, there are others that I have chosen to comment on throughout the study rather than discussing them in particular chapters, since they recur in a number of novels. The 'unhomely home' is significant here. Originating in Freud's reference to the etymological relation between the terms *unheimlich* and *heimlich* and the connection they display,[54] it evokes a domestic space that, though ostensibly warm and secure, is disturbed by secrets and the return of repressed fears and desires. The implications that it evokes of a tension or clash between the familiar and the unfamiliar, the homely and the strange, make it particularly relevant to queer existence. Writers treat the motif in contrary ways. Whereas Hensher, Purdy and Tóibín portray the hetero-patriarchal home destabilized by the revelation of homosexual secrets from within, Leavitt and Waters foreground the reverse. They represent the domestic life of the gay couple disrupted by the intrusion of homophobic influences and ideologies from the public world outside. In

Queer Phenomenology, Ahmed registers the motif's importance in her remark that whereas 'for some queers homes are already rather queer spaces, full of the potential to experience the joys of deviant desire' (p. 176), for others they represent sites of 'discomfort and alienation' (p. 11).

Royle, paraphrasing Schelling's words, describes how 'Uncanny feelings are very often generated by strange sights, unveilings, revelations, by what should have remained out of sight';[55] this is another motif relevant to queer existence that appears in several of the novels reviewed below. Unlike many people whom society regards as 'other' and abject – such as blacks, the disabled and the elderly – who display visible signs of difference, the homosexual and lesbian generally reveal none. The 'invisibility' of lesbians and gay men, Iris Marion Young argues, helps to explain the phenomenon of homophobia and the feelings of 'border-anxiety'[56] that it reflects. The fact that no physical or mental signs differentiate the homosexual from the heterosexual, and that the boundary between their sexualities is permeable, indicates that anyone can be gay, triggering in the heterosexual fears about his own sexuality. In several of the novels discussed below the unexpected sight of a lesbian or gay couple engaging in sexual contact generates in the heterosexual spectator, or the spectator who assumes himself to be heterosexual, a sensation of profound uncanniness. The outcome of this differs from text to text. Whereas in Donoghue's *Stir-Fry* it prompts the observer to reassess her own sexuality, in Grimsley's *Dream Boy* it triggers in him a rush of homosexual panic culminating in an act of physical assault. The unmasking of a male-to-female transsexual in Magrs's *Could It Be Magic?* provokes in the spectators a similarly violent reaction. Episodes of this kind occupy a central position in the novels in which they appear. They alert attention to the fact that many heterosexuals continue to regard the queer individual and his physical presence as alien and threatening. They also indicate, of course, the vulnerability and precariousness of queer existence.

Sexual/textual differences

A question that I raised at the start of this chapter that I have not yet had the opportunity to address is what differences, if any, are apparent between contemporary lesbian and male gay narratives in their treatment of the uncanny? The majority of critics, nervous perhaps of engaging in essentialist generalizations, avoid exploring topics of this kind. However this study, focusing as it does on both kinds of fiction, provides an opportunity to investigate it and move towards some answers, however tentative and provisional they may be given the limited number of novels reviewed.

A useful starting point for this enquiry, one that avoids essentialist conjecture, is to consider the different historical and cultural circumstances that furnish the context for male gay and lesbian existence and identification. Earl Jackson, summing this up in the starkest terms, states: 'Although marginalized, male gay sex is still recognisable under patriarchy. Lesbianism is inconceivable.'[57] As he implies, whereas male gay sexuality has been suppressed by society instituting laws and devising brutal or humiliating penalties for their infringement, lesbianism in many periods and cultures has been rendered well-nigh invisible. The phallocentric equation of the female genitals, since they are less overtly visible than the male, with a 'nothing' or an 'absence'[58] and the erroneous view that female sexual desire is necessarily responsive rather than active, combined with women's relegation to the domestic sphere of the home and their frequent social and economic powerlessness, have made laws prohibiting lesbian relations on the whole unnecessary. As Butler, defining the contradiction that lesbian sexuality signifies in phallocentric culture, perceptively observes, 'Lesbianism is not explicitly prohibited in part because it has not yet made its way into the grid of the thinkable, the imaginable, that grid of cultural intelligibility that regulates the real and the nameable'.[59] She continues her analysis of the relegation of lesbianism to the 'domain of unthinkability and unnameability' (p. 20) by asking the question that reflects a paradox crucial to many women's lives: 'How, then, to "be" a lesbian in a political context in which the lesbian does not exist?' (p. 20). This contradiction, and the sexual-textual strategies that writers employ to interrogate and represent it, feature prominently in some of the novels that I discuss. They are apparent in the references that Donoghue, Smith and Waters make to lesbian invisibility, and the attention they pay to the silences and taboos to which female sexuality is subject.

Male gay and lesbian writers have understandably responded in different ways to these disparate forms of disenfranchisement and oppression, especially in relation to the representation of sexual practice and the body. While both groups employ narrative strategies evoking 'excess', a concept that as indicated above has uncanny connotations, the representational tactics they choose to employ tend to differ. Male gay writers, intent on differentiating homosexual sexual practice from heterosexual, frequently write about sex and the body in a manner that is notably explicit. Earl Jackson endorses this; he argues that 'We need literary, visual and performative media that document the ways our sexual practices distinguish us from heterosexual while affirming us as individuals and communities' (p. 146). He advises male gay writers to prioritize in their fiction forms of sex that society regards as transgressive, including sado-masochism ('S & M') and public sex (anonymous sexual encounters in public places such as parks and toilets). They are 'excessive' in that they exceed convention and, as a result, can provoke controversy.

However, though effective in foregrounding the specificity and physicality of male gay sex, this strategy can give rise to problems. As well as appearing to fetishize sexual practice and giving the impression that the writer endorses phallocentric values by privileging a visual economy, it can result, if treated clumsily, in the narrative collapsing into a repetitive series of sex acts involving a predictable interplay of fragmented limbs and body parts.[60] In addition, sexual images of this kind, if read in the context of present-day media and IT culture that relentlessly bombard the spectator with images of sex and the body, run the risk of becoming over-familiar and tedious and losing their novelty. Leavitt, Purdy and Hollinghurst, three writers who introduce explicit accounts of sex and refer to public sex and S & M, succeed, in fact, in avoiding these problems. They successfully interweave references to sex with the narrative or, in the case of Leavitt, employ them in a humorously parodic manner to critique the protagonist's narcissistic preoccupation with himself and his sexual prowess.

Writers of lesbian fiction encounter difficulties of a different kind in representing sex and the body. As well as confronting the problem of lesbian invisibility, they have to contend with the contrary one of heterosexual male voyeurism. This, as pictures in porn magazines and on the web illustrate, constructs the lesbian as sexually voracious and objectifies and commodifies the lesbian couple, reducing them to items of male sexual titillation and consumption. In order to resist this scopic focus and its propensity to objectify or pathologize the lesbian, writers have traditionally avoided introducing explicit accounts of sexual practice and employed, instead, strategies of metaphor and metonymy. These frequently invoke, as the fiction of Donoghue, Smith and Waters illustrates, reference to phenomena with uncanny associations such as dreams, darkness and spectrality that exceed the perspectives and value systems of the material world. They echo Luce Irigaray's thesis that 'the predominance of the visual is particularly foreign to female eroticism ... and woman's entry into the dominant scopic economy signifies her consignment to passivity since it consigns her to the role of "a beautiful object of contemplation"'.[61] Judith Roof, endorsing Irigaray's perspective, recommends the lesbian writer to depict 'sexuality as hidden or masked, but revealed in the removal of the layers of that mask, and female sexuality as everywhere at once – as two in one and radiant'.[62] Representational strategies of this kind are, of course, likewise open to criticism; they can be accused not of being too blatant and explicit but, on the contrary, of being imprecise, over-romantic and lacking in somatic specificity. In positive terms, however, in addition to generating passages of writing that are experimental and metaphorically inventive, they serve to interrogate the linguistic and intellectual limitations of phallocentric culture, challenging its scopic focus by representing lesbian sexuality and subjectivity, to cite Jill Dolan, 'as excessive to representation's conventional codes'.[63]

The differences between male gay and lesbian representational practices summarized above are substantiated to a degree by the novels that I discuss. Exceptions occur, however, indicating that writers are by no means hidebound by convention and tradition. Hensher in *Kitchen Venom*, in representing his protagonist John's sexual encounters with the prostitute Giacomo, avoids depicting the two men's sexual practice explicitly but instead signals it indirectly through the hints furnished in their conversation. He also evokes, instead of overtly describing, John's increasing infatuation with Giacomo's body, sensuously describing the touch of Giacomo's skin as resembling 'rough silk falling through the hands'.[64] Other male writers juxtapose reference to the physical and material world with reference to the economy of the invisible and spectral, and the emergence of the repressed fears and desires that the latter metaphorically evokes. Purdy in *Mourners Below* intersperses his description of his youthful protagonist's sexual encounter with the girlfriend of his brother who has been killed in the war with the portrayal of the brother's spectral intervention in the scene – or what the protagonist, mourning his death, interprets as such. Leavitt creates a similar juxtaposition. He describes the episode of public sex that his protagonist is enjoying while cruising on Hampstead Heath being unexpectedly interrupted by the momentary appearance of the face of his deceased lover in spectral form.

Writers of lesbian fiction also on occasion reject convention and historical precedent by representing lesbian sexual practice explicitly. Waters in *Fingersmith*, as well as introducing a vividly detailed account of Sue and Maud's lovemaking – and so foregrounding the importance of sex to lesbian relations and differentiating her own treatment of the topic from that of earlier writers – creates a powerful (and excessive) rhetoric of repetition and doubling. She portrays the sexual encounter that takes place between the two women twice, firstly from Sue's point of view and secondly from Maud's. More strikingly still, she advertises her interest in the topic of lesbian sexual representation and the debates it has triggered by introducing reference to one of its most controversial features: the production of lesbian erotica by lesbians themselves. Winterson too displays an interest in lesbian representation and the contradictions it involves. She centres *The Power Book* on a love affair between two women situated in virtual reality, exploring, along with the excursions into fantasy that it promotes, its problematic aspects and ambiguities.

Other differences between lesbian and male gay narrative besides those mentioned above also emerge, reflecting their disparate sociopolitical and cultural contexts and histories. Writers of lesbian fiction, influenced by the feminist revision of popular fictional genres initiated by writers such as Angela Carter and Margaret Atwood in the 1970s and 1980s, frequently structure their narratives on motifs and storylines appropriated from fairytale and Female Gothic. Maria in Donoghue's *Stir-Fry* dreams of flying like a witch over the city of Dublin, while Mala, the protagonist of Mootoo's *Cereus Blooms at*

Night, is stigmatized as a witch;[65] Ali in Winterson's *The Power Book* enjoys, in an episode recalling the Arabian *A Thousand and One Nights*, a love affair with a beautiful princess in Istanbul; and Maud in Waters's *Fingersmith* lives, as if enthralled by hetero-patriarchy's evil spell, at the country house of Briar waiting like the Sleeping Beauty for Sue to penetrate the thorny barrier of social privilege entrapping her and awaken her with a same-sex kiss. Episodes in Donoghue's and Mootoo's texts echo the motif that, as a result of Sandra Gilbert and Susan Gubar's groundbreaking critical study, we term today 'the madwoman in the attic'.

Another difference apparent between the female and male writers discussed in this study is that the former refer to a rich tradition of lesbian/feminist theoretical writing, both Anglo-American and French. As we shall see, Galford, Mootoo, Waters and other writers make fruitful use of these discourses, interweaving in their texts concepts of sisterhood, female commonality, mother-daughter relations and the Irigarayan concept of a suppressed maternal genealogy.

Hensher, Hollinghurst and Leavitt, in contrast, rework stories about the city and its culture appropriated from urban legend or Victorian Gothic. They recast from a present-day viewpoint the motif of homo-erotic doubling associated with nineteenth-century Gothic and queer the topic of the pleasures and dangers of metropolitan life. Grimsley and Kenan, employing a rural setting, rework tales of the haunting of the American countryside by the spectral traces of the brutalities of slavery and the acts of genocide perpetrated on the indigenous population. Other topics that male gay writers prioritize include, as exemplified by the fiction of Hensher, Leavitt and Hollinghurst, cross-class relationships and public sex. Tóibín and Magrs also focus on the AIDS pandemic, describing the fears that it arouses in the individual and its devastating effect on the male gay community.

The Trinidadian-Canadian Mootoo, the Caribbean Thomas and the African American Kenan, while treating many of the themes cited above, enrich contemporary queer fiction with additional topics and narrative forms. They investigate the intersection between sexuality and race and explore interracial attachments and relationships, teasing out their positive and problematic features. Reference to the oppressive effects of white colonization and domination also assumes prominence in their novels.

Queer fiction, and the strategies that the writers who produce it employ, are of course by no means static but exist in a state of continual flux. The differences between lesbian and male gay interests and narrative strategies outlined above are proposed tentatively and are by no means conclusive. Other differences too may strike the reader as he encounters the novels treating secrets, spectrality, place and space, and the monstrous, discussed in the chapters that lie ahead, and explores in imagination the world that they create – the world of the 'queer uncanny'.

2

Secrets and their Disclosure

❧

I discern a woman
I loved, drowning in secrets, fear wound round her throat
And choking her like hair . . .[1]

Secrets and sexuality

The topic of secrets and their disclosure, the focus of this chapter,
features prominently in discussions of the uncanny, while also playing
a key role in theoretical and fictional texts treating lesbian and gay
themes. Freud, having opened his essay on 'The Uncanny' by tracing
the semantic changes that the term *heimlich* has undergone in moving
from signifying 'familiar and agreeable' to denoting its *unheimlich*
opposite 'concealed and kept out of sight', cites Schelling's observation
that the term *unheimlich* refers to 'everything that ought to have
remained . . . secret and hidden but has come to light'.[2] Theorists
writing subsequently develop these ideas in different ways. Royle
describes the uncanny as involving the subject in 'a secret encounter',[3]
while Nicolas Abraham and Maria Torok, reworking Freudian theories
of the return of the repressed and the death instinct, formulate the
concept of transgenerational haunting. They posit the idea of a secret
– they term it evocatively the phantom – that the subject unknowingly
inherits from his parents and exists encrypted in his unconscious,

revealing its presence indirectly through its destructive effect on his psyche.[4] This, as we shall see, is pertinent to one of the novels discussed below.

Secrecy, and the significant role it frequently plays in the lives of lesbians and gay men, is a key theme in queer and lesbian feminist theory. Sedgwick, exposing the hypocrisy and double standards that frequently operate in phallocentric culture, describes male homosexuality as signifying an open secret that society treats as unspeakable.[5] Butler, referring to lesbianism, gives an even bleaker analysis; she depicts female same-sex relations, as indicated in the previous chapter, as signifying 'the production of a domain of unthinkability and unnameability'.[6] Castle, writing from a lesbian feminist perspective, endorses her view.[7] Accusing Western literature of acting as 'a kind of derealization machine', she sardonically observes: 'Insert the lesbian and watch her disappear!' (p. 6).

Two interlinked topics relating to secrets and their revelation that feature prominently in queer theory are the closet and homosexual panic. The latter, as Sedgwick describes in commenting on the form of paranoid Gothic, signifies the state of emotional paralysis or rage induced in the subject by fear of being sexually propositioned by a member of the same sex or discovering feelings of homosexual desire in himself and dreading their disclosure. She argues that panic of this kind is triggered by 'the double bind'[8] in which patriarchy entraps the male: while insisting that he should bond socially and form friendships and professional ties with other men, it forbids him to engage in sexual relations with them. Halberstam develops Sedgwick's analysis with reference to the secret lives led by characters in Victorian Gothic. Discussing Robert Louis Stevenson's *The Strange Case of Dr Jekyll and Mr Hyde* and Wilde's *The Picture of Dorian Gray*, she observes that 'Secret selves, in Gothic, denote sexual secrets, secrets of the closet, more often than not'.[9]

Whereas the connections between homosexuality and secrecy in eighteenth- and nineteenth-century texts have received critical attention, the role that they play in present-day fiction has been relatively neglected. However, as the novels reviewed here illustrate, they have generated some interest from writers. The notion of homosexuality as unspeakable and taboo, along with reference to the closet and the homosexual panic relating to it, reappear in new and topical guises in contemporary fiction, with lesbian invisibility also to the fore. They are central, as one might expect, to the coming-out novel, exemplified here by Emma Donoghue's *Stir-Fry*, that portrays the protagonist recognizing and disclosing her lesbian sexuality, as well as to novels such as Philip Hensher's *Kitchen Venom* that explore the protagonist's fear of being outed. They also feature in AIDS narratives and works of lesbian and gay historical fiction. Novels describing the destructive effect of the AIDS pandemic on the gay community are frequently structured, in fact, around a double secret: the protagonist's HIV-positive status and, relating to this, his homosexuality. He strives to conceal the former from people who wield emotional or economic power over him, such as family members or employers, only to find that it comes to light with the effect of revealing, by implication, the latter. Colm Tóibín's *The Blackwater Lightship* portrays the protagonist entrapped in just this predicament.

Lesbian and male gay historical novels are also on occasion structured on a double secret, the secret represented by the past itself and that of the hidden lives of the men and women inhabiting it. Although, as Michel Foucault argues, all forms of history operate in terms of difference and discontinuity,[10] the history of male and female same-sex relations is particularly fractured and difficult to decipher due to the absence of records and the strategies of concealment to which people living in earlier periods often felt forced to resort. In recreating episodes from queer history, writers frequently focus on characters who seek to hide their sexuality by passing as heterosexual. Both David Leavitt's *While England Sleeps* and Sarah Waters's *The Night Watch* portray hidden lives of this kind, investigating their formation and sociopolitical context.

New approaches to the coming-out novel

Donoghue's *Stir-Fry* and Hensher's *Kitchen Venom* are interesting texts with which to open this study since, though they differ significantly in content and social context, they both develop a form of fiction that has recently provoked controversy. This is the lesbian and gay coming-out novel. Though it remains popular with readers, the genre has been denigrated by critics writing in the past two decades as simplistic and politically immature. In order to appreciate the two writers' treatment of the topic of secrets and their disclosure, we need to refer to the debates that both the coming-out novel and the sociopolitical ideas underpinning its construction have generated.

The coming-out novel originated in the 1970s and 1980s, the era of the gay liberation and lesbian feminist movements and their championing of identity politics as the key route to sexual liberation. The popularity the genre has enjoyed with writers and readers and its ability to flourish and survive reflect the fact that it is a highly adaptable form of fiction that addresses powerfully, if on occasion simplistically, topics of major psychological and political significance to lesbians and gay men alike. It has achieved international status among English-speaking writers, being exemplified by novels as disparate in context as *A Piece of the Night* by the British Michele Roberts, *A Boy's Own Story* by the American Edmund White, *Zami* by the African American Audre Lorde and *All That False Instruction* by the Australian Joan Riley.[11]

Despite its popularity, however, with the advent of queer theory and the postmodern perspectives that it inscribes, the coming-out novel has become the target of criticism. Critics writing from a queer viewpoint accuse it of endorsing the concept and regulatory effect of identity politics, as well as promoting the binary divisions heterosexual/homosexual and ignorance/knowledge. Comments voiced by Judith Roof criticizing the lesbian version of the form for asserting 'the victorious truth of lesbian identity' and promoting a 'politics of visibility'[12] typify this critique. Angus Gordon, in addition, while acknowledging the radical aspect of the coming-out novel reflected in the challenge it directs at the conventional heterosexual dénouement of narrative, attacks it from another angle. He complains that the trajectory it inscribes, in celebrating the protagonist's departure from the closet, inevitably positions his pre-gay existence as a period of unhappiness, resulting in the 'foreclosure of the desire to return to a time before one's queer identity was made irrevocable by the act of coming out'.[13] He sees versions of the form that focus on the period of adolescence as particularly problematic in this respect.

These criticisms are endorsed by theorists who, writing from a postmodern perspective, interrogate and problematize the act of coming out itself. Sedgwick, while acknowledging the political value of disclosing one's gay sexuality, inserts a note of caution by drawing attention to the ambiguities and problems inherent in it. She alerts attention to the fact that coming out, rather than taking the form of a single definitive act, as some of the literature of the gay liberation movement optimistically implies, tends to be on the contrary a never-ending process, one that can be as stressful as a life lived in the closet if not more so. And, far from following a clearly defined trajectory, it is often disturbingly random. As she writes: 'Every encounter with a new classroom of students, to say nothing of a new boss, social worker, loan officer, landlord, doctor, erects new closets which exact from gay people . . . new requisitions of secrecy or disclosure.'[14] She also refers to 'the potential for serious injury' (p. 80), emotional, social or physical, that coming out can involve both for the gay subject himself and the people, such as parents and friends, to whom he reveals his sexuality.

Sedgwick's analysis of the problematic aspects of coming out is developed by Butler from a psychoanalytic viewpoint. She argues that because sexuality has its roots in the unconscious, it can never be made fully transparent: '[since] part of what constitutes sexuality is to some degree precisely that which does not appear and that which, to some degree, can never appear, sexuality is to some degree always closeted, especially to the one who would express it through acts of disclosure.'[15] As a result, the individual's revelation of his gay identification seldom brings the sense of freedom he anticipates it will. She criticizes the binary opposition of inside/out, entrenched in Western culture, for generating this futile hope.

Queer theorists, as well alerting attention to the problematic aspects of coming out, also take a fresh look at the phenomenon of the closet, investigating its social and psychological complexities. Sedgwick argues that refusing to reveal one's sexuality is in fact as much a per-formative act as revealing it, since '"closetedness" itself is a perform-ance initiated as such by the speech act of silence'.[16] Lisabeth During and Terri Fealy go a step further. They investigate the emotional compensations and creative spin-offs that the individual can enjoy by refusing to disclose his gay sexuality and passing as heterosexual. Associating the closet with the 'distinctive aesthetic'[17] of artifice and mimicry stemming from the cultural perspectives of Oscar Wilde that flourished prior to the gay liberation movement, they investigate the rich language of verbal innuendo, counter-codes and inversion that members of homosexual and lesbian subcultures have developed in order to communicate with their fellows while avoiding revealing their secrets to the world at large. Affrica Taylor argues that the lesbian or gay subject, by exploiting this aesthetic, can transform the heterotopic location of the closet from a 'vulnerable site of shameful hiding' to 'a performance space ... a powerful site of deliberate ruse – the site of the wild card and mischievous joker'.[18] He can subtly utilize the protective camouflage that passing affords to expose and critique the performative dimension of heterosexuality.

The queer critique of the coming-out novel, and the problematization of the act of coming out and identity politics that it inscribes, are of course not unchallenged. Defenders of the genre point out that the trajectory it depicts is useful psychologically and socially since it offers readers 'a model for respecting and nurturing their own lives'.[19] They also argue that the improvements in the situation of lesbians and gay men in the West that have taken place in recent years have been achieved chiefly in the name of identity politics, as a result of individuals confronting prejudice and bravely disclosing their sexual identification. Many of us who, in the climate of extreme homophobia operating in the 1970s and 1980s, took the risky step of coming out certainly remember the event as an act of personal triumph and, despite Roof's critique of the response as mistaken, the declaration of 'a victorious truth'! As John D'Emilio, drawing on personal memories, movingly recalls,

> For a gay man or a lesbian of that time, I don't think that it was possible to experience anything of comparable intensity. In a psychological sense it was an act of 'revolutionary' import. No manner of political analysis could convince someone who had come out then that he or she wasn't turning the world inside out and upside down.[20]

The debates relating to the coming-out novel and identity politics outlined above are relevant to this study since they have influenced queer fiction, generating in the 1990s the production of a new, intellectually complex version of the genre. Writers contributing to it interrogate the psychological and sociopolitical significance of the act of coming out and take a fresh look at the phenomenon of the closet. They illustrate the latter's performative dimension and, in contrast to earlier writers, explore the attractions that it holds for the gay subject as well as its oppressive aspects. Donoghue's *Stir-Fry* and Hensher's *Kitchen Venom*, both published in the 1990s, exemplify this trend.

The two novels, though both set in the 1980s, display significant differences. Whereas Donoghue portrays her female protagonist's discovery of her lesbian sexuality in the context of 1980s student life in Dublin, Hensher situates his male protagonist's fears about being outed in the elitist, masculinist world of the House of Commons in the homophobic context of the Thatcher government. However, the two novels also share common features. Both writers illustrate the attractions, as well as the stresses, of a closeted lifestyle. Whereas Donoghue explores the playful use of verbal parody and sexual innuendo that the closet can generate, Hensher, while emphasizing the insecurities and fears that it breeds, examines its existential import and describes the perverse sense of enjoyment that his protagonist draws from concealing his sexuality. Yet although they acknowledge the dangers that disclosing one's sexuality can involve for the individual and the pragmatic uses and attractions of the closet, the two writers steer their narratives towards foregrounding the importance of achieving sexual openness if circumstances permit and illustrate the confusions and disasters that can arise from hiding one's sexual orientation.

Both writers, in addition, introduce uncanny imagery and perceptions to evoke the feelings of alienation and fear, as well as the sensation of jouissance, that queer existence can involve in heteronormative society. They also effectively exploit the political dimension of the coming-out novel, employing it to investigate those oppressive institutions that, by promoting a climate of homophobia, coerce lesbians and gay men into concealing their sexuality. Donoghue centres her criticism on the Roman Catholic Church, exposing the way in which, by perpetuating Judaeo-Christian taboos, it renders lesbianism unspeakable and invisible. Hensher examines the social structures of those twin bastions of British upper-class male power and privilege, the public school and the House of Commons. He illustrates their destructive effect not only on men but also on the lives of women who are unfortunate enough to be caught in their wake.

Donoghue structures *Stir-Fry* on the contradiction that is according to Butler integral to lesbian existence: 'How, then, to "be" a lesbian in a political context in which the lesbian does not exist?'[21] In order to investigate this question, Donoghue inverts the conventional structure of the coming-out novel. Whereas examples of the genre generally open by foregrounding the queer protagonist's isolation and alienation and conclude on a positive note with her locating some form of supportive same-sex community, *Stir-Fry* operates the other way round. The seventeen-year-old protagonist Maria Murphy is portrayed living from the start with her two flatmates Ruth and Jael who are in a lesbian partnership. The problem is that she fails to recognize this fact. The Roman Catholic culture in which she has been raised and the homophobic climate of 1980s Ireland render her flatmates' sexuality inconceivable and invisible to her. She deciphers their secret only after some time has elapsed when, in an episode positioned as the uncanny climax of the novel, its content is made blatantly obvious.

Ruth and Jael's decision not to divulge their partnership to Maria is represented by Donoghue as pragmatically motivated. When they had acted in an upfront manner with a former prospective lodger, the revelation of their lesbianism not only drove her away but almost led to their eviction from the flat as well. As well as refusing to take the flat-share, she had threatened to out them to the owner of the property with the aim of terminating their tenancy. This is the first of many instances of homophobia, ranging from verbal abuse to violence, that Donoghue describes as typifying Dublin society in the 1980s. In consequence, the two women, though uneasy about keeping silent, decide this time to act cautiously and leave Maria to decipher their secret for herself. Rather than divulge their sexuality, they therefore drop a trail of verbal clues that Maria, had her upbringing been less narrow, would probably have interpreted. Their conversation bristles with double entendres and humorously parodic references to the role of outcast and monster that, as lesbians, they occupy in Dublin society. Jael refers to herself as 'the Wicked Witch of the West'.[22] Puckering her face into a troll-like mask, she jokingly describes herself as a vampire who survives by sucking the blood of virginal freshers (p. 14). Ruth echoes her grotesque self-portrayal, playfully punning on the word 'friend' and addressing her as 'fiend'

(p. 63). These and other examples of the humorously pointed repartee in which the couple engage represent the closet less as a hiding place than, to cite Taylor, a 'site of deliberate ruse' associated with 'the mischievous joker'.[23] Their exchange of witticisms and bawdy innuendos is offensive as well as defensive in intent. As the weeks pass and they begin to regard Maria as a friend, their repartee becomes increasingly flamboyant and sexually suggestive. It teasingly challenges her to decipher the clues it contains, open her ears and recognize the truth.

The affection that Ruth and Jael feel for Maria is ironically reflected in the way that they begin to include her in the domain of abject beings that, from a heteronormative viewpoint, they themselves inhabit in Dublin society. Jael, engaging in carnivalesque raillery, humorously calls her 'a bog-trotter' and, when Maria explains that her name is pronounced 'Marya', mockingly observes that it rhymes with 'pariah' signifying 'outcast' and 'deviant' (pp. 11–12). Here, as well as hinting at the risk to her reputation that Maria is running in living with two social outcasts, Jael unconsciously signals the course that the narrative will take. Living with the couple and eventually perceiving their lesbian sexuality furnishes Maria with a route to recognizing or rather, for this is how Donoghue describes it, *constructing* her own. She falls in love with Ruth and – after a number of narrative twists and turns in the course of which the potential for injury that coming out can involve emerges and the vampirish Jael who, we discover, has frequently been unfaithful to Ruth is exorcized and banished from the both the household and the text – is portrayed, in the final chapter, about to become Ruth's lover.

Maria discovers her flatmates' sexuality purely by chance. Returning home one night, she accidentally catches sight of them through the bead curtain slung across the door sitting on the kitchen table, traditionally the centre of heterosexual family life[24] but here subversively recast as the site of lesbian love, sharing a passionate kiss. Royle's reference to the ability of 'strange sights, unveilings, revelations, by what should have remained out of sight'[25] to generate a sense of the uncanny in the spectator sheds light on her response. The interplay between the familiar and unfamiliar, the mundane and the strange, that the scene evokes, gives it a surreal dimension, plunging her into a maelstrom of confused emotions. She thinks distractedly:

31

It wasn't her fault; she was in no sense spying. She couldn't help but see the shape they made. Her eyes tried to untangle its elements. Ruth, crosslegged on the table, her back curved like a comma, and Jael, leaning into it, kissing her. There was no wild passion; that might have shaken her less. Just the slow bartering of lips on the rickety table where Ruth chopped garlic . . . The kiss, their joined body on the table, all seemed to belong to a parallel world. She had the impression that no noise from behind this shifting skin of beads could reach them. (p. 68)

Maria's initial response to the sight of her the two women kissing is to blame herself for failing to recognize their sexuality; she punishes herself with the thought, 'What ludicrous naivety, even for seventeen. How could she not have known?' (p. 69). Then, remembering the narrowness of her upbringing and convent education and the silence always maintained about homosexuality, effectively erasing it, to cite Butler, 'from the grid of cultural intelligibility that regulates the real and nameable',[26] she abruptly shifts tack. She thinks, 'embarrassment swinging to anger, the question reversed: how the hell was she meant to know?' (p. 69).

Though pondering it obsessively in private, Maria keeps to herself the fact that she is sharing her home with, as the nuns at school would have termed them, 'two active homosexuals' and 'mortal sinners' (p. 77). Instead of revealing her discovery of their sexual secret to her flatmates, she broods on it in silence like a witness to an un-speakable crime. She projects on them the role of monstrous Other, envisaging them in imagery appropriated from Gothic fantasy. The portrait of them she sketches one evening strikes her as resembling 'a two-headed monster in a fairy-tale, the kind of the thing the hero had to fight . . . or a gargoyle, with two tongues for waterspouts' (pp. 125–6). However, on deciphering the second secret that haunts her – her growing feelings of attraction for Ruth – she is forced to recognize that her own sexuality is not as orthodox as she had assumed. The discovery enables her to redeem the two women from the domain of the abject and acknowledge their full humanity. The transformation from monstrous to human that they undergo in her eyes resembles the uncanny metamorphosis that concludes the folktale 'Beauty and the Beast' and Angela Carter's well-known feminist recasting of it.[27]

Donoghue, in fact, advertises these intertextual connections by representing Maria playfully addressing Jael as 'beast' (p. 95).

Another strategy that Donoghue employs to represent Maria conquering her sexual prejudices is to invert the pejorative significance of imagery of the monstrous feminine and employ it in a celebratory light. The fantasy image that Maria creates of herself, flying triumphantly over the city of Dublin at night 'black air between her legs, the office windows glinting as she skimmed by' (p. 28), relates her to the figure of the witch, an icon of feminist empowerment. And, while strolling through Dublin city centre, she finds herself unexpectedly admiring the statue of Anna Livia described by Donoghue as 'a reclining giantess in bronze . . . a monster really all out of proportion' (p. 87). Maria's ability to appreciate the statue's appearance reflects her burgeoning feelings of love and desire for Ruth, the representative of 'the monstrous feminine' with whom she shares her home. She discovers that, as Ahmed writes in *Queer Phenomenology*, 'It takes time and work to inhabit the lesbian body. The act of tending toward other women has to be repeated, often in the face of hostility and discrimination, to gather such tendencies into a sustainable form.' (p. 102).

Reference to the uncanny dimension of place and space plays a key role in the novel, with Donoghue foregrounding the ambiguously homely/unhomely associations of the attic flat where the three women live. The flat, towering above the neighbouring houses 'high as the gulls' (p. 85), metaphorically represents 'a lesbian space',[28] while its residents' marginalized social situation associates it with the title of Sandra Gilbert and Susan Gubar's study *The Madwoman in the Attic*. At night it assumes a surreal appearance, with the staircase bathed in shadow and the kitchen table, where Maria first glimpses her two flatmates kissing, appearing to be uncannily 'floating in a pool of yellow light on top of the city' (p. 84). The flat's interior reminds Maria, in addition, of a 'Victorian theatre' (p. 85). The term signals the heterotopic role of performance site that it plays in the personal drama of lesbian love that the three women enact together.

The novel concludes with the three packing up their belongings and leaving the flat, with the resultant erasure of its significance as a lesbian space. Donoghue moves at this point from exploring the social and linguistic intricacies of the closet to setting the scene for Maria's act of coming out. She portrays her embarking on a quest to seek Ruth who, mistakenly believing that Maria is attracted to Jael, has temporally returned to her family home. Maria's decision to follow her and declare her love is described as prompted by passion rather than reason, with Donoghue portraying her 'moving like a sleepwalker' to find Ruth (p. 230). The simile, developing the references scattered throughout the text to instances of the intrusion of the unconscious into everyday life such as dreams, fantasies, double entendres and slips of the tongue, vividly evokes the mysterious processes of the emergence of same-sex desire that Donoghue perceptively explores in the novel.

In contrast to Donoghue's *Stir-Fry* that represents Ruth and Jael's decision to conceal their sexuality as pragmatic, aimed at avoiding problems with prospective tenants, Hensher's *Kitchen Venom* portrays the protagonist John's closeted existence as psychologically motivated. Although John's decision to keep his homosexuality secret at first appears to be prompted by expediency – he is married and works as a House of Commons clerk – the reader soon perceives that his motivation is more complex than this. Although, as Hensher describes, he 'wanted sex with a man, there was something he wanted more . . . What he most wanted was a secret to keep. He relished secrecy, and he created it around him.'[29] Instead of being secretive because he is homosexual, he is 'homosexual because that was what best suited his secrecy' (p. 47). This agrees with D. A. Miller's suggestion that the individual's decision to keep a facet of his life secret does not necessarily reflect its special nature since, when eventually revealed, it often turns out to be disappointingly mundane. It reflects, rather, his existential attempt to resist definition by making himself 'radically inaccessible', as Miller writes, 'to a culture which would otherwise entirely determine him'.[30] It reflects his 'paranoid perception that the social world is a dangerous place to exhibit the inner self (p. 203).

We first encounter John attending the funeral of his wife Helena with whom he has lived for thirty years. The funeral is a formal, emotionally chilly event, with his adult daughters Jane and Francesca the only mourners to express grief. Hensher describes John's closeted existence as resembling a masquerade that takes the form not of playful sexual innuendo and repartee as in *Stir-Fry* but of maintaining a rigid facade. A family friend attending the funeral who, like everyone else there, is unaware of John's sexual orientation grimly compares the social mask he wears, in its appearance of corpse-like passivity, to 'a coffin'. She wonders 'if there's anything private behind' it (p. 17). Like the automaton Olympia in E. T. A. Hoffmann's story 'The Sandman' in Cixous's critical analysis,[31] John gives the impression of uncannily blurring the border between life and death.

The one occasion when John partially drops his mask is when he is in the company of Giacomo, the beautiful young Italian sex worker whom he has visited at his flat in Earls Court once a month for the past two years. Though he is becoming increasingly fond of Giacomo and senses that the attraction is mutual, John tries to keep the relationship on an impersonal, financial basis. Butler, describing normative masculinity as constructed on the disavowal of homosexual desires, argues that 'When they do emerge on the far side of the censor, they may well carry the mark of impossibility with them, performing as it were, the impossible within the possible'.[32] This sheds light on John's situation. Although he enjoys sex with men, the repressive nature of his public school education and his institutionalized existence in the British parliamentary system make him incapable of expressing feelings of tenderness and love.

As well as passing as heterosexual, John daily enacts another form of masquerade, one with a grotesque aspect that it is beyond his power to change. This is the role of hunchback with which he was born. Representing his deformity in terms of a dark version of carnival with Gothic resonances, he bitterly describes the people who stare at him in the street and at social functions as 'the audience at the pantomime', with himself in 'the Quasimodo costume he could not take off' (p. 122). He depicts the hump on his back as representing the 'repository of everything vile and murderous and poisonous that was in him' (p. 122). The hump also operates as an image for the dangers inherent in his closeted existence and the potential for injury that the secret of his sexuality, waiting to emerge, encrypts.

The pairing of John, middle-aged and physically deformed, with the attractive young Giacomo, combined with the linking of their names, introduces an instance of uncanny doubling. It evokes the pairing in Victorian Gothic of characters who are physically deformed with their conventional-looking counterparts, such as Hyde and

Jekyll or Victor Frankenstein's creature and Victor. John also exemplifies a twentieth-century version of the paranoid Gothic male since while participating in an erotic same-sex relationship, he features ambiguously as both the victim and agent of violence. Whereas the description of his hump as 'a killer behind him' (p. 133) inflicting a 'strangling' tension on his body portrays him as victim, Hensher subsequently reverses this role and describes him assuming agency. He portrays him committing a murder.

The murder that John commits is predictably provoked by a clash occurring between his public and private lives, triggering in him the fear that he will be outed and the secret of his sexuality come to light. He discovers that his young colleague Louis, who is also gay, has learnt of his homosexual relationship and is himself attracted to Giacomo. John's anxieties are further exacerbated by being unexpectedly assaulted by a beggar in the street. The beggar, after verbally abusing him as a 'fucking hunchback faggot' (p. 215), punches him in the face and steals his wallet. John seeks refuge after the event at Giacomo's flat. Giacomo, who is starting to envisage him less as a client than a possible 'sexual partner' (p. 177), tends the black eye that the beggar has inflicted upon him. Moved by the fact that he has sought his help, in an outburst of spontaneous emotion he discloses his affection and feelings of tenderness for John by suggesting that they might perhaps live together. The unexpectedness of the proposal and the erotic and emotional intimacy it implies disorient John. They strike him with the uncanny significance of something that should have remained unspoken and hidden but has inappropriately and disturbingly come to light. Succumbing to an attack of homosexual panic, registered in a sudden fit of 'stomach-clenching terror' (p. 220), he loses control and, on the spur of the moment, strangles Giacomo.

Although John murders Giacomo in order to protect the secret of his sexuality and the resistance to social definition it signifies, the act ironically has the reverse effect. As he himself quickly recognizes, when the murder is discovered, Louis, knowing of his relationship with Giacomo, will no doubt suspect him of committing it and out him as a homosexual and a murderer to the police. And since, as indicated above, Giacomo represents in certain respects his double, he also kills a key aspect of himself. Contemplating the metropolis as the location of furtive sexual encounters and the risks they involve, exemplified by 'queer acts after night fall, and violence in silence', he fatalistically observes: 'And at the end of all the desires and the violence and the murder ... there was a man killing what he most wanted and loved, because it was what he most wanted and loved' (p. 240).

In paradoxically 'killing what he most wanted and loved', John parodically re-enacts the stereotype of 'the tragic homosexual' associated with Oscar Wilde's 'The Ballad of Reading Gaol' and the fiction of Honoré de Balzac and Jean Genet.[33] Querelle, the protagonist of Genet's *Querelle de Brest*, who perversely kills his lover Vic in a ritualized display of sexual energy, appears particularly relevant to John's situation. However, unlike Genet who depicts Querelle as the transgressive outsider defying convention, Hensher deliberately deflates any romantic or heroic connotations that might dignify John's crime. He portrays him retiring to bed after the murder with an attack of flu where, surrendering to inertia and self-pity, he morbidly pictures his lover's corpse lying undiscovered in the flat. Elisabeth Bronfen supplements Kristeva's reference to the abject significance of the corpse by describing it as representing the double of the deceased.[34] This is pertinent to Giacomo. His putrifying corpse with, as Hensher gruesomely describes, the liquids oozing onto the carpet and insects feeding on it, doubles grotesquely with the physical perfection of his body when alive. It recalls Dorian Gray's grotesquely ageing body doubling with the beauty of his portrait.

John's obsession with keeping the secret of his sexuality intact, as well as prompting him to commit a murder, impacts destructively on the lives of his two daughters Jane and Francesca. Both women exhibit symptoms of disturbance, with their actions appearing to be dominated by repressed emotions that they can neither define nor control. Their frequent bickering erupts in one episode into a fit of outright violence when Jane attacks Francesca with a kitchen knife and then, so Hensher implies, stabs herself. The automaton-like behaviour of the two women, as well as displaying connections with the social mask that their father habitually wears, relates them to the marionette Olympia in Hoffmann's story. Although they are ignorant of the sexual secret that John conceals, they perceive that they are emotionally damaged and that he is somehow to blame. Jane, on overhearing her mother once observe that her family had feared that if she married him any children born of the union would inherit his deformity and 'be crippled', nods her head in silent agreement. She thinks obscurely to herself, 'They are, they are' (p. 129).

The two women's traumatized behaviour is clarified by reference to Abraham and Torok's theory of transgenerational haunting and the transference of a transgressive secret ('the phantom') from the parent to the child's unconscious that they claim can occur. They argue, controversially, that 'what haunts us are not the dead but the gaps left within us by the secrets of others'.[35] Their thesis is pertinent to John's relationship with his two daughters and the destructive effect that his obsessive desire to conceal the secret of his sexuality has on them.

Hensher's novel, as well as exploring homosexual panic, has socio-political relevance, providing an indictment of the British class system and the rigid codes of masculinity that it promotes. By setting the novel in the era of the Thatcher government, Hensher evokes memories of Section 28,[36] one of its many oppressive legacies. His critique of Margaret Thatcher's policies is reflected in his occasional references to her and her Cabinet, as well as in the novel's title. The phrase *Kitchen Venom* is applicable both to the hypocrisy and intrigue that characterized the House of Commons in the 1980s and to the deceitful atmosphere of John's affluent upper-class home where, having deceived his wife for thirty years, he lives in a tense relationship with his two emotionally crippled daughters.

Double secrets: AIDS narratives

According to Emmanuel S. Nelson, 'Much of the energy of gay writing since the mid-eighties has been directed at formulating re-sponses to the crisis that AIDS has generated'.[37] The attempt by writers to register the enormity of the pandemic and describe its devastating effect on individuals and the gay subculture, as well as to challenge the homophobia and negligence evinced by the pharma-ceutical companies and governmental agencies, inspired in the 1980s and 1990s a new form of queer fiction: the AIDS narrative. Fiction of this kind, though differing radically in tone and perspective from that produced in the 1970s with its hedonistic celebration of gay life and sex, reveals connections with the novels published in the earlier period of the 1950s and early 1960s. It echoes on occasion the representation of the homosexual as an abject outcast 'living out a tragic destiny of loneliness and shame'[38] found in the novels of Genet and David Storey. A problem, in fact, confronting the writer who seeks to treat the gay community's encounter with AIDS is how, while acknowledging the suffering it involves, to avoid appearing to endorse the connection of homosexuality with disease and death that typifies both earlier traditions of homosexual fiction and the homophobic attitudes of the moral right.

AIDS fiction raises other questions too. As Alan Sinfield observes, 'Writing about AIDS is difficult. How to match the scale of the thing? How to avoid appearing to use it?'[39] Brookes comments perceptively on the choice of approaches available to the writer. Should he treat the pandemic with a degree of 'distance' and, while acknowledging the suffering it inflicts, continue to explore other facets of gay existence? Or should he instead employ an apocalyptic rhetoric with the aim of assaulting the reader's emotions and opening his eyes to the horror of the crisis?[40]

Whichever approach the writer decides to employ, the fiction he produces frequently introduces reference to uncanny perceptions and motifs, with secrets and their disclosure assuming prominence. The association of AIDS with secrets and silence, and the determination of activists to challenge it, is registered in the slogan 'SILENCE = DEATH' on the poster that the New York organization ACT UP used in its 'fight-back' campaign protesting at the Reagan government's failure to confront the crisis. In equating silence with death, ACT UP aimed to expose the government's refusal to permit the advertising of strategies of safe sex and allocate adequate funds for drug-testing and medical research. Activists demanded an end to 'the murderous regime of silence and disinformation';[41] they insisted that both the pandemic's existence and the authorities' negligence should be publicized and brought to light.

Silence and breaking it also inform AIDS narratives on a personal plane, in the protagonist's disclosure of his HIV status to lovers, friends and family. The topic of death that haunts this fiction also has connotations of secrecy. According to Derrida, '*death* is always the name of a secret'. He argues that the language we employ in referring to it is 'nothing but the long history of a secret society, neither public nor private but on the border between the two'.[42]

Another topic with uncanny connotations that fiction focusing on AIDS inscribes is uncertainties and instabilities relating to personal identity and embodiment, reflected in the individual's 'doubt as to which his self is', a topic that Freud discusses in 'The uncanny'.[43] This is relevant to the HIV-positive individual who is conscious of the changes that are occurring in his body, as well as, very probably, in his personal and professional life. Society's propensity to treat him as abject, combined with the gay community's promotion of a counter-discourse contesting this, also has uncanny significance. Edelman exposes the slippage that took place in the 1980s from the recognition of AIDS as contagious to the 'pervasive homophobic misconception of gay sexuality as contagious – as something one can catch through contact with, for instance, a teacher who is lesbian or gay'.[44] This served to revive the pre-Stonewall view of homosexuality as a disease, encouraging its pathologization.

Colm Tóibín's *The Blackwater Lightship* and Sarah Schulman's *People in Trouble*, the two AIDS narratives selected for analysis here, treat the motifs described above very differently. Tóibín, focusing on the personal dimension of the pandemic, explores, in an austerely spare style that suits his bleak subject matter, the impact that it has on a family living in rural Ireland. Schulman in contrast locates *People in Trouble* in 1980s New York and describes the crisis partly from a lesbian point of view. Employing a wider canvas than Tóibín, she situates her three key characters' troubled relationships in the equally troubled context of the New York queer subculture as it strives to contest the homophobia and negligence evinced by the City authorities.

Secrets and their disclosure inform the narrative structure of Tóibín's *The Blackwater Lightship* as well as its content. The novel opens on an enigmatic note with Helen, the sister of the protagonist Declan – who, as she is shortly to discover, is terminally ill with AIDS – witnessing her young son Magnus experiencing a nightmare. Roused from sleep by the sound of his whimpering, she finds him 'crying

out hoarsely and fending off some unknown terror with his arms'.[45]
His inarticulate cries indicate his regression to the pre-linguistic
domain of the semiotic, reflecting the intrusion of the uncanny into
the domestic sphere of the home and family life, rendering it unfamiliar and strange. They look forward to the frightening encounter
with sickness and death that awaits Helen, her mother Lily and her
grandmother Doreen when they discover to their horror that Declan
is terminally ill.

The opening four chapters of the novel trace Declan's step-by-
step disclosure of the secret of his illness and, by implication, his
homosexuality, to his family. He has postponed revealing both until
now, in what turn out to be the final weeks of his life, for fear of hostile
reception to the news. The only relative to whom he has risked coming
out is his sister Helen, and she has no idea that he is HIV-positive.

Homosexuality, the reader discovers, signifies to the older members
of Declan's family the ultimate taboo and they regard it, and everything relating to it, as unspeakable. His mother Lily refuses to utter
the words 'homosexual' and 'gay' but insists on referring to the gay
community as 'them' and addressing Declan's friend Paul obliquely
as 'one of you' (p. 142). The euphemisms and circumlocutions in
which she engages furnish a source of black humour in the narrative,
with Paul interjecting as a mocking refrain, 'She means homosexuals'
and, a moment later, 'I think she means homosexuals again' (p. 142).
His defiant repetition of the word gives it a performative dimension,
flaunting it in Lily's face. Employing the strategy of resignification
that Butler recommends as a tactic to challenge the abject treatment
of the homosexual, Paul subversively redeploys the word that she
refuses to speak.[46] He himself, we learn, has experienced similar
prejudice. Describing his parents' response to the discovery of his
sexuality, he sardonically remarks that the expression of horror on
his mother's face indicated that she would have preferred to hear
that he had joined the IRA. The latter, though illegal and dangerous,
represents a tangible threat and is regarded as an organization comprising 'real' men, whereas homosexuality, in contrast, signifies an
unknown horror and has connotations of effeminacy.

Declan's disclosure of his terminal illness and sexuality to his family
is represented, as a result of the two topics being considered unspeakable, as tortuously indirect. It takes the form of a chain-like

process in which one individual uneasily passes on the information to another, in the manner of M. R. James's uncanny tale 'Casting the Runes'. This has the effect of impeding the flow of the narrative and, as is the case in nineteenth-century Gothic novels such as Charles Maturin's *Melmoth the Wanderer* that treat topics encoded as taboo, the reader recognizes 'the difficulty the story has in getting itself told'.[47]

Helen is the first of the three women to receive the news of Declan's illness. His friend Paul, acting as intermediary, arrives unannounced at the school where she teaches and conveys it to her. With his words plunging her from the familiar, everyday world into the scarily unfamiliar, she agrees to accompany him to the hospital in Dublin where Declan currently resides. Declan's summoning her to his bedside reflects more than just brotherly love. Lacking the courage to inform his mother Lily directly of his illness and sexuality, he asks Helen to disclose the news to her; and though her own relationship with Lily is emotionally problematic, she feels unable to refuse his request. While dreading the encounter with Lily, she also resents the fact that Declan has confided his illness to his gay friends Paul and Larry and accepted help from them while he has left her, who had acted as his protector when he was a child, out in the cold. She thinks despondently, 'Declan had replaced his family with his friends. She wished he had thought of her as a friend' (p. 34). This introduces a topic that recurs frequently in AIDS narratives, the tensions and jealousies that erupt between the AIDS patient's biological relatives and the members of his queer family.

In order to postpone the encounter with Lily, Helen first visits Doreen in her house in the remote coastal village of Cush. Doreen, now in her eighties, is portrayed as a strong, feisty woman with independent views. Helen's young son regards her, in fact, as a witch. Having previously surmised that Declan might be in some kind of 'trouble', Doreen responds relatively calmly to the news of his sexuality and illness. His mother Lily, on the contrary, reacts indignantly. Though distressed to discover that her son is gay and terminally ill, she resents the fact that he has not informed her directly of these facts. She lacks the self-awareness to perceive that it is her failure of understanding that has prevented him. With their disclosure to Lily, the secrets of Declan's sickness and sexuality have completed their roundabout journey and reached their goal. It concludes appropriately in an encounter with the figure of the mother whose body, Freud observes, represents the original familiar/unfamiliar 'home of all human beings'.[48]

The major part of the narrative takes place in Doreen's house at Cush where Declan, on being temporally discharged from hospital, expresses the wish to stay. The visit represents for both him and Helen an act of uncanny repetition since they had previously lived there as children when their father was terminally ill. The remote coastal location of the house, combined with the unhappy childhood memories it evokes, links it to the concept of the homely/unhomely house, its ostensible warmth undermined by discord and emotional tensions. Declan admits that the location 'gives him the creeps', adding wryly that, in his present predicament, 'I need these creeps' (p. 115).

Kristeva describes the subject's encounter with the abject and the feeling of the uncanny that it generates as serving to 'disturb identity, system and order'[49] and, as Tóibín illustrates, Declan's illness disturbs and destabilizes his family's and his friends' emotional life as well as their external routine. Relations between his two familial groups, his biological relatives and his gay friends, predictably erupt in conflict. Lily, resenting the fact that Paul knows more about her son's medication than she does, tries to assert what she sees as her privileged role as his mother and orders him on one occasion to leave the house. He defiantly refuses, insisting that he takes his instructions from Declan, not from her. Gradually, however, the two groups strike up an uneasy truce. Unlike Lily who treats Paul and Larry with deliberate rudeness, Doreen warms to the two gay men. She treats them with a mixture of authority and banter, referring to them sarcastically as Declan's 'evil friends' (p. 225) and countering Paul's raillery and playful quips by ridiculing him as 'a young pup' (p. 226). The two groups, as Tóibín perceptively illustrates, though differing in gender and sexuality nonetheless share common experiences. Like the house where they reside, positioned precariously on the edge of the cliff, both live on the social margins. The gay men have encountered sexual prejudice while the women are victims of gender discrimination and ageism. Confronted by Declan's imminent death and the thoughts of their own mortality that it evokes, they find their reserve crumbling and start divulging their personal secrets and anxieties. As a result, the narrative is temporarily transformed into a network of personal anecdotes and life stories. Paul and Larry describe the difficulties they encountered in coming out to their families, while Doreen reminisces about her husband's terminal illness and ponders Irish superstitions relating to death.

Helen too is haunted by 'memories and echoes' (p. 260) from the past. Strolling on the beach with Larry, she acknowledges the anger she feels towards her mother Lily for having left her and Declan as children with Doreen when their father was terminally ill, as well as for selling the family home on his death. She experiences a sudden onrush of *déréliction*, a deep sense of maternal loss that, as Irigaray describes, leaves the female subject feeling emotionally abandoned. Her resentment towards her mother is illuminated by Irigaray's analysis of the way phallocentric culture separates mother and daughter, causing them to live 'never in touch with each other, lost in the air, like ghosts'.[50] Helen also reveals her anger towards Doreen for having attempted to coerce her into returning to rural Wexford to teach in a convent school after she completed her studies in Dublin. Disclosing the repressed feelings of hostility towards the two women that her distress at Declan's proximity to death has brought to the surface, she harshly admits that they represent 'parts of myself that I have buried, that is who they are for me, both of them, and that is why I still want them away from me' (p. 188).

Doreen's homely/unhomely house, ostensibly welcoming but disturbed by Helen's feelings of resentment at her mother and grandmother as well as by Lily's distress at her son Declan's homosexuality and terminal illness, unites the topos of the maternal with the imminence of death. The house symbolically signifies, in this respect, both womb and tomb. Pamela Thurschwell, elucidating Freud's linking of the two topics in 'The uncanny', observes that 'home is the womb'. She explains that the womb, as 'the earliest home of all of us, may logically seem like a terrifyingly deathlike place, which predates our existence'.[51]

Another house that, preserved in Helen's memory, assumes significance in the novel is the family home where she lived as a child and that Lily chose to sell. Helen pictures 'the house empty and ghostly, like a ship under water, as though it had been left as it was on the last day she saw it' (p. 118). While recognizing the irrationality of the hope, 'she believed that some day she would some day go back there, that it would be her refuge, and that her mother, despite everything, would be there for her and take her in and shelter her and protect her' (pp. 119–20). Declan too looks to Lily for protection. On experiencing a sudden attack of pain, he instinctively calls, 'Mammy, mammy, help me, mammy' (p. 258). His cry to his mother for help, as well as echoing Helen's fantasy image of her childhood home as a maternal refuge, uncannily repeats the appeal voiced by her son Magnus on experiencing a nightmare in the opening chapter.

As indicated by Helen's comparison of her lost childhood home to 'a ship under water', Tóibín underpins the novel's focus on mutability and death with reference to the sea, exemplified both by the ocean itself, representing the random destruction of nature, and the eponymous Blackwater lightship. Although the latter no longer exists, Lily remembers it from her youth and speaks of it nostalgically. Helen, while walking on the beach, contemplates the sea, envisaging it metaphorically as 'untouchable and monumental' (p. 260) and contrasting it with the futility and ephemerality of human concerns.

It is, however, the changes occurring in Declan's physical condition as he approaches death that furnish the key image of mutability and mortality in the novel. Emmanuel S. Nelson laments the fact that the AIDS pandemic 'has made the body of the gay male an object of massive public curiosity' by representing it 'as a site of mysterious and fatal infections'. He sees it as the task of the gay writer to rescue the male gay body 'from this unprecedented ongoing textual abuse'.[52] Tóibín, acting on his recommendation, sensitively limits his portrayal of Declan's body to the changes it undergoes that indicate his declining health, such as the loss of sight in one eye. This also has symbolic import since, in signifying castration, it signals the end of his sex life.

Unlike Tóibín who writes deliberately austerely, Schulman employs a more varied style, interspersing realist description with passages of figurative writing. The queering of the myth of the apocalypse, with which she opens *People in Trouble*, preserves the emphasis on death and social disintegration that it traditionally inscribes while – as is usual with present-day secular versions of the motif – omitting reference to the positive theme of a new beginning.[53] She writes rhetorically: 'It was the beginning of the end of the world, but not everyone noticed right away. Some people were dying. Some people were busy. Some people were cleaning their houses, while the war movie played on television.'[54] In representing the AIDS pandemic as signifying a secret that, though known to the gay subculture, is perceived only gradually by heterosexuals, she signals the focus on secrets, both personal and social, and their disclosure that pervades the novel as a whole.

Schulman also structures her narrative very differently from Tóibín. Whereas Tóibín's narrative is centrifugal in design, portraying Declan, his relatives and friends leaving the locations where they live and work to meet in the remote coastal village of Cush, Schulman's is centripetal. It moves, in a manner resembling the feminist fiction of the 1970s and 1980s such as Marilyn French's *The Women's Room* (1977) and Marge Piercy's *Braided Lives* (1982), from a focus on sexual politics exemplified by personal relationships in the private sphere of the home to the role they play in public life. Bisexual Kate, lesbian Molly with whom she is having an affair, and Kate's heterosexual husband Peter are portrayed temporarily putting their personal lives on hold and leaving their apartments to observe or participate in the life of the gay community in the public world of streets, bars and – reflecting the focus on sickness and death – hospitals, churches and cemeteries. The narrative movement outwards into the social world agrees with Alan Sinfield's observation, voiced in relation to the AIDS quilt, that 'the significance of AIDS art *is collective*'.[55]

The two storylines, personal and sociopolitical, that Schulman constructs are closely interlinked, with the emotional tensions and conflicts erupting between Molly, Kate and Peter reflecting in microcosm the feelings of unease and hostility that divide gay and heteronormative communities in general. Heterosexual individuals and groups are described responding ambivalently, with mixed feelings of fascination and fear toward their lesbian and male gay counterparts, while the latter strive with varying degrees of success to resist being patronized as victims or typecast as abject outcasts.

Secrets feature prominently in Schulman's representation of the triangular relationship between Kate, her husband Peter and her lover Molly. Kate assumes that her love affair with Molly is a secret, but discovers it to be an open one when she unexpectedly learns that Peter knows of its existence. The fact that his wife is having an affair with a woman does not initially worry him. As Schulman ironically remarks, commenting on the male tendency to trivialize and devalue female attachments, 'Since it was with a woman ... he'd expected Kate to break it off' (p. 9). Kate, though she has initiated the relationship with and become increasingly sexually infatuated with Molly, at first shares Peter's dismissive view. She is as astonished as he is at the importance that, as the weeks pass, it starts to assume in both their lives. She thinks naively, 'It just snuck up on both of them' and, revealing her prejudices, 'If it had been a man it never would have gotten this far' (p. 70).

Kate's ignorance of lesbianism takes other forms too. She is surprised to discover, on accompanying Molly to a lesbian club, that there are other married women there besides herself. She is also startled to perceive the transformation that the relationship with Molly is effecting on her own subjectivity and the repressed aspects of her psyche that it liberates. As she dramatically tells Peter, 'You think that the trouble we're having is because of her, but the truth is that it is about me. Me. I'm changing!' (p. 153). Kate is an artist, and the new sense of independence and awareness of sociopolitical issues that she learns from Molly, who devotes much of her time to participating in AIDS demonstrations and supporting male gay friends who are sick, influences her work. She angrily dismisses her past paintings as too far removed from the 'sex and violence' (p. 16) of city life. She eventually gives up painting altogether and, to the alarm of her agent who questions its financial viability, creates a complex installation that she reflexively entitles 'People in Trouble'. Its title furnishes a gloss on the themes that the novel treats, alerting the reader to the cultural dimension of the AIDS crisis.

Homosexuality also represents something of a secret to Peter. As is typical of the individual's encounter with the abject, it simultaneously repels and fascinates him. On accidentally meeting Molly in the street, he scrutinizes her critically and, with a sense of relief, dismisses her as ugly and unfeminine: 'She has a moustache, he thought. *And she's fat. Not fat exactly but definitely out of shape*' (p. 107). Typecasting her on account of her lesbianism as a manipulative, strident man-hater, he thinks: 'This one swaggered. He'd have known she was gay immediately. As soon as there was any real difference of opinion she'd be a real bitch, not conceding anything to a man, just for the principle' (p. 107). The unexpected meeting with her none-theless arouses him sexually. He enters a local cinema and, having a purchased a ticket for the film, enters the men's toilet. Schulman describes how 'Once inside, he stood in the stall sweating, holding his balls and rocking back and forth' (p. 107).

Peter's response to the gay male community in the grip of the AIDS pandemic reflects a similar mingling of fascination and disquiet. While admiring men who identify as gay both for their creative abilities and what he terms their 'trick' (p. 59) of concealing their sexuality and rendering it invisible, he himself, ironically, is deceived by it. Sitting in a cafe watching a group of people enter a church across the street, he fails to recognize that the spectacle that he is witnessing is a funeral service for the victim of AIDS, a common event in 1980s New York. Impelled by curiosity, he enters the church. Once inside, however, he experiences a sense of suffocation and, overcome by the smell of incense, the proximity of the corpse and his discomfort at being an outsider, feels that he is about to faint. He recovers his equilibrium only when he is outside.

Schulman recasts from a sociopolitical viewpoint the motif of secrets and their disclosure that informs the narrative centring on Kate, Molly and Peter in the storyline of the AIDS pandemic that she interweaves with it. In addition to exposing the climate of hypocrisy and secrecy surrounding the pandemic, she describes the demon-strations that 'Justice', a fictional version of the actual New York ACT UP, organizes to expose and challenge it. Molly's friend Scott, in a speech echoing the slogan 'SILENCE = DEATH' on the ACT UP poster, urges the gay community to encourage pharmacists in the city to stock books with information about safe-sex practices since the New York authorities, regarding the topic as inappropriate, discourage this. Meanwhile his co-worker Jeffrey criticizes a number of New Yorkers who are HIV-positive for promoting a climate of silence and denial by refusing to acknowledge their homosexuality. Ironically proposing that 'We should change the name of this country to the United States of Denial' (p. 75), he insists that 'This epidemic will never be taken care of properly until people can be honest about sex' (p. 75).

Schulman also depicts death itself as signifying a secret since many New Yorkers appear unaware of its presence in the city. As Molly, highlighting how easy it is for the healthy to be blind to the suffering of the sick, observes, 'New York is a death camp for thousands of people, but they don't have to be contained for us to avoid them. The same streets that I have fun on are someone else's hell' (p. 113). The tension and divisions between the gay and heterosexual communities are exemplified by the description of the funeral of one of Molly's friends who has died of AIDS. The biological family of the deceased and his gay friends cluster together in separate groups and avoid conversing.

Where Tóibín challenges the sensationalization of the AIDS-infected body by avoiding describing it in any detail, Schulman adopts a different strategy. Interweaving realist writing with metaphorical, she portrays the activist Scott, now terminally ill, 'propped up in bed with his hair brushed out loose round his shoulders'. She strikingly adds, 'He looked like the Madonna, even though his skin was coming apart' (p. 145). By incongruously juxtaposing the realist description of Scott's painfully fractured skin with the simile of the Virgin Mary, she foregrounds the contradictions of the physically grotesque and patient suffering that he epitomizes. She concludes her portrayal of him with a disturbingly physical recasting of the uncanny motif of doubling: Molly admits that she finds it 'hard to believe that this raw bleeding skin was Scott and not just something laid on top of him' (p. 145).

The emphasis on death and social disintegration that dominates the novel's concluding chapters recapitulates the apocalyptic mood of the opening pages. Replying to Molly's complaints about the gay community's apathetic response to the pandemic, Scott's partner James, clarifying the novel's title, despondently observes that 'Suffering can be stopped. But it can never be avenged, so survivors watch television. Some deaths are shocking, some invisible. We are a people in trouble, we do not act' (p. 228).

History/mystery

Approaches to queer history have altered significantly since the 1970s, the period when, influenced by the advent of the gay liberation and lesbian feminist movements, research and publications in the field began to multiply. Influenced by theorists such as Michel Foucault, Jeffrey Weeks and Martha Vicinus, researchers no longer focus in essentialist terms on 'changing attitudes to an unchanging "gay people"'.[56] They represent different sexualities and lifestyles as socially and historically constructed, influenced by a variety of economic and political factors. Recognizing that lesbian and gay identities as we are familiar with them today are relatively recent in origin, they examine the terms 'tom', 'sapphic', 'sodomite' and 'invert' that people living in earlier periods employed, investigating their sexual and social nuances. They acknowledge that, as Laura Gowing observes, 'the terms we [now] use to define ourselves have no precise historical equivalents: every word used in relation to same sex acts in the past has its own history'.[57]

The field of queer historical research bristles with controversy, with 'social constructionists' and 'essentialists' debating the validity of applying the term 'homosexual' to people living in earlier centuries. This prompts Caroline Gonda and Chris Mounsey, criticizing the extreme form of social constructionism that some theorists advocate, humorously to observe that 'where once it was impossible to write about homosexuality in history because theirs was "the love that dare not speak its name" and about which respectable people did not speak, to write about homosexuals in history has again become problematic'.[58]

Other changes in approach to queer history are also in evidence. Although a Foucauldian emphasis on discontinuity still tends to dominate research, a move is now afoot to investigate the connections, as well as the differences, between past and present eras, with Valerie Traub describing how 'resemblances shimmer unsteadily and unevenly, moving closer or receding, depending on the axes of definition that inform one's perspective or capture one's attention'.[59] Researchers also investigate the differences between lesbian and male gay homosexual history. Since literacy and access to publishing have generally been the prerogative of upper-class men, there is a dearth of information about lesbian lifestyles and sexual and cultural practices, as well as those of the working classes.

These developments have understandably influenced the writing of queer historical fiction, with many of the novels published since the 1980s displaying a new intellectual rigour. Writers treat the formation of their characters' sexualities in the sociopolitical and economic context in which they lived and, instead of representing history as a seamless web that unfolds smoothly through time, tease out the contradictions and incoherences that the discourses informing it display. Instead of seeking to offer the reader positive role models and 'celebrate moments of courage and pleasure', as was the often the aim of writers working in the 1960s and 1970s, they investigate 'the difficulties of the queer past'[60] and explore the different forms that prejudice can take. Lesbian and male gay fiction though, like the coming out novel, sometimes ignored or disparaged by academic critics on account of its populist appeal, has nonetheless established a rich cultural legacy. It holds obvious attractions for lesbian and male gay writers and readers, helping to remedy their sense of exclusion from mainstream historical records and furnishing an insight into the lifestyles and sexual practices of the past.

A pertinent context for discussing Sarah Waters's *The Night Watch* and David Leavitt's *While England Sleeps*, the two examples of historical fiction reviewed here, is Homi K. Bhabha's discussion of postcolonial historical narrative in the context of the Freudian *unheimlich*, with its focus on 'the reinscriptions of the unhomely moment'[61] and the interplay between the familiar and unfamiliar that informs it. Bhabha recommends the writer of historical fiction to employ a form of writing that fragments and destabilizes narrative continuity by inter-relating the present with the past and juxtaposing private events with public ones. This, he argues, serves to connect 'the traumatic ambivalences of a personal, psychic history to the wider disjunctions of political existence' (p. 15), foregrounding the interaction between private and public spheres. He argues that this 'does not merely recall the past' representing it as 'an aesthetic precedent' frozen in time but renews it, 'refiguring it as a contingent "in-between" space that innovates and interrupts the performance of the present' (p. 10).

Waters and Leavitt both locate their novels in the London of the first half of the twentieth century. Waters focuses on the 1940s, the period of the Second World War and its aftermath, while Leavitt treats the earlier period of the 1930s. By disrupting the chronological order of events, they foreground both the connections and dis-continuities between past and present, illustrating the instabilities and contradictions they display. Investigating the difficulties that their characters experience in forming and maintaining same-sex relationships in the shifting sociopolitical climate of the period, one rendered turbulent by war, they illustrate how the impingement of sociopolitical forces on the private world of the home impacts on their characters' lives, involving them in deceit and uneasy silences.

Unlike Hensher and Tóibín who explore the destabilizing effect that the presence of a homosexual individual has on the heteronormative family, Waters and Leavitt investigate the way in which lesbian or male homosexual relationships and domestic life are disrupted by homophobic influences from the public world outside. Waters explores the stresses that the post-war pathologizing of lesbianism imposed on female same-sex partnerships, utilizing imagery of invisibility and darkness to evoke the closeted lives that her characters feel forced to lead. Leavitt explores the difficulties that his upperclass male narrator experiences in coming to terms with his homosexuality in the context of 1930s conventions of class and masculinity and the homophobia engulfing Europe in the wake of fascism. He also humorously describes the narrator's unconvincing attempts to pass as heterosexual. In treating these topics, the two writers demonstrate how, to cite Bhabha: 'The borders between home and the world become confused; and, uncannily, the private and public become part of each other' (p. 13).

Discontinuity and contradiction are strongly in evidence in Waters's *The Night Watch*. By chronologically inverting her characters' narratives and commencing the novel in 1947 and concluding it in 1941, she enables the reader, by travelling back in time, to perceive the shifts in the sociopolitical climate that contribute to the formation of their subjectivities and lives. This strategy enables her to demonstrate how, to cite Bhabha, 'The "past-present" becomes part of the necessity, not the nostalgia, of living' (p. 10). By introducing a range of different sexualities and relationships, including lesbian, homoerotic and heterosexual, and describing the disparate forms of oppression they encounter, she also moves towards deconstructing the binary opposition homosexual/heterosexual. This, as well as agreeing with queer perspectives, develops, as we shall see, a focus on the connections existing between women from different classes and with different sexualities.

As well as reworking Rich's concept of 'lesbian continuum', it recalls the feminist fiction produced by writers such as Marge Piercy and Marilyn French in the 1970s and 1980s, with its emphasis on female commonality and sisterhood. It also illustrates the connections between lesbian feminist and queer discourses, endorsing Linda Garber's argument that 'lesbian feminism provides an intertext for queer theory'.[62]

Historians generally treat the period 1941–7, in which Waters sets *The Night Watch*, as exemplifying an era of wartime 'deprivation' followed by one of post-war 'recovery'. Waters however problematizes this model, particularly with reference to her lesbian characters Kay and Helen. The upper-class Kay spends the war years working in an ambulance unit in central London assisting victims of the bombing raids. Like her work-mate Mickey, who also identifies as lesbian, she is treated as a valued member of society and, in the camaraderie that the war engenders, enjoys a positive identity and role. The two women also enjoy the privilege, one that they recognize with hindsight was transitory, of doing a 'man's job' and dressing as they choose. As ambulance workers they have first-hand experience of the ravages the bombing raids inflict on the metropolis. Driving through the derelict streets at night in a battered old vehicle, Kay remarks on the 'odd sort of haunted feel'[63] that pervades the city: 'When the guns stopped, the atmosphere could be even weirder . . . The place was uncanny: quieter, in its way, than the countryside would have been' (p. 180). By 1947, however, with peace declared and a climate of so-called 'normality' restored, attitudes to women's role in society have drastically changed. With her partner having left her for another woman and the ambulance unit in which she previously worked disbanded, Kay feels herself reduced, to cite the term Castle employs to represent the lesbian's role in hetero-patriarchal culture, to a 'non-person . . . or a sinister bugaboo'.[64] Now it is her, not the cityscape, that Waters portrays in spectral imagery. She describes how, living alone in rented accommodation, Kay 'haunted the attic floor like a ghost or a lunatic . . . She'd sit still for hours at a time – stiller than a shadow, because she'd watch the shadows creeping across the rug. And then it seemed to her she might really be a ghost' (p. 4). These spectral allusions, as well as recalling Castle's account of the way the lesbian is culturally '"ghosted" or made to seem invisible' (p. 4) by heteronormative culture and the associations with the title of Gilbert and Gubar's study *The Madwoman in the Attic*, evoke her relegation, as Butler writes, to 'a domain of unthinkability and unnameability'[65] and its abject effect.

However, whereas Kay's lack of role and social recognition reduce her to a position of invisibility, her resistance to post-war dress codes makes her suffer paradoxically from an excess of *visibility* that marks her as marginal and eccentric. Referring to her characters' literary interests, as she frequently does in her fiction, Waters portrays Kay, on visiting Mickey at the garage where she works, glancing at the novel she is reading. It is H. G. Wells's *The Invisible Man* (1897). Kay picks it up, and her eye falls on the following passage:

> 'But you begin to realise now', said the Invisible Man, 'the full dis-advantage of my condition. I had no shelter – no covering – to get clothing was to forgo all my advantage, to make of myself a strange and terrible thing. I was fasting; for to eat, to fill myself with un-assimilated matter, would be to become grossly visible again.' (p. 96)

In this intertextual reference Waters utilizes Wells's account of the difficulties experienced by his protagonist, a scientist who invents a formula to render people invisible and unwisely tests it on himself, to illustrate the contradictions in terms of image and dress in which lesbians were caught in the post-war period. If, like Kay, they continued to dress in a butch manner, they were regarded as socially unacceptable. Like Wells's Invisible Man who, muffled up in his bandages, is treated by onlookers as 'a strange and terrible thing' and jeered at by children as a monstrosity, Kay strikes people as 'grossly visible' and, despite her upper-class accent, meets with derision. On visiting the local bakery, she is greeted by the assistant with the mocking question, 'Don't you know the war's over?' (p. 94). It is provoked, she recognizes, by her trousers and masculine haircut. As Mickey admits, the reason she herself works in a garage is that it is one of the few places where she can dress in a butch style without arousing ridicule.

Helen, Kay's former partner, also experiences problems relating to the visibility/invisibility dilemma, though of a different kind. She is now in a relationship with Julia Standing, a writer of detective fiction whose novels are beginning to attract public acclaim. Julia's status as a successful writer, however, instead of winning her the freedom to dress and behave as she likes, does the reverse. As Helen despondently remarks, 'Now that Julia's books were doing so well, they had to be more careful than ever' (p. 48). The two women live together, and the effort they make to conceal their relationship from the prying eyes and ears of neighbours inhibits their lives. They cannot employ a 'char' to clean since if they did the secret that they share a bed would come to light. Their pleasurable ritual of taking a bath together on Saturday mornings is also spoilt by the fact that they have to keep their voices down in case the neighbours overhear them talking. And, in striving to conceal their sexuality to protect themselves from the lesbian stigma, they ironically lay themselves open to a different form of prejudice. Helen overhears the neighbours, discussing the fact that they are unmarried, insultingly describe them as 'eunuchs' (p. 46).

Helen and Julia are associated throughout the novel with the un-canny motifs of invisibility and secrets. Walking through London at night during the bombing raids shortly after their initial meeting, they hear an explosion in the distance and take shelter behind a wall. 'Now we're invisible', Julia whispers (p. 349). The remark acts as a prelude to their first kiss, their physical invisibility symbolically representing their social invisibility as lesbian lovers.

Unlike Kay who refuses to change her dress style to suit the con-ventions of the post-war era, Helen and Julia make an effort to conform to feminine dress codes. They conceal their lesbian partnership by performing the feminine masquerade described by Irigaray as 'what women do in order to participate in man's desire, but at the expense of renouncing their own'.[66] In fact Helen, who is insecure and prone to jealousy, thinks that Julia performs it a little too well. Contrasting the publicity photos of her in a magazine with her everyday appear-ance when lounging around the flat, she thinks bitterly that they 'made her look glamorous – but not glamorous in the way she really, effortlessly was . . . They made her look *marriageable*' (p. 137). The photos portray Julia in a typically artificial pose of heterosexual femin-inity, resembling the image that the automaton Olympia in Hoffmann's novel employs to attract suitors.

Two other characters hiding transgressive secrets whom Waters portrays are Duncan and his sister Viv. Helen first encounters Duncan after the war while working with Viv in a 'lonely hearts' bureau. Though aware that 'he had some queerness or scandal attached to him' (p. 17), she deliberately refrains from enquiring further for, as Waters writes, employing the 'dark' imagery that pervades the novel, she had 'one or two things in her own life that she preferred to keep in darkness' (p. 18). Duncan's earlier life, as Waters reveals by the strategy of tunnelling back into his past that she employs, reveals connections with blood and the corpse that link him with the uncanny and the Kristevan abject. In his teens, in protest at the carnage of the war, he formed a suicide pact with his friend Alec in order to avoid military conscription. However, whereas Alec abides by the pact, cutting his throat with a razor, Duncan does not die. Instead, he finds himself imprisoned for the duration of the war in Wormwood Scrubs. On telling his story to Fraser, the conscientious objector with whom he shares a cell, he is overcome by an onrush of memories and experiences a brief 'violent glimpse of the scarlet kitchen in his father's house' (p. 405) where Alec had killed himself.

Another topic, besides death and the corpse, that links Duncan to the uncanny is his uncertainty about his sexual orientation. Though he angrily rejects the identification 'homosexual' that his fellow prisoners project on him and expresses disgust at the camp behaviour of the effeminate homosexuals, he finds the proximity of Fraser's body lying in the bunk above him, as Waters describes, simultaneously disturbing and strangely alluring:

> Duncan opened his eyes and gazed into the perfect, velvety blackness of the cell. There was a depthlessness to it that was so queer and unnerving, he put up his hand. He wanted to remind himself of the distance between his and Fraser's bunk: he'd begun to feel as though Fraser was nearer than he ought to have been; and he was very aware of his own body as a sort of duplication or echo of the one above . . . (p. 285)

Waters's reference to 'the perfect darkness' of the cell evokes the subliminal nature of Duncan's attraction to Fraser and its taboo aspect. Duncan's perception of his body eerily doubling with Fraser's equivocally registers both his sense of identification with him and his secret feelings of erotic attraction.

In a subsequent episode, when the noise from the falling bombs is particularly loud and oppressive, Duncan manages to overcome his feelings of anxiety about male physical contact and allows Fraser, who admits to finding 'this bloody war' (p. 408) scary, temporarily to share his bunk. In the climate of fear that the bombing raid generates, he instinctively puts his arm round him, and Waters movingly describes how the two men 'settled back into an embrace . . . as if they weren't two boys, in a prison, in a city being blown and shot to bits; as if it were the most natural thing in the world' (p. 411). Her description of their embrace interrogates the binary division between homosexual and heterosexual to queer effect.

Waters's portrayal of Viv likewise problematizes this division. Instead of foregrounding the differences between the heterosexual Viv and the lesbian Helen and Kay, she focuses on the experiences that the three women share and the interaction their lives display. The secret that Viv attempts to conceal is, like Helen and Kay's lesbian partnership, sexual in nature and puts her on the social margins. In a period when extramarital sex is regarded as scandalous she is surreptitiously engaging in an affair with a married man. Just as Helen avoids divulging to Viv her 'perverse' relationship with Kay, so Viv refuses to disclose her adulterous affair with the male Reggie. As Foucault observes, emphasizing the sexual–political significance of secrets and silences as well as their performative aspect: 'Silence itself – the things one declines to say, or is forbidden to name, the discretion that is required between speakers – is less the absolute limit of discourse than an element that functions along the things said.'[67]

Viv's feelings of excitement at the illicit nature of the relationship with Reggie turn to panic when she discovers that she is pregnant. She obtains a termination from a back-street abortionist but, on returning home, finds herself bleeding profusely and is forced to summon an ambulance. It is Kay who, in her role as ambulance worker, arrives to take her to the hospital. Waters utilizes the encounter between the two women to illustrate female solidarity and support. When Viv inadvertently reveals that she has deliberately terminated her pregnancy, Kay, instead of reporting it to the nurse and prompting her to inform the police, tells her that Viv has suffered a miscarriage. Waters further describes how Kay 'put her own hands together' and 'worked them as if wringing them for a second, then produced a little circle of gold. She did it so swiftly and so subtly, it was like magic' (p. 388). She slips the ring on Viv's finger, thus deceiving the hospital staff into assuming her to be married. This uncanny ruse transforms the ring, traditionally a symbol of heterosexual marriage, into a token of feminist sisterhood.

Leavitt's *While England Sleeps*, though set in the 1930s, resembles Waters's *The Night Watch* both in its London location and its exploration of the way in which conflicting sociopolitical discourses and the insecurities they generate impinge on the characters' personal lives and relationships. In consequence, as Bhabha writes, 'The public and private become part of each other' (p. 13), with the effect of rendering the queer subject's personal and domestic life tense and *unheimlich*.

In contrast to Waters, however, Leavitt employs quirky, satiric humour as an instrument of sociopolitical comment, portraying his upper-class narrator Brian Botsford as a naive and, on occasion, comic figure. The strategy of interleaving past and present that Leavitt employs to illustrate the problems that unforeseen changes in the sociopolitical climate can cause the homosexual commences in the opening chapter, with Brian cast in the role of hapless fall guy. Leavitt locates the chapter not in the London of the 1930s, in which he sets the major part of the novel, but twenty years later in 1950s Hollywood. As Brian explains to the reader, the reason he has the leisure to write the memoir that the novel represents is that an ugly shift in American politics has unexpectedly brought to an abrupt end to his successful career as a scriptwriter of screwball comedies. Having moved from London to Hollywood ten years earlier to escape arrest for cottaging, he once again finds himself in trouble with the authorities since, on account of the communist sympathies he professed in his youth, his name features on the McCarthy blacklist. His memoir, he explains, will tell 'the story of why I briefly had Communist leanings'.[68] He adds, with the aim of whetting the reader's appetite and signalling the novel's focus on sex and romance: 'The answer – in brief – was love' (p. 3).

Brian's youthful adventures in 1930s London, to which Leavitt now retrospectively turns, develop the portrayal of the homosexual as the victim of conventions and political cross-currents beyond his control. Although Brian is strongly attracted to men and has had a number affairs with fellow students while studying at Cambridge, his upper-class background and the pressure exerted on him by his Aunt Constance, a writer of romantic fiction on whose cheques he depends for support, dictate that sooner or later he should marry. Expressing astonishment at the fact that though aged twenty-three he is still single, Aunt Constance indicates that she sees it as her mission in life to find him an attractive young bride. Brian too, ironically considering his obvious enjoyment of sex with men, regards marriage as his destiny. As he explains with hindsight:

> Although I'd gone to bed with probably three dozen boys, all of them either French or English, never with a woman, nonetheless – and incredible though it may seem – I still assumed that a day would come when I would fall in love with some lovely intelligent girl, whom I would marry and who would bear me children . . . I pretended that my homosexuality was a function of my youth, that when I 'grew up' it would fall away, like baby teeth, to be replaced by something more mature and permanent. (p. 92)

However, it is the imperative of sexual desire, not Aunt Constance's advice, that dictates Brian's behaviour in the early chapters of the novel. Ignoring financial considerations and social taboos, he embarks on a whirlwind love affair with Edward, a nineteen-year-old youth from a working-class family and a committed communist. He first encounters Edward at an 'Aid to Spain' meeting at which the Republican representative John Northrop vigorously addresses the audience. It is one of many similar political meetings that, as Brian wryly observes, took place in the 1930s 'in basements . . . with mildewed walls and few bare bulbs hanging from the ceiling, which gave them a dim, ecclesiastical glow' (p. 37). Feeling instantly attracted to Edward, he courageously crosses what he describes as 'even in this Communist haven, an irrevocable gulf of class' (p. 38) and, braving public opinion, engages him in conversation. The two men discover that they share an interest in politics and contemporary theatre. They leave the meeting together and, after taking a stroll, end up at Brian's flat where, unable to suppress their passion, they engage in energetic sex. Leavitt's account of the event, as well as illustrating Brian's patronizing attitude towards his working-class lover, playfully registers the physical absurdities to which the fumbling first encounter between the two men, combined with the urgency of desire on Edward's part, gives rise.

The serendipitous aspect of his meeting with Edward captures Brian's imagination. After he has left the flat, Brian pleasurably ponders 'the mysterious ... almost spectral' (p. 49) manner in which they had met and daydreams romantically about travelling with Edward in Europe. Far from being deterred by his lover's working-class background and lack of formal education, he positively welcomes his 'rawness' (p. 50). As Sinfield writes, referring to the treatment of the topic in earlier fiction, 'The cross-class liaison was not just a convenience, it was a turn-on. For many middle-class and upper-class men, lower-class people were sexy *as such*.'[69] Leavitt, however, criticizes Brian's tendency to exoticize his working-class lover and his exaggeratedly romantic portrayal of him. He playfully parodies the sentimental clichés and superior stance he adopts towards his 'bit of rough' and the image of 'natural man' that, though he knows Edward to be an intelligent autodidact with a good knowledge of politics and literature, he insists on projecting on him.

Further chance encounters occur between the two men. They strike Brian as delightfully fortuitous, illustrating how, as Freud and subsequent theorists describe, coincidences can promote a sense of the uncanny.[70] One takes place on the London Underground where, since it furnishes the setting for a play he is writing, Brian is thrilled to discover that Edward works as a ticket inspector. He ascribes heterotopic significance to the tube system, transforming it in his imagination from a mundane means of transport to 'a simulacrum of connectedness' (p. 64) concluding in same-sex romantic meetings.

The two meet frequently, and Edward, perceiving that the liaison represents more than a mere fling, introduces Brian to his parents and sister Lucy. She turns out to be lesbian and, though he assigns her only a minor role in the novel, Leavitt portrays her confidence about her sexuality and the ease she shows in mixing with people from different social backgrounds as a distinct contrast to Brian's nervousness about being recognized as queer by his aunt and upperclass friends.

As well as describing the London tube system in a romantic light, Brian depicts it uncannily representing 'another London, subterranean and sinister and Gothic' (p. 64). The dark portrayal prefigures the problems that undermine his relationship with Edward. They arise shortly after the latter has accepted Brian's invitation to move into the flat and live with him. Leavitt describes how the discourses inscribing homosexuality in the period and the contradictions they display impact destructively on the two men's partnership. In contrast to Brian's socialist friends who regard same-sex relationships idealistically as a blueprint for a classless society, homosexual acquaintances from his public school days ridicule effeminate queers as sissies. A letter he receives from a friend in Germany conveys frightening news about Nazi homophobia, and he notices that British attitudes too are becoming increasingly repressive. The class differences between Edward and himself cease to appear alluring and instead exacerbate his anxiety. As a result, when Aunt Constance, whose cheques he continues to spend, introduces him to Philippa, a young woman who she hopes will make him a suitable wife, he agrees to meet her.

Assuming Philippa to be unaware of his affairs with men, Brian does his best to live up to her expectations of heterosexual masculinity and reinvent himself as an appropriate suitor. His attempted sexual self-transformation resembles the 'colonial mimicry' (p. 122) that Bhabha, recasting Freud's reference to the automaton Olympia's mimicry of femininity, portrays the black subaltern adopting. Brian turns himself into 'a mimic man almost the same, but not quite' (p. 87) as the heterosexual male he seeks to emulate. The difference between the two, however, becomes blatantly apparent when Philippa, characterized by Leavitt as intelligent and sexually experienced, indicates that she recognizes from Brian's sexual performance that he lacks experience with women. After generously remarking 'You're wonderful, I adore you', she adds lightly but perceptively, 'It's just that I could tell that you didn't quite know your way around. Yet. It was as if you were constantly having to consult a map' (p. 146). She also lets on that she knows of his homosexual past, forcing him to recognize that the closet he has been hiding in is a glass one.[71] Overcome by embarrassment, he refuses her invitation to stay the night and speedily makes his escape. On arriving at the tube station he enters a public toilet to wash what he coarsely describes as 'her strong smell' (p. 147), a telltale sign of his infidelity, from his hands. While standing at the urinal he has an erection and accepts the offer, voiced jokingly by a working-class youth, to 'take care' of it. He then takes the tube back to his flat where Edward, unaware of his double infidelity, patiently awaits his return.

The episode represents one of several incidents of public sex situated in London toilets and heaths in which Leavitt describes Brian engaging. The immense importance that Brian attaches to these anonymous sexual encounters is indicated by his exaggeratedly romantic description of them. He refers to 'the rare, elusive camaraderie' (p. 155) between men that he regards them as signifying and dwells on the way they momentarily liberate the individual from what he rather pretentiously terms 'the rush and whistle of time' (p. 155). In addition to furnishing another example of the interplay between private and public spheres that the novel treats, these anonymous sexual encounters shed light on the difficulty Brian experiences in achieving a sense of personal and sexual autonomy in the homophobic and class-obsessed climate of the period. Anthony Giddens controversially argues that anonymous sex of this kind, since it 'permits power in the form only of the sexual practice itself' with 'sexual taste being the sole determinant, expresses an equality between the partners'[72] that seldom exists in other forms of sex. The anonymous encounters in which Brian engages appear to offer him a brief interlude of freedom, illusory perhaps but nonetheless emotionally significant, from the rigid conventions of masculinity and class that entrap him.

Brian's sex life moves increasingly into the area of farce when, instead of taking Philippa's hint and terminating the relationship with her, he decides, in a desperate attempt to accommodate to heterosexuality, to continue it. He becomes entrammelled, as a result, in an ever-increasing web of deceit. While lying to Edward to excuse his absences from home, he also lies to Philippa, insisting that although he has engaged in a few brief affairs with men he has 'never had a real male lover' (p. 151). Far from enjoying this double life, he admits that 'shuttling between the two left me feeling sexually exhausted. At no time in my life had I had so much sex, or enjoyed sex less.' (p. 152) He finds himself making love with his two partners not for pleasure but 'in order to ward off any suspicions either might have as to the existence of the other' (p. 152). The stresses of the situation understandably affect his sexual performance. He experiences difficulty in getting an erection with Edward, and in order to achieve a climax with Philippa has, as he describes, 'to summon into my mind images of fornicating men' (p. 152). Pondering the mysteries of desire, he thinks gloomily, 'Why couldn't I transform my lust for hairy chests into a lust for pincushion breasts?' (p. 153). The pressure he experiences to conform to heterosexual masculinity destroys his pleasure in sex with both partners, illustrating how, as Bhabha writes, 'The recesses of domestic space become sites for history's most intricate invasions' (p. 13).

Influenced by the then fashionable discourse of eugenics and determined to put his own sperm to good use, Brian compounds his mistakes by rashly proposing marriage to Philippa with the aim of starting a family. She unsurprisingly rejects his proposal, suggesting, with unconscious irony, that she thinks he might be happier in a relationship with a man. Her comment finally prompts him to perceive the truth. Admitting that 'while the prospect of a homosexual life still frightened me, I knew it could not be worse than a life built around delusion' (p. 181), he hurries back to his flat in the hope of repairing his damaged relationship with Edward. His change of heart however comes too late. Edward is no longer there. Hurt and humiliated by Brian's neglectful treatment, he has left for Spain to fight for the Republican cause.

The concluding chapters, describing Brian's desperate search for Edward in civil-war Spain, illustrate even more radically the impact of history and politics on the characters' personal lives. John Northrop, the champion of the Republican cause whom Brian had last encountered at the Aid for Spain meeting in London, tells him that Edward, far from proving to be an exemplary soldier, has deserted from his battalion. He brands him a traitor and a coward and, having heard of his relationship with Brian, pompously denounces homosexuality as 'a corrupt aberration' (p. 211). Crudely equating the political with the personal, he accuses Brian of exploiting Edward, 'the way the bourgeoisie has been exploiting the working class for generations' (p. 210). Brian angrily dismisses his words.

On eventually locating Edward in military confinement, Brian finds him disillusioned with the war and its egalitarian ideals. He describes the battalion to which he was assigned as riddled with hypocrisy and complains that the 'the upper-class boys' (p. 226) use their working-class comrades as servants, treating them as expendable in battle. Although he portrays Brian succeeding in rescuing Edward from the firing squad to which he has been sentenced, Leavitt resists the temptation to conclude the narrative on a positive note; instead, he portrays Edward dying from typhoid on the journey back to England. The final image Brian has of him occurs, in fact, some years later when he is unexpectedly reunited with Edward in spectral form. While enjoying a spell of cruising on Hampstead Heath one night, he momentarily glimpses the face of the man with whom he is having sex; he describes how 'Suddenly a streak of light passed over his face, fleeting as a moon beam through a break in clouds. For a millisecond Edward's eyes stared into mine' (p. 292). This encounter with his deceased lover, as well as reflecting the surfacing of his repressed feelings of guilt and desire, makes an appropriate conclusion to the incidents of public sex in which Brian has engaged throughout the novel. The movement into fantasy that the episode involves ironically implies that only when death has stripped Edward of his working-class associations and transformed him into a ghostly imago can Brian regard him as an equal. The reunion, however, is tantalizingly brief since it is predictably interrupted by the sound of footsteps heralding the arrival of the police, intent on clearing the Heath of homosexual activity. Once again sociopolitical forces beyond his control invade Brian's personal space, disrupting his love life.

The novels discussed in this chapter illustrate some of the roles that secrets and their disclosure play in contemporary queer fiction, demonstrating their varied treatment and uncanny significance. Secrets relating to sexuality and personal relationships understandably assume prominence, their eventual revelation frequently reflecting society's perception of that which 'ought to have remained . . . secret and hidden but has come to light'.[73]

Delineations of the closet in the novels reviewed above are notable for their complexity. Rather than describing it merely as a place of shameful hiding, as tended to be the case in the fiction published in the 1970s and 1980s, writers investigate its psychological and social nuances, exploring the attractions and practical uses that it offers the lesbian and gay individual, as well as its oppressive effects. Donoghue represents the closet in *Stir-Fry* as a performance space of playful innuendo and verbal wit, while Hensher describes it in *Kitchen Venom* as an existential site to which the subject retreats in a paranoid attempt to avoid cultural and social definition. The concept of 'the glass closet', explored by Sedgwick,[74] receives attention from Leavitt.

Secrets relating to sickness and death also achieve prominence, as illustrated not only in the AIDS narrative exemplified by the novels of Tóibín and Schulman but also in Waters's and Leavitt's historical fiction. In Waters's *The Night Watch* Duncan's association with his friend's suicide casts a profound shadow over his life, conferring on him an uncanny aura of mystery and scandal.

Leavitt's decision in the final chapter of *While England Sleeps* to disrupt the realist style he has employed throughout the novel by portraying his narrator Brian encountering the ghost of his deceased lover, or what he perceives as such, while cruising on Hampstead Heath illustrates the ability of the uncanny to infiltrate – in a manner that is intellectually significant and atmospherically effective – forms of fiction, comic in style, with which we least associate it. It also appropriately introduces us to the topic of the next chapter: the role that spectrality and the double associated with it play in contemporary queer fiction, whether lesbian, male gay or transgender. The literary treatment of the two motifs, as will become apparent, is highly varied. Ranging from the scary and disturbing to the playful, it provides further insights into the situation of the queer subject and the part that perceptions and motifs relating to the uncanny play in queer existence.

3

Queer Spectrality

❧

The direct figure of the uncanny is the Ghost.[1]

Spectral fictions

The key role that spectrality plays in the theorization of the uncanny and novels inscribing it is indicated by Castle's description of the Freudian uncanny itself as signifying 'a sort of phantom, looming up out of darkness',[2] a fantasy imago stemming from the unconscious that returns to haunt us. The figure of the ghost is particularly rich in metaphorical significance, both traditional and postmodern. As well as evoking connotations of invisibility and fluctuations in visibility – the 'now you see it, now you don't' effect familiar from Gothic film – it can operate as an image for liminality and border-crossing, as illustrated by its ability to traverse the boundaries between inside and outside, present and past and, even more mysteriously, life and death. Cixous portrays the ghost existing in a limbo region, 'neither alive nor dead' but 'erasing the limit between the two states'.[3] The connection it displays with death and the corpse also relate it to the Kristevan abject.

Another meaning that the ghost acquires on account of its connection with ideas of return and repetition is that of the double or copy. This is exemplified not only by its role as the uncanny double of the deceased but also, as poststructuralist theorists discuss, by its relation to cultural representation and reproduction – literary, cinematic and pictorial. Neil Cornwell's observation that 'ghostliness is cognate with reproduction and non-originality'[4] gestures towards the spectral dimension of narrative and textuality. Since all texts emerge from others, they appear culturally haunted by them.

The ghost, in inhabiting both spiritual and material dimensions, also carries associations of ambiguity and contradiction, attributes that help to explain its prominence in queer theory. Fuss and Butler utilize the concept of 'homo-spectrality' to explore the contradictions and interaction between homosexual and heterosexual economies and investigate the ambiguities of 'inside/out' (inside the closet but outside heteronormative society) that the queer subject has traditionally experienced.[5] Contradiction also informs Castle's image of the 'apparitional lesbian' that she employs to investigate the spectralization of the lesbian in nineteenth- and twentieth-century literature. Writers, Castle argues, intended the representation of the lesbian in spectral imagery to disembody her and negate her desire for, as she asks, 'How better to exorcise the threat of lesbianism than by turning it into a phantom?'[6] The spectralization of the lesbian, however, has the reverse effect, since it indicates the ability of her desire to survive society's efforts to suppress it and, like the ghost, *return*. As Castle writes: 'Only something very palpable – at a deeper level – has the capacity to "haunt" us so thoroughly' (p. 7).

The connotations and operations that different theoretical discourses assign to the ghost return and re-emerge, in a manner resembling its own fluid movement, in the novels discussed here. In recasting them, writers of queer fiction experiment with different narrative forms, some pioneered by Gothic writers. The ghost story is among the most popular and receives innovative treatment in James Purdy's *Mourners Below* and Ali Smith's *Hotel World*.

Another fictional form with spectral connotations discussed in this chapter, one that interrelates metafiction, queer theory and Gothic critical studies, is 'the phantom-text'. Associated with Derridean theory[7] and utilized by Wolfreys and Susanne Becker[8] in their analysis of Gothic narrative, it illustrates the way in which strategies of intertextuality connect contemporary fiction to literary and cinematic texts produced in the past. Sarah Waters's *Fingersmith* and Christopher Bram's *Father of Frankenstein* illustrate its uses for lesbian and male gay representation.

The chapter concludes with reference to the double, another motif associated with the Gothic. Writers employ it to investigate different forms of psychological division and fragmentation reflecting the phenomenon of 'the doubling, dividing and interchanging of the self' discussed by Freud.[9] It furnishes a vehicle, as Stella Duffy's *Beneath the Blonde* and Patrick McGrath's *Dr Haggard's Disease* illustrate, to represent the sense of cross-gendered identification that the transsexual and transgender subject can experience.

Ghost stories and queer hauntings

The ghost story is one of the most tricksy of Gothic fictional forms, capable of tying the protagonist, and on occasion the reader, in phenomenological and intellectual knots and confronting him with riddles. While some examples, such as James Herbert's novel *The Fog* and M. Night Shyamalan's film *The Sixth Sense*, tease us by initially failing to make clear which characters are alive and which phantoms, others raise interpretative problems that permit no clear solution and continue to perplex readers. How should we interpret the story? As a tale of supernatural visitation or a psychological narrative in which the spectral visitor signifies a figment of the protagonist's disturbed imagination, an instance of what Haggerty, discussing Henry James's *The Turn of the Screw*, calls a work of 'explained gothic'?[10] Does the ghost signify, as Neil Cornwell writes citing three key possibilities, 'illusion, allusion or delusion'?[11]

These questions are pertinent to the two novels discussed here. Whereas Purdy's *Mourners Below* teases us about whether we should read it as a tale of spectral visitation or a work of 'explained gothic', Smith's *Hotel World* reveals ambiguities hinging on the figure of the narrator. Smith selects as narrator the ghost of a young girl who has recently recognized her lesbian sexuality, and problems confront the reader in determining the significance of her spectral invisibility and liminality. Do they diminish her power and agency or do they on the contrary, by locating her in an uncanny dimension that exceeds the material, enhance them? And what, if anything, do they indicate about the living lesbian?

Mourners Below opens with the protagonist Duane Bledsoe, a seventeen-year-old youth living in rural North America in the 1940s, receiving a visit from the ghosts of his two half-brothers Justin and Douglas who have recently been killed in the war. Shortly after his father Eugene receives the telegram with the news of their death, the two men appear in spectral form at the foot of Duane's bed 'looking at him eagerly, imploringly'.[12] They are unusually colourful for ghosts since he romantically describes them as resembling 'blue and pink smoke, their eyes like beautiful light violet pools in which water lilies grow' (p. 13). The encounter with them both fascinates and scares him for, while introducing an explosion of luminous colour into his drab, grief-stricken world, it simultaneously, like the Kristevan abject, 'disturbs system, identity, order'.[13]

Duane plucks up the courage to ask the two ghosts what they want but receives no reply. When on a later occasion they materialize in the garden outside his window, they appear to be about to speak. However he is prevented from hearing what they say since, in his eagerness to reach them, he rushes from the room and in the first of a series of down-to-earth episodes, humorous in tone, with which Purdy punctures the narrative, falls head-first down the stairs and suffers a spell of concussion.

Although Duane is the only character who sees the ghosts frequently, Estelle Dumont, the beautiful young widow who lives nearby and with whom Justin had been having an affair before he left for the war, claims to have done so once. According to the version of events she gives towards the end of the novel, the ghost of Justin visited her and instructed her to host a lavish party to commemorate him, insisting that she invite Duane to attend. Estelle, portrayed by Purdy as something of a femme fatale, holds the party and in the erotically charged atmosphere generated by the music and wine seduces Duane. On finding that she is pregnant from the encounter, she decides to give the baby to Duane and Eugene to raise. The novel concludes with Estelle marrying Duane's tutor who has long harboured a passion for her, and Duane and Eugene agreeing to care for the baby. It turns out by a stroke of good fortune to be a boy, ensuring as a result the survival of the patrilineal family line, endangered by the death of Duane's half-brothers.

Read with reference solely to the plot, the novel tells a story, albeit a rather odd one, focusing on the hetero-patriarchal family unit and illustrating the lengths to which its members will go – even returning from the grave – to ensure its survival. The spectral Justin, aware of his father's fear that with his and his brother's deaths 'their house fell' (p. 7), intervenes in the situation and solves the problem by proxy. By instructing Estelle to hold the party, he sets the scene for her one-night stand with Duane. Acting as a sort of spectral match-maker, he encourages Duane to get her pregnant in his stead, in this way promoting the birth of a son and heir.

This heteronormative reading, however, though faithful to the novel's storyline, ignores a key feature of its telling. This is Purdy's reference to the homosexual attachment between Duane and Justin. If we take this into account, the novel emerges as an 'explained ghost story' treating the psychological production of phantoms, with Duane's spectral visitors representing figments of his adolescent imagination. It investigates the interaction between the homosocial and homosexual, identification and desire, anticipating in this respect the interests of present-day queer theorists such as Sinfield and Butler.

Several factors contribute to Duane's fantasy production of the ghosts of his two half-brothers. One is Eugene's insensitive handling of the bereavement he and his son have suffered. Instead of sharing his grief with Duane and encouraging him to mourn, Eugene conceals his emotions under a mask of masculine reserve. The housekeeper Mrs Newsom, to whom Duane confides his spectral encounter, refers critically to Eugene's 'close-mouthed and distant' (p. 16) behaviour. She remembers that it was his inability to express emotion that had caused his wife, Duane's mother, to desert him for another man, leaving Duane without maternal care at a formative stage. Eugene's insensitivity is also apparent in the attempts he makes to coerce Duane into achieving adult masculinity before he is ready by insisting that he give up ice-skating, a pastime he enjoys, in exchange for the sport of boxing that he dislikes. And on learning from Mrs Newsom that he has been seeing ghosts, Eugene humiliatingly accuses Duane of being a sissy. Even worse, as Purdy later reveals, he deliberately conceals from Duane the letters that his mother has sent him during her absence.

However, though Eugene's insensitive behaviour is certainly relevant, the factor that appears chiefly responsible for Duane's fantasy creation of the ghosts of his half-brothers is the emotionally intense and ambiguous relationship that he had formed with them when they were alive, with Justin especially. Purdy describes how the two men tried to compensate for the absence of a mother by helping look after Duane and giving him treats such as accompanying him to the local cafe to eat ice cream and taking him for a spin in their new car. As a result, he finds their deaths devastating and feels, as he admits, seriously 'unlooked-after' (p. 11). Describing them as 'heroes' and 'giants' (p. 91), he expresses anxiety that he will fail to attain their physical and mental stature. Remembering how, before they joined the military, they used to measure his height against the wall, he nervously surmises that they may have returned from the dead with the express purpose of 'measuring him with some heavenly measuring tape . . . if they care about measuring in heaven' (p. 54).

Duane's relationship with Justin, however, as well as involving feelings of admiration and identification, also reveals a significant sexual element. Sinfield, challenging Freudian perspectives, argues that 'the confounding of the distinction between the desire-to-be and the desire-for is endemic in same-sex passion'.[14] This is certainly the case with Duane, as is illustrated by the shifts in role and identification he experiences in his sexual encounter with Estelle at the party she hosts. While making love with her, he moves from identifying with Justin, thinking 'it was just like Justin had come to her again, but let me act' (p. 229), to believing that he is the object of Justin's passion – that 'Justin had turned into a woman and [given] him this tenderness, this strong affection' (p. 207). As he confusedly tells Estelle, 'I'm me, you understand, or I'm him' (p. 213). Estelle's kisses also arouse in Duane repressed memories of Justin's erotic attentions, causing him to relive the occasion when Justin had kissed him on the mouth, giving him 'a fiercer kiss than any man would give a girl . . . a death kiss' (p. 215). Duane's association of the kiss with death, as well as referring to Justin's demise and possibly to his own feelings of guilt at the homosexual and incestuous aspect of the relationship, evokes the connection between the erotic and death that as Jonathan Dollimore explains has traditionally haunted homo-sexuals.[15]

The memories of his relationship with Justin that Duane's sexual encounter with Estelle arouses are strongly physical. Drinking wine from her mouth, he remembers how, when wrestling with him in the fields, 'heavy thick drops [of sweat] from Justin's chest had come down first upon his own mouth and then fairly blinded his eyes' (p. 212). They also reveal a sadomasochistic element. He remembers the disturbing occasion when Justin, sexually infatuated with Estelle and desperately proclaiming 'I've got to have her, or I'll die' (p. 135), had instructed him to hammer thumbtacks into his chest and take his blood-soaked shirt to her as proof of his love. Though initially refusing to perform the gruesome task, Duane eventually complied. Purdy's account of the episode is psychologically and sexually ambiguous. While it ostensibly portrays Duane playing the role of go-between in Justin and Estelle's heterosexual romance, his act of hammering tacks into Justin's chest transforms the episode into an S & M encounter between two men.

Rosemary Jackson observes that the uncanny 'exists only in relation to the familiar and the normal. It is tangential ... on the edge of something else.'[16] In keeping with this, Purdy renders Duane's fantasies and memories of his erotic relations with Justin particularly vivid by juxtaposing them with a series of mundane, humorously described domestic incidents. As Angus Wilson observes in his review, the novel ingeniously intermingles the 'horrible and sad' with the 'wildly funny'.[17] Although, as indicated by his fits of weeping, Duane finds the bereavement and his spectral encounters with his brothers distressing, they do little to quell his healthy adolescent appetite for food. Purdy portrays him, in intervals between bouts of grieving, consuming with evident relish large quantities of roast beef, ice cream, custard pie, devil's cake and other culinary goodies. He also amusingly describes Eugene's ham-fisted attempts at cooking and the unappetizing meals that he serves up when – having foolishly dismissed Mrs Newsom from his service for permitting Duane to accompany her to a service at the Catholic church in order to light a candle in his half-brothers' memory – he is forced to fend for himself in the kitchen.

Mrs Newsom, as well as being a first-rate cook, also proves a supportive friend to Duane. In an attempt to alleviate his anxiety about 'seeing things' (p. 55), she takes him to visit the family medical practitioner Dr Cressy. The latter, though he expresses amusement at the fact that Duane should see 'his young brutes of brothers . . . who gave off such a profusion and odour of sweat' (p. 65) when alive, floating around in spectral form, does his best to set his mind at rest. By portraying Dr Cressy as an affluent bachelor who has surrounded himself with a 'staff' of young men with no set job-description who 'have been in trouble with the law' (p. 65), Purdy indicates that he is both homosexual and rich enough to ignore public prejudice. While serving Duane large helpings of homemade jelly roll that he consumes with evident pleasure, Cressy tells him that he himself has 'enjoyed almost everything, even oftentimes the unpalatable and unpleasant' in the course of his life. He suggests that the ghosts that Duane sees, rather than being harmful, may if regarded from a liberal viewpoint merely be 'different'. He advises him that encountering them 'is nothing to be alarmed about – and if you enjoy seeing them come back . . . don't *interdict* them' (p. 73). He also comforts him with the thought that 'Long after you are dead and gone, some other man or boy will see what you have felt and seen. Nothing that happens is outlandish or out of the ordinary. The people who think so are fools, but of course fools rule the world' (p. 72). His observations are as applicable to homosexuality as they are to spectral visitation, and they prompt the reader to perceive the metaphorical connection that Purdy makes between the two.

Purdy also contrasts Cressy's radical views with the bigotry rife in the local community. He describes how Duane, on leaving Estelle's house after the party in the early hours of the morning, is brutally assaulted by two yobs who, ridiculing his evening dress and 'fair hair' (p. 218) as effeminate, proceed to strip him of his 'fancy clothes'. They then pour a tin of black paint over his head and brutally rape him with a broom handle.

Mourners Below, if read as an 'explained ghost story' as indicated above, illustrates the utilization of spectral visitation as a vehicle to represent the return of repressed same-sex desires, disturbing but at the same time enriching the protagonist's life. The one possible problem with this reading, the fact that Estelle as well as Duane claims to have seen the two ghosts, does not present a significant obstacle to it. She makes the claim towards the end of the novel when, as Purdy emphasizes, Duane's spectral encounters with his half-brothers have become common knowledge in the neighbourhood and Estelle already knows that she is pregnant. It is therefore possible to discount it as a fabrication she invents in order to explain her one-night stand with Duane and persuade him and Eugene to adopt the baby. Mrs Newsom and Dr Cressy, the two characters whose interpretation of events Purdy appears to endorse, both regard the ghosts as fantasies. Cressy in fact diagnoses Duane as suffering from 'a very highly developed case of the imagination' (p. 73).

This reading also sheds light on another queer feature of Purdy's decidedly queer novel, the exceptionally colourful appearance of the two ghosts. It can be interpreted as evoking the 'excess' that homosexuality signifies when regarded from a hetero-patriarchal viewpoint. Their fluctuation in visibility, another aspect of their appearance that Purdy emphasizes, reflects the propensity of heterosexual society – though forced on occasion to recognize the existence of homosexuality – generally to ignore it and erase it from the field of vision.

In contrast to Purdy's *Mourners Below* which is written in the third person and focuses on the protagonist's encounter with the spectral, Smith's *Hotel World* is narrated by a ghost, that of the nineteen-year-old Sara Wilby. She is represented having fallen to her death in a lift shaft at the Global Hotel, the 'Hotel World' of the novel's title, while working there as a maid. She returns to haunt the site of her death and, although she is unable to make contact with the world of the living, her portrayal illuminates the topic of lesbian storytelling and is relevant to lesbian social invisibility.

Elisabeth Bronfen compares storytellers in general to 'revenants' since they 'feed off previous "inanimate" texts' and, in addition, 'the liminal realm between life and death' that they inhabit 'inspires and produces fictions'.[18] The association of the writer with spectrality is especially applicable to the queer storyteller since, as Fuss observes: 'Homosexual production emerges [in heteronormative culture] as a kind of ghost writing, a writing which is at once a recognition and refusal of the cultural representation of "the homosexual" as phantom other.'[19] It both investigates and challenges the homosexual's social invisibility and the ambiguous 'inside/out' position, in the closet but outside mainstream society, that he has traditionally occupied.

The spectral Sara also acts as a mouthpiece for other themes besides queer storytelling. They include the precariousness of life and society's readiness to typecast as abject people who live, in terms of sexuality, class or disability, on the social margins. With reference to the former topic, an emphasis on mortality and mutability pervades the novel. Contemplating the residents of the city in the north of England where the narrative is set, Sara recasts the *carpe diem* motif associated with classical and early modern literature from a female viewpoint. Employing the semiotic linguistic form that Smith assigns to her since she mediates between the realms of the living and dead, she tells them, 'Remember you must live. Remember you most love. Remainder you mist leaf.'[20] According to Irigaray and Bronfen, phallocentric culture, while permitting men to confront and contemplate their death, allows no such act of sublimation to women since it is women themselves who in this male-supremacist system represent matter and mortality.[21] By portraying Sara and other female characters in the novel commenting on their own death and that of others, Smith effectively challenges this phallocentric perspective.

Like Purdy who describes the ghosts of Duane's half-brothers as ambiguously immaterial yet vividly coloured, Smith foregrounds Sara's liminal position, situated as she is between the spiritual and the material. She describes her in one particularly uncanny episode burrowing down into the earth to converse with her own corpse, representing her physical double. In registering her connection with it, Sara acknowledges her relation to the abject since Kristeva depicts the corpse as 'the utmost of abjection ... death infecting life', signifying 'imaginary uncanniness and real threat'.[22]

Sara's musings on mortality and her reference to the importance of enjoying life to the full are rendered particularly poignant by her own premature death which cut short her hopes of emotional and sexual fulfilment. Smith portrays her, shortly before she fell to her death in the lift shaft, experiencing a happier kind of 'fall'. She fell in love with a girl of a similar age to herself who worked in a shop selling and repairing watches, the reference accentuating the novel's focus on time and mutability. Sara did not know the girl's name and, although she loitered outside the shop in the hope of meeting her and even saw her pass close by, lacked the courage to speak to her. As she despondently observes, 'She looked straight through me as she passed me as if I simply wasn't there. Falling for her had made me invisible' (p. 23). Sara's invisibility in terms of her lesbian desire anticipates her invisibility as a ghost, recalling Castle's discussion of 'the apparitional lesbian' and her 'history of derealisation'.[23]

In referring to the premature nature of Sara's death, Smith introduces another topic with uncanny connotations. Freud, commenting on the double, refers to 'all the unfulfilled but possible futures to which we still like to cling in phantasy, all the strivings of the ego which adverse external circumstances have crushed'.[24] However, although Sara's fantasies of love remain unfulfilled, there are indications in the final pages that the girl shares her feelings of attraction. She has noticed Sara standing outside the shop and, though too shy to address her, experiences reciprocal stirrings of desire: 'She can feel small wings moving against the inside of her chest, or something in there anyway, turning, tightened, working' (p. 235).

In addition to exploring Sara's subjectivity and emotional life, Smith widens the scope of the narrative by treating the topic of female commonality associated with the feminist fiction of the 1970s and 1980s. She connects Sara, in terms of her marginal situation as a ghost, to the socially marginalized women whom she sees frequenting the hotel and its environs. They include the homeless Else who sits in the street outside begging, her body wracked by a cough, and the hotel clerk Lise who, though suffering from a life-threatening illness, compassionately offers her a room for the night. Another woman with connections to the hotel is Penny. Although she now works as a publicity agent and rents a room there while travelling, in her youth she had kleptomaniac tendencies and stole from department stores.

However, the character who is closest to Sara emotionally and whose trajectory Smith prioritizes is her younger sister Clare. Angered by society's refusal to confront death, Clare criticizes the mourners at Sara's funeral for the way, embarrassed by her symptoms of grief, they shy away from her, giving her 'this funny sideways look' (p. 198). With the aim of investigating the circumstances of Sara's death, Clare visits the hotel anonymously and, in order to gain access, puts on the uniform Sara wore while working there, thus transforming herself into her double. On locating the entrance to the lift shaft where Sara died in an upstairs corridor, she finds it concealed by a wooden panel. The attempt to 'paper over the cracks', performed on the instructions of the manager, that this represents acts as a metaphor for society's efforts to sanitize the event of death and conceal the fissure that it makes in the fabric of existence. In representing an attempt to avoid confronting death or be reminded of it, it signifies, from the perspective of Lacan and Slavoj Žižek, the refusal to confront the Real.[25]

Clare, however, refusing to be deterred, removes the panel with a screwdriver and throws a clock down the lift shaft to measure the drop. In so doing, she uncannily repeats the event of Sara's fall. Gazing down the shaft, she wonders 'What would it take to fill that cavity?' Moving into the realm of metaphysics, she thinks: 'Even if they knocked down the whole of the hotel & that lift shaft was taken apart & wasn't there anymore it would still somehow be there though you couldn't see it' (p. 200). The empty shaft, concealed from public view and described by Sara as 'a void that no one can fill' (p. 199), appears symbolically to represent the absence and irrevocable loss that the death of a loved one creates.

The hotel itself, frequented by Sara's ghost, also assumes symbolic import. Interpreted in the context of Anthony Vidler's concept of 'the architectural uncanny'[26] and the transformation of the *heimlich* building into the *unheimlich* that he describes, it represents both haunted house and crypt. In this respect it creates a female inflected version of other buildings in Gothic fiction of a similar kind, such as Edgar Allan Poe's House of Usher.

The phantom-text

According to Derrida, all forms of writing have spectral connotations since, as well as being legible beyond the grave and continuing to signify and 'act' after the writer's death, they involve strategies of repetition and return. He observes: 'In representation, the present, the presentation of what is presented comes back, returns as a double effigy, an image, a copy, an idea as a picture of the thing henceforth at hand, in the absence of the thing.'[27] Introducing the concept of the 'phantom-text',[28] he describes how intertextual references to earlier writers and the rhetorical figures they employ create ghostly 'traces', in this way serving to 'phantomize the text itself' (p. 80).

The concept of the phantom-text, as critics illustrate, is particularly relevant to Gothic, a genre that prioritizes both spectrality and intertextuality. Since writers frequently appropriate and recast motifs and storylines from earlier contributions to the genre, strategies of repetition and return, with their uncanny significance, play a key role in the texts they create. Wolfreys describes 'the ghost of another text haunting and inhabiting the [Gothic] narrative' and demonstrates how intertextual allusions interrupt and complicate its flow, creating 'the sense of the unfamiliar within the familiar'.[29] Vijay Mishra remarks on the different 'levels of uncanny duplication at work in the Gothic'[30] and investigates the contribution to the 'chain of repetition' (p. 55) that each new reading of the precursor text creates. Jodey Castricano concentrates on exploring narrative structure; she describes Stephen King's repeated portrayal of the return of characters from the grave in *Pet Sematary* creating 'the uncanniness of an economy of revenance'.[31]

Works of queer fiction that recast storylines and motifs from earlier literature are also rich in intertextual reference and create sexually radical versions of 'the phantom text'. Christopher Bram's *Father of Frankenstein* and Sarah Waters's *Fingersmith*, the two novels discussed here, though differing significantly in content, both rework from a queer perspective episodes and storylines from canonical nineteenth-century Gothic texts. By 'reading against the grain of the "master works" of Western culture',[32] they establish a dialogue with the precursor text, interrogating and revising its ideological perspectives. By teasing out its covert allusions to male or female same-sex relationships, they expose the repressed aspect of Victorian culture, while simultaneously filling in the gaps that it displays. Their act of rewriting is ambivalent, combining an act of homage with a sexual-political critique.

Bram's *Father of Frankenstein* creates a fictional account of the final days in the life of James Whale, the homosexual director of the two acclaimed cinematic adaptations of Mary Shelley's novel – *Frankenstein* and *The Bride of Frankenstein* –that appeared in the 1930s. In focusing

the novel on Whale and his Frankenstein films, Bram selects a topic
admirably suited to queer recasting. Although Whale himself dismissed
critical attempts to interpret his films with reference to his sexuality,
critics today recognize their contribution to queer cinema through
covert references to homosexuality and scenes representing 'misfit
outsiders pitted against hostile mobs'.[33] Bram builds his portrayal of
Whale and the contradictions informing his life around intertextual
references to the relationship between Victor Frankenstein and the
creature he constructed, as represented in both Shelley's novel and
Whale's own cinematic productions. He portrays Whale remarking
on the fact that 'People are always confusing the Monster with its
maker'.[34] Whale's reference to the common slippage alerts attention
to Bram's portrayal of him as interrelating in his subjectivity and
situation facets of both figures.

Father of Frankenstein opens with Whale, having been hospitalized
after suffering a stroke, recuperating at his Hollywood villa in Palm
Springs in the care of his Mexican housekeeper Maria. Maria, though
she laments the fact that he is 'a bugger' (p. 167) and therefore unlikely to achieve salvation, is nonetheless deeply devoted to him.
Bram intersperses episodes from Whale's earlier life – describing
him socializing with film stars and fellow directors and working
with Boris Karloff and Elsa Lanchester on the set of the Frankenstein
films – with episodes set in the present. The latter portray him coming
to terms with the debilitating effects of his stroke, conversing with
his former lover David Lewis and striking up an unlikely friendship
with the ex-marine Clayton Boone whom he employs as his yard-
man. The final chapters depict him succumbing to despair and
secretly formulating a plan to end his life that, on account of the
disturbing and incurable neurological effects of his medical condition,
he finds increasingly intolerable.

It is in this interplay of episodes between past and present that
the conceit on which Bram structures the novel emerges. This is
the portrayal of Whale acquiring as uncanny doppelgängers the two
characters from Shelley's novel that he himself had brought to life
on the silver screen: Victor Frankenstein and his creature. In fact
the opening episode of the novel initially tricks the reader into thinking that he is watching a scene from Shelley's novel or one of Whale's
films. Against an eerie backdrop of thunder and lightning we see a

figure with flattop haircut resembling Karloff in the role of the creature standing in a garden watched by a shadowy figure in an upstairs window who could well be Victor Frankenstein. However, as we shortly discover, they are not Shelley's characters but the yard-man Boone in a summer storm with Whale watching him from above. The episode alerts attention to the role that strategies of doubling and uncanny return play in the novel, with Whale's personal trajectory consistently haunted by the Frankenstein story.

Doubling is also in evidence in the twin images of his skull that Whale sees when he returns to the hospital to learn the results of his brain scan. Gazing anxiously at the screen, he perceives 'Two skulls, one faces forward. The other is in profile, turned toward the first as if gazing at a spouse or lover' (p. 75). The images evoke the element of uncanny doubling that Frankenstein's relationship with his creature embodies. Whether we interpret the relationship between the two figures as exemplifying 'the entanglement of mastery and slavery'[35] or 'the male–male homoerotic bond'[36] that Frankenstein, to his cost, refuses to acknowledge, the concept of doubling, as critics illustrate, is undoubtedly central to it.

Bram utilizes Whale's relationship with his two uncanny alter egos as a vehicle to illuminate the contradictions of his situation. Whale's role as the director of the Frankenstein films and the fame that it won him connect him with Victor Frankenstein and his creative powers. The student of film history who arrives unexpectedly to interview him respectfully describes his villa as 'the house of Frankenstein' (p. 29), while the retrospective portrayal of him conversing with Karloff and Lanchester on the film set similarly illustrates his intelligence and creative abilities. As Bram describes, 'He is very happy here, fully engaged, intensely alive . . . He feels enlarged by a studio soundstage, his imagination magnified, his wit and love of theater turned into secret powers' (p. 152). The stories that Whale tells his yardman Boone about his experiences in the First World War and his early years in Hollywood reflect similarly attractive qualities, winning Boone's grudging respect. Though regarding his homosexuality as repellent and scary, and initially ridiculing him as an 'old English fairy' (p. 63) and a pathetic 'old coot' (p. 66), Boone is impressed to discover that he is the director of two famous horror films. He thinks admiringly: 'This man made *Frankenstein*' (p. 74). He decides in consequence to tolerate his employer's perverse sexuality and the fact that he acts 'a little weird and creepy' (p. 74).

Other facets of Whale's representation, however, relate him not to Victor Frankenstein but, poignantly, to the creature that Franken-stein constructed. Important here is the transformation into a grotesque monster and malfunctioning automaton that Whale feels he is experi-encing as a result of his stroke. Employing imagery relating to the war, he grotesquely portrays himself, on account of his damaged neurological system, as resembling 'a city during a blackout, all manner of deformed, forgotten creatures coming out to wander its pitch-blacked streets' (p. 137). In addition to experiencing intermittent pains, problems with speech and disturbingly turbulent dreams, he suffers from a neurological manifestation of the return of the repressed that takes the form of hallucinating smells. He encounters 'sniffs of things from forty or fifty years ago' (p. 8) and, evoked by them, previously experienced emotions. The neurologist at the hospital, explaining these sensations to him in layman's language, employs metaphors of electricity and spectrality. He tells Whale that 'Whatever was killed in your stroke appears to have short-circuited the inhibitory mechanism' (p. 77) resulting in 'parts of the brain firing at random' and generating 'olfactory phantoms' (p. 77) and 'ghost pains' (p. 78). The problems that Whale experiences with speech and memory, and the reference to electricity that the consultant uses to explain them, again connect him with Frankenstein's creature. Electricity was regarded by nineteenth-century intellectuals as a 'life science or, more than that, as the science of life itself'.[37] Reference to it features in both Shelley's literary and Whale's cinematic representations of the technologies that Victor Frankenstein employs to inspire life into the creature.

As well as establishing Whale's metaphorical connections with Frankenstein's creature by means of the strategies described above, Bram portrays him explicitly identifying with the creature. Watching *The Bride of Frankenstein* on television in the company of Maria who, shocked by the film's grotesque images, makes disapproving noises throughout, Whale is struck by the creature's pathos. He finds the words he utters, 'Love death, hate living' (p. 133) painfully pertinent to the frustrations of his own situation and his thoughts of suicide.

Bram ingeniously extends the Frankenstein intertext and the concept of doubling that it inscribes to Whale's relationship with Boone. It is, in fact, Boone's physical resemblance to Karloff in the role of the creature in the Frankenstein films that first provokes Whale's interest in him and prompts him to invite him into the villa to take tea. Boone's powerful physique and strongly contoured head, with its broken nose and flattop haircut, transform him, in Whale's eyes, into a present-day version of the creature. Whale playfully thinks of him as 'his monster – a monster with a dick' (p. 250). He mentally adds him to the company of his two other 'monsters', Karloff and Lanchester, the latter eulogistically described by him in the role of the creature's mate that she performed as 'uncanny, perfect' (p. 146). He is sexually attracted to Boone and, though aware that having sex with him is out of the question on account of both Boone's homophobia and his own poor health, he persuades him to pose for a series of sketches, including on one occasion in the nude. Bram's emphasis on the erotic attraction that Whale feels to his 'monster' Boone echoes the homoerotic subtext of the two Frankenstein films. Though portraying Frankenstein in a predominantly heterosexual light by foregrounding his relationship with Elizabeth and avoiding representing him as emotionally attached to the creature, Whale hints at his possible homosexuality by linking him with Fritz and, more significantly, with the overtly queer Dr Pretorius. In this way, as Michael Eberle-Sinatra describes, 'he replaces Victor's homosexual interest in the creature with another man'.[38]

Haggerty, constructing a queer reading of Shelley's *Frankenstein* in the context of Sedgwick's theory of the paranoid Gothic, argues that it is Frankenstein's foreclosure of 'the secret (homoerotic) desire that the creature represents'[39] that triggers the series of violent events in which the two figures subsequently become enmeshed. Succumbing to melancholy on account of Frankenstein's rejection, the creature proceeds to enact revenge by killing the people he loves. Whale's relationship with Boone moves in a similar manner into a scenario of violence, though one that remains chiefly on the plane of fantasy. Determined to end his own life, Whale projects onto Boone, on account of the latter's powerful physique and his earlier career as a marine, the roles of 'classic American killer' (p. 84) and a 'monster, more authentic than Karloff' (p. 139). Aware of Boone's paranoiac aversion to homosexuality, he attempts, by propositioning him sexually, to coerce him into experiencing a fit of panic in the hope that he will retaliate by lunging out with his fist and killing him. This perverse stratagem fails, however, provoking a scene not of tragedy but of bizarrely black farce. The foresighted Maria, aware of Whale's sexual preferences and intent on protecting him, has previously advised Boone to remain calm if Whale should make a sexual pass at him. Besides, Boone himself has no wish to injure his new-found friend and the acclaimed director of the Frankenstein films. Though puzzled and hurt by Whale's efforts to provoke him to violence, he staunchly refuses to retaliate. Whale is therefore left to take responsibility for ending his own life. The novel concludes with him doing so by drowning himself in the swimming pool at the villa.

The motif of doubling on which Bram structures the novel – established both in his portrayal of Whale acquiring Frankenstein and his creature as uncanny doppelgängers and the intertextual references to Shelley's literary and Whale's cinematic texts that he builds into the narrative – is particularly to the fore in the episode in which he portrays Whale watching *The Bride of Frankenstein* on television in the company of Maria. Scenes in the film intriguingly duplicate episodes from Shelley's novel in celluloid form. Bram also ingeniously utilizes the episode to introduce a debate about Whale's cinematic productions and the early experiments in Gothic horror they exemplify. Watching the film again after so many years have elapsed, Whale responds to it ambivalently. While telling himself that it was just 'a bit of fun, an elaborate joke at the expense of the studio who insisted he made a sequel' (p. 131), the interest that the student of film history shows in his work unsettles him, making him wonder if his own modest evaluation of it is correct. Watching the reels unwind, he finds himself having second thoughts about his achievement. With an uncertainty new to his appraisal of the film, he thinks, 'He wasn't saying anything serious here. Was he?' (p. 131)

Like Bram's *Father of Frankenstein* that recasts from a queer perspective elements of the Frankenstein narrative, as exemplified both by Shelley's novel and Bram's cinematic adaptations, Waters's *Fingersmith* queers storylines and episodes appropriated from a selection of texts with

Gothic affiliations and recasts uncanny motifs of doubling and spectrality. Utilizing as intertexts episodes from novels by Wilkie Collins and Charles Dickens, in particular ones relating to the Gothic and the sensation novel, she reworks their representation of female sexuality and woman's socially and economically oppressed position from a lesbian viewpoint. Her choice of material suits the phantom-text she constructs. Eleanor Salotto, arguing that 'Gothic narrative is obsessed with returns and the multiplot' and the production of 'specters',[40] cites as examples Collins's *The Woman in White* and Dickens's *Bleak House*, the two precursor texts to which Waters chiefly refers. Salotto describes how in them, 'narratives proliferate much like an army of ghosts' (p. 7). Waters's treatment of narrative, as suits the genre of historiographic metafiction that her novel exemplifies, is similarly rich and profuse.

Waters's recasting of material from nineteenth-century Gothic in *Fingersmith* in no way cramps her own imagination. Discussing her writing in a television interview, she observed that, although as an historian she finds the invisibility of women in same-sex relationships in the Victorian era and the lack of documentation of their lives frustrating, as a creative writer she welcomes it since 'Because there are those gaps, it gives me more liberty to make things up'.[41] *Fingersmith* illustrates, possibly more vividly than any of her other novels, her inventiveness at 'making things up' as she modestly puts it.

Hutcheon describes the writer of historiographic metafiction as 'reshaping material (in this case the past) in the light of present day issues'.[42] Waters makes effective use of this strategy, interweaving in her narrative topics relevant to present-day lesbian culture that forge a link with her lesbian and feminist readership. As the title *Fingersmith* with its punning reference to both writing and lesbian sexual practice signals, lesbian sexual representation is to the fore in this respect.

The plot of *Fingersmith* hinges on the class reversal that occurs between Sue Trinder, who – though a lady by birth – works as a pickpocket in the London area of Borough, and Maud Lilly, the daughter of a working-class baby-farmer who is raised as a lady in the country house of Briar. It describes the sexual attachment that develops between the two women and explores the difficulty they experience in breaking free from the male puppet-masters who control them and achieving autonomy and agency. The strands of their individual stories intertwine and then separate, converging again in the final chapter.

Waters signals in the opening chapters that she is engaging in a dialogue with Victorian fiction. Her description of Sue Trinder's London home in Lant Street echoes Dickens's description of Fagin's den in *Oliver Twist*, creating a matriarchal version of his male-dominated criminal establishment. The baby-farmer Mrs Sucksby who runs the gang of thieves entertains Sue with stories of Nancy's relationship with Bill Sykes. Reference to spectrality also occurs, with the three knocks on the front door that herald the arrival of Richard Rivers ominously reminding Sue of 'the knocking on a door in a play, when the dead man's ghost comes back'.[43] Her comment alerts attention to the role that the return of the repressed plays in the novel with the narrative haunted by traces of the past, both historical and literary. It also signals the importance that role-play and performance will assume in it.

Rivers, colloquially known as 'Gentleman' on account of his upper-class pretensions, comes to the house in Lant Street with the aim of persuading Sue to assist him in his courtship of the heiress Maud Lilly. In an act of deception, recalling that perpetrated by Sir Percival Glyde in Collins's *The Woman in White*, he plans – so he tells her – to marry Maud and subsequently dispose of her in a mental asylum with the aim of gaining possession of her inheritance. In actual fact, as Sue later discovers to her cost, it is she, not Maud, whom he intends to dispose of in this ruthless manner. Unaware of his duplicity, she agrees to accompany him to Maud's home in the provinces and, by acting as her personal maid, assist him in promoting the love affair.

Maud lives as a ward in the care of her tyrannical guardian Christopher Lilly at the country house of Briar. As well as employing her to collate his extensive collection of erotica, Lilly scandalously coerces her into reading passages aloud to his gentlemen friends. Briar evokes echoes of other houses in Victorian fiction associated with female isolation and entrapment. While its name recalls Thornfield House in Charlotte Brontë's *Jane Eyre*, the role that it plays as the location of male conspiracy and the dreary stretch of water adjacent to it connect it to Blackwater Park in Collins's *The Woman in White*. It is here that Sir Percival Glyde and his co-conspirator

Count Fosco fabricate their plot to separate his wife Laura from her half-sister Marian, who is deeply attached to her, and imprison her in a mental institution to gain possession of her fortune. Sue, in contrast, is not Maud's half-sister but her maid. This, in turn, relates Briar to other country seats in Victorian fiction where maids and their mistresses form emotionally complex attachments. A key example is Chesney Wold in Dickens's *Bleak House*, the location of the emotionally fraught trio of Lady Dedlock and her two personal maids, the naive Rosa and the passionate, jealous Hortense. Echoes of these involvements shadow the relationship that develops between Sue and Maud.

In contrast to Collins and Dickens, however, who represent the female attachments they describe primarily in terms of affection and romantic friendship and relegate them to the margins of the text, allowing them to become buried by narratives focusing on the hetero-patriarchal family, Waters foregrounds the sexual aspect of Sue and Maud's relationship. She also prioritizes their storyline, permitting it to challenge and eventually supplant the masculinist-inflected narrative treating Gentleman and his fortune-hunting. Irigaray, commenting on woman's role as an object of exchange performing the feminine masquerade that phallocentric culture assigns to her, ironically observes, subversively parodying Lacan, 'Woman? She "doesn't exist"' . . . She acts out the role that is imposed on her. The only thing really expected of her is that she *keep intact the circulation of pretence by enveloping herself in femininity*.'[44] This is the role Maud initially enacts, trapped as she is between Lilly's and Gentleman's exploitative treatment. Gentleman, commenting on the notoriety that Maud's readings of Lilly's erotic texts have brought her in metropolitan society, mockingly remarks: 'They speak about you in the shady bookshops and publishers' houses of London and Paris . . . as of some fabulous creature: the handsome girl at Briar, whom Lilly has trained like a chattering monkey, to recite voluptuous texts for gentlemen – perhaps to do worse' (p. 224). Sexual-textual politics operate visibly here, with society linking the female subject's sexual conduct to the immoral literature she reads. Gentleman's words, in addition, portray Maud in the role of 'monkey' and puppet, uncannily ventriloquizing the words men put in her mouth in a manner resembling the automaton Olympia in E. T. A. Hoffmann's 'The Sandman'.[45]

The uncanny is also in evidence in the attempt that Maud makes to liberate herself from the chain of male power entrapping her by deflating Gentleman's arrogant assumption that she is captive to his sexual charms. When she indicates that it is Sue, not him, to whom she is erotically attracted and therefore has not 'the heart' (p. 276) to betray her, he cannot conceal his astonishment. He mutters incredulously, 'You've a heart, instead, for little fingersmiths? Oh, Maud …' (p. 276). An observation voiced by Dianne Chisholm, in discussing Balzac's 'The Girl With the Golden Eyes' that portrays the hero making a similarly disconcerting discovery about the same-sex desires of the girl he is amorously pursuing, helps to explain Gentleman's discomfiture. As Chisholm argues: 'The uncanny is the effect produced when, instead of serving as a mirror image of masculine sovereignty and reflecting precisely what the male gaze intends to see – masculine self identity – the mirror of femininity reflects back the desire of another – a woman, his castrated counterpart.'[46] The upsetting effect that Maud's admission of her erotic attachment to Sue has on Gentleman demonstrates that lesbian desire, though socially marginalized and frequently invisible, can nonetheless intervene on occasion, 'jamming the machinery'[47] as Irigaray expressively puts it of the phallocentric economy. Although in this instance Maud loses courage and complies with Gentleman's scheme to imprison Sue in a madhouse, Waters concludes the novel by portraying her rejecting male manipulation and achieving personal autonomy.

The concepts of the 'return of the repressed' and the '*unheimlich* place of the female genitals' representing 'the former *Heim* [home] of all human beings' (p. 368), discussed by Freud in 'The uncanny', play a key in Waters's account of Sue and Maud's trajectory. Underpinning the two women's quest for self-determination, as is often the case in lesbian fiction, is a narrative focusing on the figure of the mother. Occupying a central place in the novel, representing its primal scene as it were, is the retrospectively described episode in which the pregnant Marianne Lilly arrives at the house in Lant Street seeking refuge from her male relatives who are pursuing her and, on the birth of her daughter, requesting Mrs Sucksby to raise her and give her an orphan girl in exchange. Although Waters postpones disclosing this event until the later stages of the narrative, veiled traces of Marianne Lilly surface earlier. The fear Sue expresses that Briar 'might certainly have ghosts' (p. 87) is in fact closer to the truth than she perceives at the time. While acting as Maud's maid, she accompanies her on the visits she pays to Marianne's grave, unaware that it is the burial place of her own mother and not Maud's as the two women then assume. She also thinks that she sees 'Maud's dead mother, come back as a ghost to haunt me' (p. 87). Although the supposed apparition turns out, on closer scrutiny, to be merely a crinoline cage, the episode indicates that Briar, like Chesney Wold in *Bleak House* where Esther is briefly reunited with her mother, operates as the location of a repressed female genealogy. Here, as in Tóibín's portrayal of Helen's emotionally tense relationship with her mother in *The Blackwater Lightship* discussed in chapter 2, Irigaray's reference to *déréliction* assumes pertinence. Irigaray describes women, separated from one another by the patrilineal family system, 'lost in the air, like ghosts',[48] and advises them to challenge their oppressed position by bonding together in friendship or love. Sue and Maud unconsciously embark on this course when they become lovers.

As well as foregrounding the sexual aspect of Maud and Sue's relationship and twice describing their sexual encounter, initially from Sue's point of view and subsequently from Maud's, Waters prioritizes the related topic of lesbian sexual representation. On making love with Sue, Maud finds her approach to her guardian's erotic texts changing, particularly the passages describing 'the means a woman may employ to pleasure another' (p. 279). On reading them aloud to Lilly, she thinks, 'I have supposed them dead. Now the words – start up, are filled with meaning. I grow muddled, stammer. I lose my place' (p. 279). Lying in Sue's arms, she mentally compares life with art: 'May a lady taste the fingers of her maid? She may in her uncle's books – the thought makes me colour' (p. 256). In linking sexuality and textuality, Waters interestingly recasts another motif that Dickens treats. Miller, discussing Dickens's account of the youthful relationship between David Copperfield and Steerforth at boarding school, suggests that exchanging stories from the novels they have read functions as a substitute for the sexual relations in which, judging from the erotic attraction between them at which he hints, the two boys might have engaged.[49] Waters, in contrast, writing in the sexually permissive climate of the present day and secure in the knowledge of her lesbian-feminist readership, feels free to treat queer relationships openly. Like her representation of Helen and Julia's relationship in the *The Night Watch*, discussed in chapter 2, her description of the sexual encounter between Sue and Maud is both explicit and richly sensual.

The eventual reunion of the two women at Briar house with which Waters concludes the novel again recasts an episode from Dickens's fiction. It echoes, in the reversal of the 'expectations' the two women have experienced, the revised ending of *Great Expectations* that, though leaving their future uncertain, portrays Pip and Estella reunited in the ruins of Satis House. It also gives an unexpected twist to the topic of lesbian sexual representation. On arriving at Briar, Sue finds Maud seated alone, writing at Lilly's desk. Lilly is now dead and Maud, having discovered her humble origins, is as she explains earning a living in the only way she knows: by producing and selling erotica. In response to Sue's objection to what she regards as the unladylike nature of the occupation, she defends the accounts of lesbian sex she is writing not just from a commercial point of view but in personal terms: 'It is filled with all the words for how I want you' (p. 547). The novel's final sentence portrays the illiterate Sue receiving her first lesson in reading, though certainly not in the manner she had envisaged. She describes how Maud 'put the lamp upon the floor, spread the paper flat; and began to show me the words she had written, one by one' (p. 548).

This episode has proved controversial, with Mark Llewellyn criticizing Waters's reference to Maud writing lesbian erotica, mistakenly in my view, as 'a possibly less than satisfactory resolution'[50] to her romance narrative. In fact, read in the context of both Waters's own interest in lesbian sexual representation and the questions and debates the topic has provoked from lesbian/feminist historians and critics, it emerges as notably appropriate. A key question that researchers debate is that of the significance of the accounts of lesbian sex that feature in eighteenth- and nineteenth-century erotic texts. Do they (as Lillian Faderman suggested in the 1970s) merely reflect male sexual fantasy and have little if anything to do with actual women,[51] or do they, as Donoghue has more recently suggested, perhaps have a degree of authenticity?[52] Donoghue also points out that although it is generally assumed that all such accounts were written by men, there is no actual proof that they were. Waters herself also questions whether the interest in these publications was exclusively male. Discussing the collection of erotic material owned by the nineteenth-century collector Henry Spencer Ashbee, who provided the model for her portrayal of Lilly, she observes that although the majority of such texts 'would have been written by men, almost certainly, I suppose women working in the sex industry and some men's wives might have read and possibly enjoyed them'.[53]

Lesbian erotic representation has also provoked controversy with reference to writing produced today. While the degree of explicitness writers of lesbian fiction should employ in describing their characters' sexual practice has aroused discussion, the topic that has generated the most heated debate is the production and publication of lesbian erotica and pornography by lesbians themselves. The mid-1980s marked a period of sexual enquiry and experimentation in the lesbian subculture, with a number of women challenging what they regarded as the puritanical attitudes of the lesbian feminist movement. Erotica and pornography, along with other previously taboo topics such as butch/femme role-play and S & M, featured on the agenda for debate. Whereas some women expressed distaste for the new erotic publications such as the magazine *Quim* and the collection *Serious Pleasure* that catered for such interests, others, as Emma Healey writes,

> began to argue that you could make a distinction between male-produced pornography and that produced by and for lesbians. It could be argued that the old arguments that porn is basically exploitative were no longer viable when it was clear that women, the usual victims of porn, were actually its consumers and audience.[54]

By moving from representing Maud being coerced by Lilly into reading lesbian erotica to him and his gentlemen friends to portraying her utilizing the example that she herself has produced to instruct her lover Sue in the rudiments of literacy, Waters encompasses in the novel both its oppressive and its arguably creative uses. She comments wittily on the controversies that erotica and porn have provoked in the lesbian community while leaving the debates they have generated open.

Transgender doubles

Discussing the motif of the double and its uncanny significance, Wolfreys describes it as 'the figure of haunting *par excellence*'.[55] Its importance, he argues, resides in its ability to evoke the 'fragmented divided self' and, by interrelating the unfamiliar with the familiar, 'remind us of the otherness that inhabits the self-same' (p. 15).

Cultural and theoretical discourses focusing on the double differ considerably in approach. Representations of the motif in Victorian Gothic, which explores from a moral viewpoint the contraries of good versus evil and reason versus passion, are as critics illustrate[56] at odds with the Germanic tradition of the uncanny exemplified by the work of Hoffmann and Schlegel, which interprets the subject's encounter with his doppelgänger in terms of a tension of opposites. Psychoanalytic approaches, pioneered by Freud and developed by later theorists, have enriched these traditions by linking the double to the return of the repressed, the fragmentation of the psyche and the tension between conscious and unconscious dimensions.

Among the different approaches contributing to the treatment of the double in fiction, queer perspectives are notably in evidence, particularly in Gothic writing. Sedgwick interprets the mysterious Gil Martin in James Hogg's *The Private Memoirs and Confessions of a Justified Sinner* as the 'eroticized, paranoid double'[57] of the protagonist Robert, while Armitt reads the female figure entrapped in the paper in Gilman's *The Yellow Wallpaper* that the protagonist seeks to liberate as representing her same-sex alter ego.[58] With reference to transgender, the topic considered here, Dale Townshend investigates queer cross-gendering in Matthew Lewis's *The Monk*, while I explore the 'gallantly boyish role' that Leonie performs in Antonia White's *Frost in May*.[59] The two writers, though both treat the topic very differently from contemporary writers, bring it to the attention of readers and open it for discussion.

Freud's reference to the concept of doubling in 'The uncanny', as indicated in the opening chapter of this study, is pertinent to both transgender (frequently used as an umbrella term for people who do not conform to accepted gender roles) and transsexuality (denoting a person who identifies with a gender different from his biological one and who sometimes employs sex reassignment surgery). He discusses the phenomenon of 'doubling, dividing and interchanging of the self' and comments on 'the doubt as to which his self is'[60] that this can trigger in the individual. Whether we regard the transgender/transsexual person as moving from one sex-identification to another or, as Sandy Stone does,[61] challenging the conventionally accepted gender binary by refusing its constraints, he subverts the traditional Western concept of a single, stable sex and the identity that is assumed to depend on it. Halberstam describes the transsexual as living in a state of cross-identification with a sense of identity that instead of stemming from the body conflicts with it;[62] while Prosser, commenting on the rift between his 'internal' and his 'exterior body' that the transsexual experiences, employs a spectral metaphor. Reading Radclyffe Hall's *The Well of Loneliness* as a transsexual narrative, he describes Stephen's story as 'haunted' by the image of the male body that he feels he should have had and refers to 'the phantom morphology in the text'[63] that this creates. These analyses, despite their differences, all 'bear witness', as Susan Stryker observes, 'to the epistemological rift between gender signifiers and their signified'[64] that the transgender or transsexual person exemplifies in challenging the assumption that gender has its basis in the body. Stella Duffy's *Beneath the Blonde* and Patrick McGrath's *Dr Haggard's Disease*, the two novels discussed in this section, investigate these ideas in fictional form.

Transgender and transsexuality can be difficult topics for writers to address on account of the transphobic treatment they have sometimes received.[65] This is exemplified by Brian de Palma's film *Dressed to Kill* (1980) and Jonathan Demme's *The Silence of the Lambs* (1990) that portray gender-ambiguous characters as perverse killers, as well as by Jean Baudrillard's prejudiced theoretical critique. Utilizing transgender and transsexuality as a metaphor for the collapse of the division between nature and culture that he sees as typifying the postmodern condition, Baudrillard accuses them of generating a horrific world of 'indifferent and undifferentiated beings, androgynous and hermaphrodite'.[66] These negative interpretations are countered, however, by affirmative ones. Donna Haraway portrays the transgender subject, exemplified by the cyborg and the hybrid interplay of masculine and feminine the figure represents, as a blueprint for contemporary feminism,[67] while Kate Bornstein celebrates the transsexual as a courageous 'gender outlaw'.[68] She approvingly contrasts the transgressively radical performance of gender mobility that he enacts with the conservative model of gender stability that the majority of the population unadventurously accept.

Duffy and McGrath, though both structure their texts (like De Palma and Demme) on strategies of intrigue and suspense associated with the thriller, avoid positioning the transsexual or transgender person in the role of criminal. They also perceptively interrogate and discuss the ambiguities and apparent contradictions that a cross-gender identification can involve. Duffy's novel takes the form of a lesbian thriller, a subgenre that emerged in the mid-1980s originating in the lesbian/feminist experimentation with popular genres, while McGrath creates a parodic version of the Gothic mystery. He inter-weaves Gothic motifs of doubling and spectrality with topics associated with crime fiction including a death in suspicious circumstances and the dissection of the corpse in the pathologist's lab. Transsexuality and transgender are topics that are understandably popular with writers of crime and mystery fiction. The challenge they direct at conventional assumptions of the integrity and stability of gender identity and embodiment, combined with the epistemelogical questions they raise, furnish admirable material for constructing the intrigue plots and the riddles relating to identity that these genres traditionally treat. If handled intelligently, they give them a new queer dimension and a postmodern topicality.

Duffy constructs *Beneath The Blonde* around an example of female-to-male transsexuality, creating a tightly structured narrative that combines reference to gender performance with the performance of musicians on stage. The novel opens with the lesbian Saz Martin, a London-based private detective, being unexpectedly approached by Siobhan Forrest, the glamorous lead singer of the popular band Beneath the Blonde, with a request to investigate the series of threat-ening anonymous letters and bouquets of yellow roses that she has been mysteriously receiving. Attracted by Siobhan's glitzy reputation and the prospect of participating in the world tour on which the band is about to embark, Saz accepts the commission.

On meeting Siobhan and the four other members of the band – Alex, Steve, Dan and Siobhan's New Zealander boyfriend Greg – Saz discovers that their relationships, though ostensibly amicable, are in fact riddled with animosities. Her efforts to trace the source of the letters and flowers are hampered both by their lack of cooperation and, more seriously, by Siobhan and Greg's insistence that she keep the investigation secret. Siobhan cites in explanation a desire for privacy but Saz suspects her of concealing a deeper motive.

With the commencement of the band's world tour and the visits to Eastern Europe and North America that it comprises, events rapidly escalate, transforming Saz's investigation from a minor crime inquiry into a hunt for a serial killer. Alex, whom she had previously regarded as a prime suspect on account of his backbiting and general nastiness, is mysteriously killed in Tallinn, while Steve's body is discovered drowned off the Los Angeles coast. Both murders are prefaced by the arrival of the customary bouquets of yellow roses.

However, shortly after these disturbing events occur Saz succeeds in making a breakthrough in the investigation. By employing the services of some London streetpeople, she discovers that the sender of the flowers speaks with a New Zealand accent. Siobhan has arranged for the tour to conclude in New Zealand in order to enable Greg to visit his relatives, and it is here that, through a combination of intelligence and luck, Saz discovers the murderer's identity. When a fresh bouquet of yellow roses ominously arrives, accompanied by a card with an inscription coupling Greg's name with a mysterious 'Gaelene', Saz confronts Greg with it – and bluntly asks him who Gaelene is. He replies, equally bluntly: 'I killed her.'[69] However, the clue to the murderer's identity hinges not on an act of homicide committed by Greg, as Duffy teases the reader briefly into thinking, but on his symbolic 'killing' of his own former female identity and double 'Gaelene'. As a girl growing up in New Zealand Gaelene had formed an intimate friendship with a fellow pupil Shona, swearing a blood bond of sisterhood and even performing a mock marriage ceremony with her. However, despite Gaelene's subsequent sex change and 'phoenix reinvention' (p. 2) of herself into 'Greg', Shona persists in regarding Gaelene as his real self. Interpreting his change of sex as a betrayal of their love, she retaliates by trying to 'liberate' him from colleagues in the band by killing them one by one. If Saz had not intervened in her murderous project, she would have concluded as she intended by killing Siobhan as well.

This plot structure, as well furnishing the frame for a tense murder mystery, the solution to which takes both investigator and the reader by surprise, furnishes Duffy with a context to explore her characters' contrary views of transsexuality and the questions and conundrums it involves. The key to the murder mystery hinges on the fact that, as Saz discovers, Greg has not one sex identity and body image – as she assumed when introduced to him in his role of male member of the band and Siobhan's boyfriend – but two. Despite his efforts metaphorically to kill and bury his former identity as Gaelene, it unexpectedly reappears, resurrected by his childhood friend Shona, like a spectral double to haunt him. Shona, playing the role of vengeful ghost, engineers its re-emergence with the aim of wreaking havoc on him and his friends. Traumatized by what she interprets as his infidelity and desertion, she remains obsessively faithful to the female identity he has rejected and, ignoring the passing of time, continues as she grimly observes to 'remember' (p. 1). Clinging futilely to the hope that 'Gaelene is still there' and that 'somewhere in that façade there is my best friend. My blood sister' (p. 237), she responds with uncanny logic to what she regards as Greg's betrayal of his blood (his birth as female, the blood bond they swore together and the information about menstruation they shared at school) by shedding blood (killing his colleagues and friends).

Greg's approach to his former identity as Gaelene, as he explains on disclosing his sex change to Saz, is of course the reverse of Shona's. Far from regarding Gaelene as his 'real' self,[70] he sees her as an obstacle to his male identity. Though born biologically female, he recognized from childhood that he was 'really' a boy and at the age of sixteen left New Zealand to travel to Amsterdam. Here, in what Duffy describes as 'a gesture, the deliberate disposal of his past' (p. 209), he cut his hair, bound his breasts with a crêpe bandage and threw away his bra and knickers, signifiers of the 'wrong body' from which he sought to free himself. Travelling on to London, he searched for therapists and surgeons who would enable him to become 'the embodiment of the man he believed he really was' (p. 219). An ambiguity in his account, one described by Prosser as signifying the 'founding dynamic' of the transsexual narrative and reflecting the 'play between transformation and continuity of the self'[71] on which it hinges, is the fact that though he speaks of himself as being male from birth, he paradoxically also describes himself as having to be constructed as male by means of surgical intervention.

Differing from the contrary views of Shona and Greg, and possibly more in consonance with that of many readers, is Saz's response to Greg's sex change. She guiltily admits that she regards it ambivalently. Though recognizing that as a feminist 'schooled in years of left wing politics' who accepts the constructedness of gender she should un-equivocally accept the fact that Greg's embodiment and identity are partly the product of technology, she confesses that she finds it 'weird' (p. 218). Listening in astonishment to his revelations, she experiences what Royle, discussing the uncanny, terms 'a crisis of the natural'.[72] She experiences, as she describes, a confusing mix of responses:'polit-ical correctness, prurient curiosity and gender dilemmas hit her smack in the face' (p. 218).

The adjective 'weird' that she employs echoes certain events she associates with Greg. One relates to the occasion when, while visiting his parents in New Zealand, she happened to glimpse a picture of a pretty little girl on display among the other family photos.When she asked who the girl was, Greg had smoothly replied,'My cousin ... She died years ago.When she was sixteen' (p. 202). Saz recognizes with hindsight that it represents his ghostly double Gaelene.

Saz's ambivalent view of Greg's sex change is further complicated by her problematic relationship with his girlfriend Siobhan.While visiting New Zealand in the company of the band and with Greg absent from the hotel, lured by feelings of sexual infatuation she recklessly accepts Siobhan's invitation to spend the night with her. When, the following day, Siobhan casually intimates that she bedded her out of curiosity and regarded the event chiefly as an interesting experiment, Saz feels deeply hurt. Her feelings of distress and humili-ation are exacerbated by Siobhan unexpectedly announcing that she and Greg have decided to marry. After the wedding ceremony Saz bitterly spells out to herself the contradictions and riddles that, in terms of sexuality and gender, the sexualities of bride and groom signify:

Siobhan had sex with a man who'd been a woman. But Siobhan was straight. More or less. Less probably. Greg had been a woman but now he was a man and he was living with a woman. Had just got married

to a woman. Greg was a straight man married to a straight woman.
So were they both really dykes? (p. 219)

Totally confused, Saz looks back nostalgically to the simpler, if nar-
rower, sexual politics that operated in the 1970s and 1980s before
transsexuality and the conundrums and paradoxes of sex and identity
it poses had emerged on the gay and feminist scene. In that earlier
period, as she describes,

> Queer just meant gay and wasn't likely to also include women who
> loved men who were once women and men who loved women who
> were going to become men and women who loved women but quite
> liked men too sometimes and men who didn't care who they loved as
> long as they were loved back and every other trans-gender permutation
> that now gathered under the fluttering and expanding rainbow flag.
> (pp. 221–2)

Duffy herself, it is interesting to note, challenges Saz's view of Greg's
sex change as particularly 'weird' by illustrating that, in this postmodern age, the majority of us have 'uncanny' bodies: hybrid combinations of nature and culture, the organic and the technological.
She compares Greg's account of the surgical operations that he has
undergone in order to achieve male embodiment with the surgery
that Saz describes herself having experienced to reconstruct her
body after the burns she suffered in an earlier crime investigation.
She also portrays Siobhan admitting that her celebrated 'body of an
Amazon Princess' (p. 31), far from being natural, is the product of
technology and rigorous exercise. Alerting attention to the physical
effort that she has to put into achieving and maintaining it, Siobhan
humorously refers to herself as one of all 'the other Barbie dolls who
wish their sculpted limbs were made from plastic and not sweat'
(p. 32). Duffy's portrayal of her dancing 'like a constructed angel'
(p. 124) at Alex's funeral wake and the contradictions the phrase
implies also evoke an uncanny interplay of inanimate and animate,
art and nature, recalling the automaton Olympia discussed by Freud
and Cixous. Duffy describes Siobhan's performance on the dance
floor as miming a seductive element of risk, with her 'teetering on
the edge of balance only to flick herself upright at the last impossible

moment' (p. 124). The precariousness of her dance movements, as well as recalling Russo's account of woman's precarious role as 'spectacle' in phallocentric culture and the problems and dangers attendant on it,[73] symbolically enacts the risk she runs as the potential victim of Shona's murderous intentions.

Among the questions about Greg's sex change that Duffy raises, one is particularly significant: is the aim of the transsexual, on achieving the gender embodiment he desires, to 'pass' or should he, as Bornstein radically argues,[74] disclose the secret of its constructedness with the aim of challenging the binary gender system? There are signs that Duffy agrees with Bornstein since she portrays Greg, his conscience troubled by the deaths of Alex and Steve, admitting that had he been honest with Saz and revealed his sex change and the existence of his ghostly double Gaelene from the start of the investigation, Saz might have have deduced the murderer's identity earlier and prevented the two men's deaths. She also pointedly portrays Saz discussing the pros and cons of homosexual coming out with a group of lesbian and heterosexual friends at a supper party she hosts. However, had Duffy portrayed Greg disclosing his change of sex and identity in the opening chapters, her narrative would have developed along very different lines, depriving the reader of an enjoyable, cleverly contrived thriller!

Not all writers who treat the topic of gender-crossing and the riddles and questions it raises centre their narratives on a transsexual or transgender individual. McGrath, in fact, employs an alternative strategy. Unlike Duffy who concentrates on the haunting of the transsexual Greg by his former female identity, he focuses *Dr Haggard's Disease* on an instance of transgender fantasy. Like Duffy, however, he structures his novel on the double, though he treats the motif very differently.

Dr Haggard's Disease takes the form of a first-person narrative recounted by the eponymous medical practitioner Edward Haggard, his surname ironically prefiguring the destructive effect that the disturbing events that he experiences have on his person and psyche. Commencing with an account of his adulterous love affair with the beautiful Frances, the wife of the senior pathologist at the London hospital where he worked as a registrar in the 1940s, the novel goes on to describe the fantasy scenario that he unconsciously fabricates in order to compensate for her death and resurrect her image.

Reference to the motif of the double first occurs in relation to the medical staff at the London hospital where Haggard initially works. Ratcliff, the husband of his lover Frances, his name echoing the Gothic writer Ann Radcliffe and David Storey's queer novel *Radcliffe* (1963), duplicates in his brutality and uncouthness the bullying behaviour of the senior surgeon Cushing. Frances has little respect for the post-mortem activities in which the the two men obsessively engage. Employing a phrase recalling the activities of Victor Frankenstein in his 'workshop of filthy creation',[75] she describes them as morbidly 'poking through the diseased bits of dead bodies'.[76] Haggard's colleague McGuiness who occupies, like him, the humble post of junior registrar, is similarly suspicious. Rhetorically asking 'what sort of doctor wants to hang around tombs all day', he darkly conjectures, 'I think there's something primitive that makes a man go into pathology' (p. 78).

Haggard, a contemplative soul with a passion for poetry, is as he himself admits unsuited to the role of surgeon. His description of himself 'hunched over a stained and battered workbench . . . in the musty closet of a laboratory at the end of the ward that stank of urine and chemicals' (p. 18) again conjures up the image of Frankenstein, evoking a shabby, unheroic image of his labours. These echoes of Shelley's novel are more than merely atmospheric. They signal McGrath's interest in the age-old topic of man's efforts to transcend the limitations of human existence by creating an uncanny double, to which he inventively gives a new transgender slant.

The location of the novel subsequently shifts from the hospital in London to Elgin, the 'romantic house' with 'steeply gabled roofs' and 'tall chimneys' (p. 7) situated in a genteel British seaside resort that Haggard inherits from an uncle. He retires there to take up the post of country doctor when his love affair with Frances comes to an abrupt end. It is terminated both by Ratcliff's discovery of it and Frances's unexpected death, an event Haggard attributes partly to Ratcliff's medical negligence.

Perched on a cliff overlooking the sea with the waves, as Haggard describes, surging wildly below, Elgin resembles in geographical situation the ill-fated house of Manderley in Daphne Du Maurier's

Rebecca. It furnishes an appropriate setting for his melancholy state of mind. His grief at Frances's death is exacerbated by the acute physical pain he suffers in his hip, the effect of the brutal physical assault that Ratcliff, furious at being cuckolded by a junior registrar, perpetrates on him at the hospital before he resigns. He experiences difficulty sleeping, and the fantastic 'riot of elaborate organicism', involving 'skulls, masks and snakes' (p. 25) that, lying awake at night, he projects onto the cracks in the plaster in his bedroom resemble the images that the narrator of Gilman's *The Yellow Wallpaper* strives to decipher. The thumping of 'the huge monster heart' (p. 26) that he thinks he hears (it turns out anticlimactically to be the sound of the ancient generator servicing the boiler that heats the house) recalls Poe's 'The Tell-Tale Heart'.

Haggard, however, does not remain without solace for long since an unexpected encounter with Frances's adult son James enables him unexpectedly to retrieve her image. James is a pilot in the RAF and, happening to be stationed at a base near Elgin, he visits Haggard to share his grief at her death. Haggard is immediately struck by what he sees as the young man's 'uncanny resemblance' (p. 5) to Frances. Gazing at him raptly, he contemplates with pleasure, similar to the kind she had evoked, what he erotically describes to himself as 'your unruly black hair, your clear, burning eyes, your white skin, red lips' (p. 13). Each visit James pays to Elgin confirms Haggard's belief in an event that, though it strikes the reader as absurd, makes perfect sense to him. He is convinced that as a result of the stresses of his life as a fighter pilot, James is suffering from a glandular disturbance and undergoing a change of sex.

Haggard's view of James's sex is confusingly schizoid. He moves from seeing him as he actually is, a handsome young man, to regarding him as female and experiencing what he euphemistically calls 'a distinct movement of sexual feeling' (p. 176) towards him. Envisaging the Nazi invasion of Britain and the spitfire James pilots being shot down in the crossfire, he pictures himself cradling his charred, dying body in his arms and consummating his desire for him/her with a passionate kiss: 'I press my mouth gently to yours and probe for your tongue with my own, probe with tiny darting flickers till I taste in your terribly burnt head the fresh sweet wetness of the living tongue within' (p. 180). The ghoulish nature of the fantasy illustrates the preoccupation with bodily decay and dismemberment which pervades the narrative and is associated chiefly with the male members of the medical profession, again recalling Shelley's *Frankenstein*.

The images that Haggard projects upon James shift disconcertingly from male to female. Picturing him struggling to repel the Nazi air attack, he sees him in the conventionally masculinist role of fighter pilot, 'a brave sick gallant boy giving your life for a hopeless cause' (p. 178). In other episodes, however, as illustrated in the description of the erotic kiss he gives him referred to above, he sees him as Frances's double and voluptuously female.

Haggard's own sexuality, like the fantasy images he projects upon James, is ambiguous, and McGrath treats it with macabre humour. Freud's analysis of the memoirs of Daniel Paul Schreber, a former member of the German judiciary whom he diagnosed as suffering from hallucinatory insanity reflected in fantasies of female embodiment, furnishes a context for its analysis. Schreber records how, having suffered from periods of depression, he awoke one morning with the unexpected thought that he would like to experience sexual intercourse as a woman – and subsequently came to believe that God was transforming him into one. Although Haggard's gender-bending fantasies differ from Schreber's in that he projects them not on himself but on his lover's son, he nonetheless reveals connections with Schreber. Like Schreber who thinks that he has a mission to redeem the world, Haggard describes himself as put on earth to witness and record James's female metamorphosis. The dreams of bodily dismemberment and castration he experiences, that appear to pave the way for his fantasy transformation of James into Frances, also recall Schreber's bizarre fantasies of his somatic fragmentation. Schreber portrays himself as existing without certain key organs, including stomach and intestines, and describes how, as well as having 'a torn oesophagus', he 'used sometimes to swallow part of his larynx with his food'.[77] Haggard, referring to the 'grotesque dreams' (p. 130) he experiences at night, elaborates: 'My thorax was open, my insides were neatly piled on my chest, and my penis was rolling around on the floor' (p. 130). However, unlike Schreber's fantasies, McGrath's description of Haggard's dreams and self-perceptions is grimly humorous, resembling in tone Mikhail Bakhtin's treatment of the comic grotesque. Gazing glumly at his reflection in the mirror and noting the destructive effect that grief at Frances's death has wrought on his looks, Haggard sees himself, with his 'too-large head atop the monstrous shoulders and the sunken hairless chest', as resembling 'a shrimp, a crested shrimp' (p. 58). His reference to his displaced organs and his descent to the animal, or rather the fishy, plane of creation, also differs from Schreber's self-portrayal. Whereas Schreber's fantasies are self-congratulatory, demonstrating his extraordinary powers of physical survival, Haggard's dreams illustrate his low self-image and rework memories of his medical superiors' humiliating treatment.

Freud's analysis of Schreber's fantasies and the 'feminine attitude' reflecting 'erotic desire' (p. 176) that he interprets him displaying toward his doctor Flechsig leads him to diagnose him as homosexual, and this at first seems a possible interpretation of McGrath's representation of Haggard. The youthful James, puzzled and shocked by the liberties that Haggard takes, clearly regards him as a predatory queer. When James is injured in a bombing raid, Haggard exploits his privilege as a medical practitioner to persuade him to submit to a physical examination. In the comedy of the absurd that ensues, Haggard, delighted to have the opportunity to assess the progress of James's sex change, cups his testicles in his hands and scrutinizes them, prompting the indignant James gruffly to protest, 'That's enough of that!' (p. 157). On another occasion Haggard pursues him to the RAF station and loudly announces, 'You're sick!' to which James pointedly retorts, 'Not me, doctor. You!' (p. 160).

If we interpret Haggard, as James and his comrades at the RAF station do, as homosexual, then it is tempting to interpret his excessive grief at Frances's death as a screen for his feelings of melancholia at his disavowal of his homosexuality. Butler, developing Freudian theory, argues that the subject's disavowed homosexuality can become incorporated in the ego as a melancholic self-identification.[78] Interpreted in this way, Haggard's meeting with James, who is related to Frances and physically resembles her, can be read as enabling him to recuperate in fantasy his lost homosexuality.

The problem with this reading, however, is that in the fantasy episodes in which Haggard responds sexually to James, such as the one culminating in the kiss, he regards him not as male but erotically female. As suits the Gothic mystery he writes, McGrath resists defining Haggard's sexuality but keeps it ambiguous. The title *Dr Haggard's*

Disease indicates this, since it can denote either the 'disease' of a sex change triggered by the stresses of life as a fighter pilot that Haggard diagnoses in James and to which he proudly gives his own name or, alternatively, the 'disease' of hallucinatory insanity from which he, like his famous predecessor Schreber, suffers. While tantalizingly hinting at the enigma the narrative encrypts, it skilfully keeps it concealed.

Day, discussing the development of the detective novel in the fiction of Poe and Collins, describes the figure of the detective, in his ability to solve the crime and restore a degree of order to society, as representing 'the hero the Gothic world needs but cannot sustain'.[79] Duffy's and McGrath's novels illustrate the difference between the two fictional forms. Whereas Duffy's thriller portrays the investigator Saz eventually discovering the murderer's identity and, in consequence, saving Siobhan's life, McGrath's Gothic mystery lacks a figure with the authority and perception capable of achieving this restoration of order. It concludes with Haggard lapsing ever deeper into delusion – and the reader too engulfed in cross-currents of intriguing but unverifiable conjecture.

The queer representations of spectrality in the novels discussed above, along with the double and the phantom-text relating to it, are notably diverse, with writers employing the motifs to explore a variety of different facets of lesbian, male gay and transgender experience. While reference to the return of repressed fears and desires, associated by Freud with the figure of the ghost, assumes prominence, dominating or underpinning several novels, other motifs associated with the Freudian uncanny – including doubling, the haunted house and the interplay between the familiar and unfamiliar – also feature. Lesbian and male gay versions of the ghost story are particularly inventive. Smith's utilization of a spectral narrator in *Hotel World* to explore lesbian invisibility and examples of marginalized femininity contrasts with Purdy's emotionally disturbing and at times humorous portrayal in *Mourners Below* of his male protagonist's encounter with the ghosts of his two half-brothers, and the interplay between homosocial and homosexual, identification and desire, that he employs it to explore.

The uses of intertextual reference to the nineteenth-century Gothic are illustrated in Bram's *Father of Frankenstein*, focusing on the life of the film director James Whale, and Waters's *Fingersmith*, an example of lesbian historiographic metafiction that recasts facets of the sensation novel and Gothic romance while also investigating the complexities of lesbian sexual representation. Other writers too make effective use of Gothic intertextuality. Reference to Mary Shelley's *Frankenstein* furnishes a link between Bram's *Father of Frankenstein* and McGrath's *Dr Haggard's Disease*, two novels that differ markedly in other respects.

McGrath's Gothic mystery and Duffy's thriller *Beneath the Blonde* employ the motif of the double to investigate the experience of cross-gendering that transsexuality and transgender involve. Duffy portrays the female identity that her protagonist Greg has rejected returning to haunt him, while Haggard gives a blackly humorous twist to the phenomenon of transgender fantasy.

Another topic to the fore in some of the novels discussed above is the uncanny associations that geographical and domestic locations, both urban and rural, can assume. It is in evidence in Smith's representation of the Global Hotel and the contrast that McGrath draws between the claustrophobic London hospital where Haggard initially works and the rural location of the house of Elgin to which he retires. The topic receives more detailed discussion in the following chapter, which investigates the queer significance of place and space and their uncanny aspects.

4

Place and Space

꙾

It is certainly desire that helps generate a lesbian landscape, a ground that is shaped by the paths we follow in deviating from the straight line. (Ahmed, *Queer Phenomenology*, p. 20)

Theoretical approaches

Attempting to chart the representation of place and space in Gothic fiction and narratives inscribing uncanny events is, as Punter points out, a contradictory project. Since the landscapes, buildings and other locations featuring in texts of this kind exist, as he writes, 'in a world where there are no maps ... Gothic itself challenges that very process of map-making by means of which we might hope to reduce the world to manageable proportions'.[1] However, while their mystery needs to be acknowledged, the role they play in the narrative also requires analysis. In novels by writers from Radcliffe to King, ancestral mansions, city streets and burial grounds, with places and spaces associated with different forms of ceremony, are important not merely for their atmospheric effect and symbolic significance. As well as furnishing a testing ground for the protagonist's wisdom or a setting for acts of violence or transgressive sex, they can evoke an image of horror or the sublime or a sense of continuity with the past.[2] In addition, as Day illustrates, the protagonist's relationship with his environment can indicate the stage he has reached in the Gothic process of uncanny 'enthralment', as he moves from feeling separate from the landscape to experiencing an 'interpenetration of subjective and objective reality'.[3]

Freud refers to the eerie effects of place and space in 'The uncanny', citing as a macabre example of the haunted house a property with a table ornamented with carvings of crocodiles, 'wooden monsters'[4] that appear to come alive at night and prowl the rooms. He also introduces a personal anecdote relating to the urban uncanny. Illustrating the compulsion to repeat and the anxiety stemming from loss of direction, he describes how, while visiting the deserted quarter of an Italian town in the heat of summer, he happened to lose his way. On trying to extricate himself from the maze of streets, he found himself accidentally returning to the same spot he had started out from. His reference to the 'painted women'[5] in the windows of the houses gives his account sexual significance, as Cixous observes.[6]

A very different familiar/unfamiliar place, one common to humanity in general, that Freud foregrounds in the essay is the womb where, as he writes in a sentence combining fairy-tale phraseology with biblical, 'Each one of us lived once upon a time and in the beginning'.[7] In his commentary on Wilhelm Jensen's *Gradiva* he develops the uncanny associations of place and space to encompass geographical location, nationality and family. He discusses the episode in the novel set in Pompeii in which the eponymous heroine, whom the protagonist Hanold assumes to be a ghost from the ancient city, requests him to speak to her not in Latin but in her native German, indicating her physicality and place of birth.[8] The episode illustrates, Derrida argues, the contribution that 'familial domesticity' makes to the uncanny, illustrating that 'haunting implies places, a habitation, and always a haunted house'.[9]

Queer theoretical discourse is also rich in references to place and space, frequently with uncanny resonance. Sedgwick's analysis of spatial imagery in her 1980 publication *The Coherence of Gothic Conventions* anticipates her utilization of it in the queer theoretical writing that she subsequently produced. She discusses in the former the treatment of motifs of liminality and live burial in the fiction of Radcliffe and Charles Maturin and, referring to Piranesi's treatment of space in his *Carceri* prints, remarks on his disturbing utilization of images of inside/outside exemplified by stairways that appear to lead to no-where and rooms lacking an entrance or exit. These images reappear in her discussion of the binary opposition inside/out in *Epistemology of the Closet*.[10] Her analysis of the risks attendant on coming out and the 'new walls springing up'[11] that the individual encounters when seeking to disclose his sexuality develops her reference in the earlier publication to the dangers experienced by the prisoner in eighteenth-century Gothic when he attempts to escape from the dungeon or monastery in which he is confined.[12] Her discussion of the closet and its oppressive aspect likewise echoes her earlier analysis of the Gothic motif of live burial.[13]

Ahmed is another queer theorist who makes perceptive use of imagery of space and place and their uncanny dimension. In *Queer Phenomenology* she describes how 'lesbian desire can be rethought as a space for action, a way of extending into space through tending towards other women' (p. 102). She also plays fruitfully on the different meanings of 'orientation', geographical and sexual. Referring to the lesbian's oblique relation to heteronormative conventions and her discovery of new sexual perspectives and ways of relating to women previously unperceived, she suggests: 'Queer orientation might be those things that don't line up, which by seeing the world "slantwise" allow other objects to come into view.' (p. 107)

Reference to space and place also features in Marilyn R. Farwell's analysis of lesbian narrative. Investigating the strategies the lesbian writer can employ to challenge the heterosexual bias of Western storytelling, she explores the subversive effect of 'lesbian narrative space'.[14] She demonstrates how the insertion of an episode focusing on lesbian sexuality and the excess it signifies in a text that is pre-dominantly hetero-patriarchal in emphasis has the effect of interro-gating and problematizing its ideological viewpoint. She cites in illustration the episode treating the sexual encounter between Morgaine and Raven in Marion Zimmer Bradley's Arthurian romance *The Mists of Avalon*.

With reference to queer fiction, certain of the novels discussed in the chapters above vividly illustrate the importance that place and space can assume as signifiers of the queer uncanny. Waters in *Finger-smith*, for example, signals by a reference to the spectral the role that Briar plays both as a *heimlich/unheimlich* house and the site of a repressed maternal genealogy. This chapter investigates the fictional treatment of other places and spaces with uncanny connotations, exploring the different meanings, literal and metaphorical, they assume. It prioritizes three motifs with Gothic associations that writers treat especially perceptively: the haunted house, the uncanny city, and places and spaces relating to ceremony and ritual. Jim Grimsley, Shani Mootoo and the other writers discussed below recast the motifs in the context of present-day lesbian and male gay existence. However, by means of intertextual reference, they permit traces of their earlier literary and cultural uses to emerge, thus connecting the present with the past.

The haunted house

The haunted house is a motif with enduring appeal for readers and spectators, receiving imaginative treatment in numerous novels and films. Wolfreys describes it as contributing to themes of 'spectral transformation' and the 'blurring of boundaries',[15] as well as symbolically evoking the ability of the Gothic to survive and return in innovative forms. He also cites Mark Wigley's thought-provoking definition of the uncanny itself as signifying a '"not-being-at-home", an alienation from the house experienced within it'.[16]

The motif is admirably suited to queer treatment since several classic Gothic texts constructed around it refer either explicitly or covertly to homoerotic themes and involvements. Henry James's *The Turn of the Screw*, Daphne Du Maurier's *Rebecca* and Shirley Jackson's *The Haunting of Hill House*, while differing in date of publication and the locations they employ, all utilize the haunted house narrative to explore the disturbing effect that same-sex desire can have on the hetero-patriarchal household. Society in the 1980s and 1990s found an additional reason to stigmatize the gay man as a polluting presence in the home. It treated him as a figure of intense fear and suspicion on account of his association with AIDS. Ellis Hanson, commenting on the frequent absence of homosexual members of the household from the iconic representational site of the family photo, bitterly observes that they feature in parental conversation chiefly as 'a crisis in Christian family politics'.[17] Referring to the exclusion of the homosexual in the public imagination from the concept of home and its connotations of security, he remarks that in the popular imagination, like the vampire or ghost, the 'gay man does not live somewhere, he lurks somewhere. He has no home. He has a haunt' (p. 336).

It is, of course, not only gay men who experience the concept of 'home' and its hetero-patriarchal cultural practices and connotations as oppressive. Women, heterosexual as well as lesbian, traditionally relegated to the private sphere and entrapped in the patriarchal ideology of domesticity, may also have this experience, as feminist theorists and fiction writers illustrate. This is pertinent to Mootoo's *Cereus Blooms at Night*, one of the texts reviewed here, since in queering the haunted house narrative and the motif of the *heimlich/unheimlich* house relating to it, Mootoo interrelates feminist with queer perceptions.

The representation of the haunted house in the novels of Grimsley and Mootoo echoes in certain respects the treatment of the *heimlich/ unheimlich* home in Leavitt's *While England Sleeps* and Waters's *The Night Watch*, discussed in chapter 2. Grimsley and Mootoo likewise tease out the problems that 'home', both as a concept and an actual domestic site, can pose the queer individual on account of its hetero-patriarchal ideology and traditions. However, unlike Leavitt and Waters who locate their fictions in London, Grimsley and Mootoo both focus on rural locations. Halberstam in *In a Queer Time and Place* complains that 'In gay/lesbian and queer studies, there has been little attention paid to date to the specificities of rural queer lives'.[18] Grimsley and Mootoo help remedy this omission, investigating the risks, physical as well as psychological, that the countryside can involve for the queer subject, as well as the attractions it holds. The locations they select and the representational strategies they employ to describe them reflect, however, very different cultural and literary traditions. Grimsley's *Dream Boy* is rooted in the conventions of North American Gothic, a form of fiction especially rich in reference to homosexuality, lesbian as well as male gay. James's 'The Real Right Thing' and 'The Jolly Corner', interpreted by John Fletcher as narratives of homosexual panic,[19] and Shirley Jackson's *The Haunting of Hill House* focusing on a lesbian attachment, are well-known examples. Homosexuality has also infiltrated the genre of American horror. This is illustrated by the way in which the descent of King's protagonist Jack Torrance into manic fits of violence in *The Shining* is exacerbated, as Steven Bruhm demonstrates, by fears of a 'homosexual invasion'.[20]

The tradition of Caribbean Gothic that influences Mootoo's *Cereus Blooms at Night*, in contrast, makes little reference to homosexuality since same-sex relationships tend to be stigmatized in the region as exemplifying white colonial decadence and reflecting the influence of the corruptly hedonistic culture of North America. It is, in fact, the view of homosexuality as a perverse foreign import that Mootoo seeks to challenge and redress. She achieves the feat of creating, as John Corr describes, 'a queer myth of origin that is simultaneously firmly connected to a Caribbean landscape and committed to a Caribbean anti-colonial politics'.[21] *Cereus Blooms at Night* is richly eclectic in the literary influences it reflects. It interweaves native Caribbean themes of witchcraft and the haunted rural estate[22] with intertextual reference to Jean Rhys's *Wide Sargasso Sea* and the interplay of Caribbean and European influences that Rhys's novel inscribes.

Though their novels reflect different cultural contexts, both writers centre their accounts of queer rural life on a critique of the hetero-patriarchal family, exposing the power structures informing it and the opportunities for paternal violence and sexual abuse that its enclosed structure promotes. Ruth Parkin-Gounelas, writing from a psychoanalytic viewpoint, describes the haunted house motif as signifying 'the site of inextricable origins and returns'.[23] It furnishes, she argues, an image of the family unit destabilized by incestuous desires and thoughts and acts of parricide or, alternatively, of the maternal body with its connotations of fecundity and protectiveness. Her reading is pertinent to Grimsley's and Mootoo's novels. Both writers treat explicitly the themes of homosexuality and incest that, represented covertly by earlier writers, have tended to operate as the repressed of the haunted house narrative. And by contrasting consensual loving gay and lesbian relationships with their abusive, coercive counterparts, they investigate the differences and connections they display, in this way preparing the ground for the positive delineation of queer familial formations.

Grimsley structures *Dream Boy* on not just one ghost-infested house but two, exploring the different forms of haunting they exemplify.

Whereas in the first the haunting is metaphorical, in the second, represented as doubling with it, an actual spectral event occurs – or what the boys who set foot in it interpret as one.

The novel, set in the 1980s, opens on a domestic note with reference to the teenage protagonist Nathan moving with his parents to a rural town in the American South. The settlement contains the customary buildings familiar to the reader from the American pastoral – church, school and farmstead – the latter being the family's new home. Behind the town lies a patch of woodland that the locals colloquially term the 'old Kennicutt Woods'.[24] Named after a notoriously brutal slave-owner who owned a plantation in the region, it acts as a reminder of the influence that the past exerts on the community, as well as the proximity of 'nature' to the 'civilization' that the town supposedly represents. That the narrative will involve the uncanny queering of this peaceful rural scene is signalled on the opening page in Grimsley's description of Nathan and his parents attending Sunday church together and the insight it gives into their different preoccupations. While Nathan's father leans forward in the pew 'thinking about salvation and hellfire and the taste of whiskey' and his mother raptly contemplates 'the body of Christ and the wings of angels' (p. 1), Nathan's thoughts focus on sex: 'He thinks about the body of the son of the farmer who owns the house his parents rented three weeks ago' (p. 2).

In the repressive climate of the era Nathan keeps his homosexual desires to himself, daring to confide them to nobody. As well as his sexuality, there is another secret, in this case an open one, that haunts the family. The three family members are aware of its content, yet do not talk about it but treat it as unspeakable. It is hinted at in Grimsley's comment, 'Nathan's father is always quiet when they move to a new town. Nathan can rest easy today' (p. 3), and by his portrayal of his mother exchanging a wan smile with her son when he enters the living room, uneasily dropping her gaze and unable to 'look him in the eye any longer' (p. 3). It is the secret of his father's sexual abuse. As well as accounting for the frequency with which the family moves home, trekking from town to town in search of a place to start anew, it explains Nathan's efforts to avoid the central area of the house by keeping to his room or busying himself in the yard. His precautions are justified since his father, far from remaining 'quiet', soon resumes his abusive behaviour, lying drunkenly in wait for Nathan on the stairs and trying to enter his room at night.

Grimsley's representation of the haunting of the family home by the father's incestuous desires reworks from a queer perspective the motif of the 'tyrannical impostures of the paternal figure'[25] and his abusive treatment of his children, generally his daughters, that features in eighteenth-century Gothic. By giving the motif homosexual significance, he also develops Haggerty's conjecture that in the Gothic, incest can act as a screen for other taboo desires, including homosexuality.[26] Grimsley employs imagery of darkness and spectrality to illustrate Nathan's association of his home with danger. Lying in bed at night Nathan sees 'the shadow of his father fall through the door' (p. 77), and, on another occasion, glimpses him 'standing in shadow' (p. 30) waiting to pounce. In trying to escape his attentions, Nathan himself becomes transformed into a furtive ghost; Grimsley describes him moving 'like a stranger in his own house, gliding through the kitchen, slipping quickly though the doorways and along the stairs' (p. 103). As occurs in eighteenth-century Gothic in which, as Ruth Perry describes, castle interiors 'with their labyrinthine internal passages stand metonymically for the body of the heroine, a body under siege',[27] features of the house act as an image for Nathan's threatened body. When, in a desperate effort to escape his father, he leaves the building and spends the night outdoors, his empty room with the unmade bed assumes the appearance of 'a haunted place' (p. 104), the rumpled sheets bearing witness to his hasty flight.

As well as representing the location of his father's incestuous desires, the house forms the context of Nathan's burgeoning homosexuality. Standing in his bedroom, he sees silhouetted in the window of the next-door property the figure of Roy, the son of the neighbouring family. The two boys attend the same school, and Nathan has seen Roy on the bus eyeing him with interest. Though sexually attracted to him, Nathan feels his desire tainted by memories of his father's sexual abuse, the only form of homosexual relations he has up to now encountered. Meeting Roy has the effect, as Grimsley sensitively writes, of 'forcing Nathan to remember things he does not want to remember' (p. 12). Nathan copes with the slippage between his father's abusive sex and the erotic attraction he feels for Roy by struggling to erase the memory of the former. Experiencing the 'painful ambivalence that characterises traumatic memory',[28] he exists in a state of psycho-logical division. Though striving to reconstruct his damaged sexuality and accept his desire for Roy, he experiences difficulty in relinquish-ing the past and its oppressive history.

The two boys' relationship, when eventually they become lovers, is fraught with problems, psychological and practical. While Nathan struggles to negotiate the difference between the consensual, loving sex he enjoys with Roy and his father's abusive attentions, Roy experiences difficulties of a different kind. Though he longs for emotional and physical intimacy, he initially regards sexual contact with Nathan as an assault on his manhood. Utilizing imagery of disintegration and rebirth, Grimsley vividly describes the conflict that, imprisoned in his carapace of masculinity, he experiences in responding to Nathan: 'Nathan leans against Roy, since it seems it is warmth that he craves. But the effect is out of proportion; it is as if he has cracked Roy's shell. Roy makes a sound as if he is taking his first breath. He pulls Nathan down to the mattress, unmindful of text-book and papers beneath' (pp. 22–3).

Nathan, though younger than Roy, is as a result of his sexual encounters with his father the more sexually experienced of the two boys. Though conscious of the difficulties and contradictions the project involves, he bravely attempts to put to positive use in his relationship with Roy the sexual experience he has acquired from his father's sexual attentions: 'The trick [he thinks] is to gain access to the knowledge he has stored inside, without remembering how it got there. To move in a way he knows will please Roy, without revealing the knowledge, which has a source' (p. 73). His efforts to practise this 'trick' sometimes misfire, as when Roy, his suspicions aroused, angrily demands, 'Where did you learn? . . . Who have you been screwing like that?' (p. 74). When Nathan, feigning ignorance, replies, 'Nobody taught me', Roy accuses him of lying. His trust turning to panic, he raises his hand as if to strike him. However, though repeatedly reminding Nathan of the need for secrecy and insisting that, despite the evidence to the contrary, he is not his 'boy-friend', he continues to pursue the relationship, becoming increasingly dependent on him emotionally and sexually.

A motif that appears frequently in eighteenth-century Gothic is the contrast between benevolent and tyrannical father figures.[29]

Radcliffe and other writers, differentiating the 'good' father from the 'bad', juxtapose reference to the former's benevolent behaviour with reference to the neglect and abusive treatment of the latter. Grimsley queers the motif, illustrating how, as his relationship with Roy strengthens, Nathan increasingly regards him not just as a lover but as a surrogate father figure, one who unlike his biological father seeks to protect him. Apart from the occasional lapses into expressions of homosexual panic or guilt-induced frigidity, Roy performs the role successfully, behaving as a 'steady guardian' (p. 105). With the advent of winter, he invites Nathan to spend the nights in the shelter of the family barn, supplies him surreptitiously with food, and, though puzzled by his refusal to sleep at home, avoids harassing him with awkward questions.

A key attribute of the fictional and cinematic representation of the ghost is its ability to cross the boundaries of inside/outside, traversing walls and material limits. Appropriating the motif for queer usage, Grimsley portrays the two boys, in an effort to pursue their relationship unobserved, leaving their homes and haunting the local countryside like a couple of phantoms. In so doing, he transposes to the present day the theme of the flight into 'the green world'[30] of nature to which male gay and lesbian lovers have traditionally resorted in both fact and fiction. Roy introduces Nathan to the local cemetery where the slave-owner Fred Kennicutt is buried. In this eerie heterotopic location they tell ghost stories and make love, enjoying a sense of freedom denied them at home. It is during these exploratory excursions, sexual as well as rural, that Grimsley introduces the second example of the haunted house that features in the novel. He describes Roy offering to show Nathan other places of interest in the area, including 'Indian mounds and camping places and a haunted house' (p. 15). By referring to Indian locations and Kennicutt's ruined plantation house, he associates the landscape with the ghosts of the massacred native American population and the black victims of slavery who symbolically haunt it. He also reworks from a queer perspective the Gothic transformation of the pastoral myth of North America as an untarnished Eden into the image of the country as a fallen world ravaged by acts of white brutality.

The novel concludes with an account of the expedition the two boys make to Kennicutt's derelict home, the 'haunted house' that

Roy seeks to show Nathan. The scattered references to the slave-owner punctuating the narrative culminate in the ghostly apparition of him that they glimpse on entering the ruined property at night. The spectral image of a 'sturdy, square shouldered' (p. 161) man they see, as well as developing the topic of white brutality towards blacks and recalling Leslie A. Fiedler's assertion that slavery signifies 'the essential sociological theme of the American tale of terror',[31] evokes other forms of male power, including paternal and ecclesiastical. Nathan thinks: 'It might be Dad taking off his clothes or it might be the preacher opening the Bible behind the pulpit' (p. 161). He also disturbingly notes – in a perception interrelating the contrary facets of masculinity, brutal and tender, that Grimsley investigates and illustrating the author's refusal to idealize the gay lovers he portrays – that the figure looks 'like Roy' (p. 161).

Roy has insisted on taking three of his schoolfriends on the trip to the ruined plantation house, and Nathan feels uncomfortable in their presence. He is particularly nervous of Burke, sensing that, though unaware of the sexual nature of their relationship, he is jealous of Nathan's emotional closeness to Roy. In the onrush of confused emotions that the encounter with the ghost generates, Roy, ignoring Nathan's protests, pulls him roughly towards him. The other boys enter the room and, in a moment of uncanny revelation, glimpse them engaging in sex: 'When the flashlight finds them, Roy is still kneeling in front of Nathan, and Nathan's pants are tangled at his ankles. The flashlight catches Roy's mouth straining over Nathan's heaving abdomen' (p. 164).

In the confusion that follows Nathan loses contact with Roy and finds himself at the mercy of the aggressive Burke. Whereas in Donoghue's *Stir-Fry* the unexpected revelation of the physicality of queer sex results in the spectator momentarily doubting the evidence of her own eyes and dismissing what she sees as 'impossible', here it provokes him to violence. In an act reflecting jealousy mingled with homosexual panic and repeating in extreme form the abusive treatment Nathan suffered from his father, Burke brutally rapes Nathan, knocking him unconscious.

On recovering consciousness, Nathan makes his way haltingly back to the town, on the outskirts encountering Roy who is out looking for him. In reply to Nathan's anguished question, 'What do we do now?' he unhesitatingly replies, 'Run away' (pp. 194–5). The monosyllabic sentences, 'They stand and go. They never look back' (p. 195) that conclude the novel starkly register the two boys' power-lessness to challenge the oppressive climate of rural America. They represent flight as the only available option.

On turning to Mootoo's *Cereus Blooms at Night*, we enter a very different fictional world from Grimsley's *Dream Boy*, geographically, stylistically and in terms of content. Mootoo locates her novel on the island of Lantanacamara, a fictional version of Trinidad, inhabited like its real counterpart by a hybrid population of the descendants of Indian indentured labourers and African slaves. Unlike Grimsley who pursues a single storyline and writes austerely without recourse to humour, Mootoo constructs a complex postmodern-style text. She interweaves multiple narratives, introduces retrospective episodes and playfully intersperses realist description with passages of fantasy and comedy. In addition, in contrast to Grimsley who concentrates on the topic of male homosexuality, she adopts a queer perspective, referring to a range of different sexualities including lesbianism, male homosexuality, transgender and heterosexuality. Sinfield, discussing the intersection of sexuality and race, observes: 'If you are a person of colour, the prominence of a mainly white model makes it more difficult to negotiate ways of thinking about sexualities that will be compatible with your cultures of family and neighbourhood.'[32] Mootoo avoids becoming entrammelled in 'a white model' of sexual relations for, while critiquing the homophobia and chauvinism informing native Caribbean culture, she also exposes the oppressive effects of white colonialism. Her text however does reveal certain thematic and structural links with Grimsley's. As well as referring to paternal sexual abuse and incest, it focuses on two different houses, both metaphorically haunted.

Both the houses are associated with the protagonist Mala Ramchandin. Traumatized as a child by her father's sexual abuse and vilified in adulthood by the local community as a 'crazy old woman'[33] and witch, she is connected throughout the narrative with the operations of the uncanny. Prior to her arrival at the Paradise Hotel for the elderly where she is sent to end her days, a cloud is seen hanging over the building, engulfing it in a spectral mist. The locals link its appearance to Mala's troubled history and her alleged murder of her father. When, on account of lack of conclusive evidence, the judge presiding at her trial declares her innocent and free to travel, the cloud mysteriously disappears, in the words of her carer Nurse Tyler 'Letting light shine in paradise once again' (p. 8).

Unlike the other nursing staff at the hotel who refuse to care for Mala on account of the malevolent influence they believe her to exert, Tyler – who is ostracized on account of his homosexuality – willingly performs the task, admitting that 'I felt an empathy for her clenched fists, defiant stare, pursed lips – an empathy that words alone cannot describe' (p. 19). He also tends the clippings of the cereus plant she has been given. As a hermaphrodite, it symbolizes the novel's focus on queer sexuality and gender crossing.

Intrigued by Mala's ability to mimic parrot calls and recognizing that, despite her rambling speech, she 'had volumes of tales and thoughts in her head' (p. 99), Tyler pieces together the fragments of her troubled history. He discovers that she and her younger sister Asha, having been accidentally abandoned by their mother Sarah when she fled the family home to live with a female lover, were both sexually abused by their father Chandin, traumatized by his wife's elopement. Mootoo employs the episode to critique the Caribbean tendency to describe all relationships according to the hetero-patriarchal familial system, however different from it they actually are. She humorously describes the local community as excusing Chandin's abusive treatment on the grounds 'that he had obviously mistaken his daughter for his wife' and explaining Mala's mother's lesbian relationship as reflecting the fact that she 'had obviously mistaken another woman for her husband' (p. 109).

Tyler has significant difficulty in accepting his homosexuality. He experiences problems, resembling those that Nathan experiences in *Dream Boy*, in negotiating the difference between what he initially regards as his own homosexual 'perversion' and the incestuous desires of Mala's father. Butler argues that the individual can only determine and 'claim' his sexuality and gender 'if social norms exist that support and enable that act of claiming'.[34] On the island of Lantanacamara homosexuality is encoded as taboo and, until he encounters the elderly Mala, Tyler lives in a miasma of guilt and shame. However, unlike the other nursing staff who treat him as freakish, ridiculing him for being 'neither properly man nor woman but some in-between, unnamed thing' (p. 71), she encourages him to accept his sexual orientation. Recognizing his pleasure in cross-dressing, she hands him some female garments and signals him to put them on, the supportive action increasing the sense of 'shared queerness' (p. 48) that he feels with her. Mootoo's reference to Tyler's gender ambiguity interconnects with her focus on racial hybridity, affirming, as Isabel Hoving writes, her 'plea to acknowledge the inevitability of sexual and racial border-crossing and the resulting intermediariness and hybridity, however ambiguous and uncanny they may seem'.[35]

Tyler's friendship with Mala benefits her too. His readiness to listen to her life story and the secrets informing it enables her eventually to recover from her traumatized state; this substantiates Ann Cvetkovich's thesis that 'Many narratives by "survivors" of incest suggest that the trauma resides as much in secrecy as in sexual abuse – the burden not to tell creates its own network of sexual wounds that far exceed the event itself.'[36]

The second example of the haunted house that Mootoo introduces, besides the Paradise Alms Hotel disturbed by rumours of Mala's witch-craft, is the family home where she lived as a child victimized by her father Chandin. Like Grimsley who underpins his representation of Nathan's experience of paternal abuse with reference to the brutal-izing effects of the American history of slavery and native genocide, Mootoo connects Chandin's abusive treatment of his two daughters with his experience of colonial domination. On being adopted as a teenager by the Reverend Thoroughly who has travelled from 'the Shivering Northern Wetlands' (p. 51), Mootoo's wittily apt term for Britain, to preach the Gospel, Chandin struggles to conform to British cultural conventions. However, on discovering that despite his efforts Thoroughly's family and friends continue to regard him as inferior, treating him as a mimic man 'almost the same, but not quite'[37] as whites, he rejects his adoptive family. He is further embittered by the elope-ment of his Indian wife Sarah with Thoroughly's daughter Lavinia with whom, in his youth, he himself had been in love. Traumatized by the two women's rejection, he starts visiting his daughters' beds at night in search of sex.

Unlike her sister Asha who manages to escape from her father's clutches and establish a new life, Mala remains entrapped in the family home. Experiencing the splitting of the self common to trauma victims,[38] she rejects her childhood identity as Pohpoh and metamorphoses into 'Mala', developing as she ages into 'a tall, upright, wire-thin woman with matted hair the colour of forgotten silver' (p. 113). The children in the neighbourhood, afraid of the evil eye they attribute to her, cross the street when passing the house, 'glancing through the fence not to see her but to make sure she does not see them' (p. 113). Their parents, crediting the rumour that she changes into a fire ball at night streaking across the sky, regard her as a ghost haunting the property. The role of madwoman they assign to her relates her to Caribbean characters in earlier works of Female Gothic such as Bertha in Charlotte Brontë's *Jane Eyre* and her literary double Antoinette, the heroine of Rhys's *Wide Sargasso Sea*.

Unlike those in the local community who associate it with fear, Mala treats the garden as a heterotopic playground and source of jouissance. Mootoo portrays her gliding like a spectre between the garden and house, slipping 'barefoot through the window as effortlessly as a moth' (p. 143). She describes how, lacking human company, she 'all but rid herself of words' (p. 126) and, regressing to the semiotic, converses with the parrots and other birds in inarticulate sounds. She enjoys the odours of urine and natural decay, interpreting them as 'the aroma of life refusing to end ... the aroma of transformation' (p. 128).

The garden itself, symbolically situated in the town of Paradise, acquires multiple meanings. These include a prelapsarian Eden evoking for Mala memories of her happy childhood before her mother Sarah and Sarah's lover Lavinia eloped, and an image of the maternal body. The latter connection is illustrated by Mootoo's portrayal of Mala curling up on the grass to sleep at night like a child on its mother's breast. Mootoo's description of the garden, as well as evoking, from a geographical perspective, a nostalgic image of the Caribbean landscape as an idyllic pastoral world, intertextually echoes Rhys's representation of the Coulibri Estate in *Wide Sargasso Sea* and its abundant plant life. Her comparison of Mala to a moth develops Rhys's utilization of the insect as an image of female transience, while her portrayal of her gliding silently through the garden recalls the description of

Antoinette at Thornfield House in the final chapters of Rhys's novel. The words that Rhys portrays Antoinette uttering on catching sight of her own reflection (or is it the reflection of her double Jane Eyre?) in the mirror – 'It was then that I saw her – the ghost. The woman with streaming hair'[39] – are as appropriate to Mala, with her spectral associations and unkempt silvery hair, as they are to her literary forbears Antoinette and Jane.

In contrast to the garden and the liberatory space it signifies, the house at its centre, the site of Mala's abusive history, is described as encrypting a grim secret. The vegetation invading it constructs a screen concealing from view the corpse of her father Chandin lying in the cellar, killed by her to put a stop to his oppressive treatment. The cellar, in furnishing Chandin's tomb, resembles the 'subterranean architecture' with mortuary connotations that Vidler describes in *The Architectural Uncanny* taking the form of 'a double architecture, one above ground, the other subterranean', creating a 'labyrinth under the soil'.[40] It is in this labyrinthine chamber that Otoh, the transgender female-to-male child of Mala's former boyfriend Ambrose, finds himself when lured by curiosity and rumours of witchcraft he stumbles down the rotting staircase and discovers Chandin's corpse lying in the cellar in a state of advanced decay.

In choosing to conclude her account of this period in Mala's life with an episode of magic realism, Mootoo develops the subversive associations of the device. As critics explain, in juxtaposing the material with the fantastic, its 'in-betweenness promotes resistance to monological political and cultural structures'.[41] In addition, by interrelating the familiar with the unfamiliar, it enacts a form of uncanny doubling. When the police, alerted by the rumours circulating in the community, enter the house to investigate the stories of the corpse in the cellar, Mala stands her ground. From the vantage point of the veranda, she instructs her fantasy childhood alter ego Pohpoh to escape. She watches the imaginary Pohpoh run out of the house and, raising her arms, ascend into the air. She jubilantly describes how 'Each stroke took her higher until she no longer touched the ground', surmounting 'even the tallest trees' (p. 186).

The profusion of intertextual allusions that abound in the novel, while linking Mootoo's description of Mala's garden to Rhys's depiction of the Coulibri Estate, also connects the house with a canonical nineteenth-century Gothic text. In representing the site of incest, exemplifying the collapse of culture into nature and containing a crypt concealing a secret relating to death, it represents a feminine-inflected version of Poe's House of Usher. While the reference in the concluding stages of the narrative to the fire that destroys the house recalls the conflagrations that conclude its three Female Gothic precursor texts *Jane Eyre*, *Wide Sargasso Sea* and *Rebecca*, the origin and intent of the fire is different in Mootoo's text. It is ignited not by a female character motivated by despair or revenge but by Otoh with the benevolent aim of destroying the evidence of Mala's murder of her father. His intervention enables her to avoid a prison senence and also prepares the way for Mootoo to achieve a comedic dénouement to the novel, integrating its various narrative strands. She concludes it on a utopian note with the description of the queer family formation comprising Mala, Tyler, Ambrose and Otoh (who has formed a partnership with Tyler) meeting at the Paradise Alms Hotel. Queer diversity and hybridity are depicted triumphing over sexual prejudice and racism.

Uncanny cities

Novels queering the topic of the 'uncanny city', exemplified here by Jeanette Winterson's *The Power Book* and Alan Hollinghurst's *The Swimming-Pool Library*, are particularly wide-ranging in the discourses on which they draw, interweaving themes and interests associated on the one hand with the Gothic and on the other with contemporary historical and sociological studies of male gay and lesbian culture. While writers of Gothic fiction, ranging from Poe and Stevenson in the Victorian era to Peter Ackroyd and Stephen King writing today, represent the city as the location of mysterious or supernatural events, historians and sociologists such as Jeffrey Weeks and Tamar Rothenberg working in the field of queer studies investigate the role that the metropolis plays in the development of male gay and lesbian identifications and lifestyles.

The construct of the uncanny city, as we are familiar with it today in Gothic fiction and film, tends to be represented in terms of extremes, with writers and directors describing it as combining images of pleasure and excess with reference to poverty and dereliction. They frequently portray it in terms of a maze of streets and alleys in which the protagonist, unable to locate the correct route and distinguish between reality and illusion, loses his way both geographically and morally. This construct, as Robert Mighall and other critics demonstrate, originated in the eighteenth and nineteenth centuries. Illustrating the mobility of Gothic locations and architecture and their tendency to transgress geographical and temporal boundaries, Mighall describes how the vaults and passages of the European castles and monasteries that feature in the fiction of Radcliffe and Matthew Lewis were transplanted to furnish imagery for the creation of a very different milieu: the alleys and shabby tenements of Victorian London.[42] They receive two of their most atmospheric fictional representations in the novels of Dickens and Stevenson's *The Strange Case of Dr Jekyll and Mr Hyde*. In *fin-de-siècle* representations of the city, Gothic themes and motifs interplay on occasion with queer, with Stevenson and Wilde utilizing the motif of the double to explore the phenomenon of the closet and the homosexual panic it generates.[43] Gothic novels produced in the past thirty years, such as Emma Tennant's *The Bad Sister* that reworks from a feminist perspective Hogg's *The Private Memoirs and Confessions of a Justified Sinner*, or Will Self's *Dorian* recasting Wilde's *The Picture of Dorian Gray*, continue this tradition, employing the motif of the uncanny city to explore lesbian and male gay subcultures.

Among studies investigating the city's queer sociological and historical significance, the other discourse on which contemporary writers draw, the work of Alan Bray and Jeffrey Weeks is particularly significant. Though they debate the date at which a male homosexual identification first appeared,[44] the two theorists agree on the contribution that an urban environment has made to it by providing a context for social networking and anonymous sexual exploration. The metropolis, though associated with poverty, violence and disease, can alternatively represent a place of opportunity and pleasure, particularly for people seeking to pursue a same-sex lifestyle. Studies by John D'Emilio[45] and David Higgs[46] investigate the queer sociocultural aspect of different cities around the globe.

Lesbian urban subculture, though it emerged later than its gay male counterpart and is less well documented, has also developed complex sociopolitical structures. Elizabeth Wilson, investigating from a sociological viewpoint the influence of a metropolitan environment on the lives of women who, until the Industrial Revolution separated the workplace from the home, frequently spent their lives within the family, describes 'the lesbian as the inhabitant of the great cities'.[47] She cites in evidence the growth of lesbian subcultures in nineteenth-century Paris and London. Essays by Rothenberg[48] and Shari Benstock[49] explore the development of lesbian social and cultural space in New York City and Paris.

Hollinghurst and Winterson interrelate in different ways elements from the Gothic and the sociological discourses referred to above. In exploring the contradictions of pleasure and danger traditionally associated with a metropolitan environment, they create present-day versions of the Gothic image of the city as 'a dark, powerful and seductive labyrinth'[50] that, having enticed the subject with promises of enjoyment, either fails to deliver them or if it does leaves him feeling disillusioned or jaded. Central to their novels is the portrayal of the protagonist as on the one hand an autonomous agent, enjoying the pleasures and enhancement of the self that the metropolis offers, and on the other subject and victim, disoriented by the city's fragmented images or disillusioned by the discovery of its seamy and ruthless underside. Their novels create, in this respect, present-day versions of the experience of uncanny 'enthralment' that Day describes as enticing the protagonist into the Gothic world.[51]

'Queer' has a reputation for being transgressive, with Michael Warner describing it 'as protesting not just the normal behavior of the social but the *idea* of normal behavior'.[52] Hollinghurst and Winterson, linking the anti-normative associations of 'queer' with ideas of Gothic transgression, both refer to forms of sex that society regards as unorthodox or morally dubious. Hollinghurst describes his upper-class narrator Will Beckwith's exploitative and sometimes violent treatment of the working-class and black youths he selects as lovers. He also foregrounds the importance that public sex assumes in metropolitan male gay subculture, with toilets in streets and pubs furnishing a cruising site. Women, for a number of reasons, do not generally have access to the public sex in toilets and parks that is a feature of the male gay scene – and nor would many wish to engage in sex of this kind. They do however have access to the alternative public space of the web and the opportunities it offers for anonymous sexual encounters and liaisons, both virtual and actual. Winterson constructs her novel around her lesbian protagonist's sexual adventures in urban locations, continental as well as British, in virtual reality. She also portrays the protagonist, in exploiting the scope that the web provides for enacting sexual fantasies, enacting a sex change.

While both writers queer motifs of Gothic enthralment and the uncanny city, they treat them very differently. Winterson creates a complex postmodern narrative interweaving different genres, including Gothic, travelogue and different forms of romance narrative. Interspersing realist representation with reference to spectrality and passages of magic realism, she describes the British and European cities she depicts in images of shifting surfaces and erotic masquerades evoking Butleresque ideas of performativity and Jean Baudrillard's theories of simulacra and the hyperreal. Hollinghurst, in contrast, constructs a vividly drawn, ostensibly realist account of his narrator Will's experience of gay life in 1980s London, describing his sexual liaisons and portraying him developing a friendship with the elderly aristocrat Lord Nantwich. The narrative he constructs, however, turns out to be less realist than it at first appears since it recasts and updates a number of motifs and structures rooted in nineteenth-century Gothic.[53]

Winterson's *The Power Book*, though not usually read in a Gothic context, utilizes spectral imagery particularly innovatively. As well as employing the spectral to represent the lesbian narrator's homely/unhomely house in the historical London borough of Spitalfields and the sense it gives of being haunted by the past, she introduces it to evoke the futuristic world of virtual reality.

The house in Spitalfields, as Winterson describes, served in the nineteenth century as the location of a curio shop. The strange assortment of items that it allegedly sold, including 'suits of armour, wimples, field boots' and 'wigs on spikes, like severed heads',[54] recall the 'suits of mail, standing like ghosts in armour'[55] and other antique items cluttering the home of Little Nell in Dickens's *The Old Curiosity Shop*. The house has criminal associations since Jack the Ripper allegedly visited it to purchase a new disguise, and its connection with the uncanny is apparent in the sound of the ghostly footsteps mysteriously audible on the stairs. Sitting at her computer one night, the owner Ali – or rather the woman who uses the name as an alias, for in the world of virtual reality it is difficult, if not impossible, to distinguish identity from masquerade – is aroused from thoughts of ghosts by an email she receives. It reads, '*Freedom, just for one night*' (p. 3) and comes from an unknown correspondent who signs herself 'Tulip'. Interpreting the words as signifying 'Just for one night the freedom to be somebody else' (p. 4), Ali, a writer by profession and as is indicated by her reference to *The Passion* a stand-in in certain respects for Winterson herself, accepts the challenge to fulfil Tulip's wish. She proceeds to create a series of virtual narratives portraying herself and her unknown correspondent meeting in different foreign venues, their identities transformed. Comparing herself to the owner of the nineteenth-century shop where, by purchasing a change of costume, 'People arrive as themselves and leave as someone else' (p. 3), she emails Tulip the message, 'Undress. Take off your clothes. Take off your body . . . Tonight we can go deeper than disguise' (p. 4). Moving from thoughts of domestic haunting to the spectral world of the web, she portrays herself and Tulip engaging in uncanny communication like participants at a seance, their 'fingers resting lightly on the keys like a couple of table-turners' (p. 26).

Derrida refers to the way in which modern 'technologies inhabit, as it were, a phantom structure'.[56] He describes the text on the computer screen as 'fantomatic' since it appears 'less corporal, more "spiritual", more ethereal'[57] than the printed page. Referring speculatively to 'that "toile" of the World Wide Web that a network of computers is weaving around us, throughout the world, but around us *in us*' (p. 12), he portrays surfers running the risk of becoming addicted to to the web since 'they can no longer do without these voyages around the world under sail – a sail that traverses or transits them in turn' (p. 12). Ali too employs maritime imagery, representing virtual reality as 'a world inventing itself' where 'daily, new landmasses form and then submerge' (p. 63). Describing the way 'found objects wash up on the shores of my computer', she explains: 'That's why I trawl my screen like a beachcomber' (pp. 63–4).

Like the world of virtual reality where 'Nothing is solid. Nothing is fixed' (p. 44), the narratives Ali invents to amuse Tulip shift and mutate. They change from furnishing entertainment to operating as a 'story of desire' and a form of 'textual erotics',[58] as she finds herself succumbing to the attraction of the romantic scenarios she herself creates and falling in love with Tulip.

Ali's perspective on the different cities to which she transports Tulip in her tour de force of virtual storytelling varies from celebratory to critical. She commences her narrative on an exotic, fairy-tale note by describing a transgender romance in the style of the Arabian *A Thousand and One Nights* set in Istanbul. Playfully portraying herself in the role of a girl who masquerades as a boy by substituting tulip bulbs for balls and a tulip stem for a penis, she describes herself embarking on a sea voyage. In the manner of the random adventures experienced by characters in early romances such as Shakespeare's *Pericles*, she is taken prisoner by pirates. Having survived various dangers, she eventually lands up at the apartment of the Italian envoy to the Turks where she meets and makes love with Tulip, portrayed here in the guise of a beautiful princess. The sexual encounter between the two women concludes, as suits the fantastic nature of the story, with an excursion into magic realism, with Ali discovering to her amazement that she is able to enjoy full sexual congress with her lover:

> Then a strange thing began to happen. As the Princess kneeled and petted my tulip, my own sensations grew exquisite, but as yet no stronger than my astonishment, as I felt my disguise come to life. The tulip began to stand. I looked down. There it was making a bridge from my body to hers . . . Very gently the Princess lowered herself across my knees and I felt the firm red head and pale shaft plant itself in her body . . . All afternoon I fucked her. (p. 22)

Winterson wittily recasts in the passage cited above the early modern concept of 'a vegetable love' (a love characterized only by growth) introduced by Andrew Marvell in his famous seduction lyric 'To his Coy Mistress'. Tulip, however, finds Ali's portrayal of her being sexually penetrated by a tumescent tulip stem a dubious compliment. Objecting to Ali's transformation of her into 'a flower-fucking princess', she playfully protests by email, '*That was a terrible thing to do to a flower!*' (p. 25)

Ali's fantasy enactment of masculinity, though Tulip fails to appreciate it, intrigues the reader, enabling her to enjoy the spectacle of gender performance. It illustrates Halberstam's observation: 'In order to find our way into a posttranssexual era, we must learn how to take pleasure in gender and how to become an audience for the multiple performances of gender.'[59]

Ali follows this dendroerotic narrative set in Istanbul with an account of a rendezvous with Tulip in present-day Paris. The romantic pleasures of the stroll the couple take by the Seine are undermined, however, by the clichéd images, appropriated from film and photography, that she employs to represent the scene. She describes how 'The broad view of the river was a cine film of the weekend, with its amateur, hand-held feel of lovers and dogs and electric light . . . Frame by frame, that Friday night was shot and exposed and thrown away, carried by the river, by time, canned up only in memory, but in itself, scene by scene, perfect' (p. 36). Here the image of the river becomes obscured by its cultural and commercial baggage. The stereotypical images and references to cinematic representation recall Baudrillard's critique of contemporary culture as 'substituting signs of the real for the real itself: that is, an operation to deter every process by its operational double'.[60] Ali's virtual storytelling appears to have transported her here into the postmodern world of the 'hyper-real' that, rather than merely duplicating or parodying the real, has the effect as Baudrillard writes of 'substituting signs of the real for the real itself' (p. 167). Ana Cecília Acioli Lima perceptively demonstrates how reference to Baudrillard's ideas illuminates the virtual reality dimension of Ali's narrative and love affair with Tulip.[61] They also illuminate the locations that furnish their context.

Against a backdrop that she describes as resembling 'a grainy movie' (p. 47) Ali accompanies Tulip to her hotel room and enjoys a night of love. However, like the image of Paris itself, her sexual encounter with Tulip strikes her as clichéd and false. On discovering that Tulip is married, she contrasts what she now regards as the tawdry reality of the love affair with the idealized image that she had initially projected upon it. Disillusioned with her web-based amour and ruefully admitting that her heart is a 'carbon-based primitive in a silicon world' (p. 40), she plaintively laments, 'The trouble is that in imagination anything can be perfect. Downloaded into real life, it was messy. She

was messy. I was messy. I blamed myself. I had wanted to be caught'
(p. 46). The contrast she draws between sex in real life and its fantasy
counterpart is, however, ambiguous, reflecting a vertiginous process
of doubling and replication. It is problematized by the fact that, as
her use of the word 'downloaded' signals, her love affair with Tulip,
though Winterson teasingly tricks the reader into regarding it as real,
is decidedly unreal. As well as featuring as a virtual reality construct
in the story that Ali narrates, it is an episode in Winterson's postmodern metafiction.

After following Tulip to the island of Capri, no longer a quiet fish-
ing village but the centre of a flourishing tourist industry, Ali returns
disillusioned with the love affair to her *heimlich/unheimlich* home in
Spitalfields. Here she is again met by the spectacle of tourism. Her
reference to 'the Dracula Tour' (p. 236) that gives visitors the opportunity to see some of the locations that Stoker describes in his novel
reintroduces the reader to London's role as the location of Victorian
Gothic, though one now cheapened by commercialization. She feels
haunted by the past, 'tight-rope walking' between the present day
and eras long since vanished, the latter exemplified by 'the Hawksmoor
church' (p. 235) across the street and her own house, haunted by the
ghosts.

As well as illustrating Ali's disillusion with her liaison with Tulip,
Winterson also portrays her, in a series of richly erotic episodes,
evoking its pleasures. Creating a complex celebration of lesbian love
centring on the uncanny motif of doubling, Ali romantically tells
Tulip, 'Sex between women is a mirror geography. The subtlety of
its secret – utterly the same but always different. You are the looking
glass world. You are the hidden place that opens to me on the other
side of the glass' (p. 174).

The final episode of the novel portrays the two women at Padding-
ton Station, on the verge of parting but dramatically rescuing their
relationship at the last moment and staying together at least temporarily. This adds a further note of ambiguity to the narrative, and
others reflecting the novel's metafictional aspect also strike the reader.
Does the tale of seduction and romance that Ali spins on the web
represent merely cheap 'telephone sex' (p. 27) or does it signify, as
she herself argues, a form of 'art' (p. 27)? Which, if any, of the couple's
sexual encounters take place in 'meatspace' (p. 161), as Ali disparagingly

terms the material world of physical sex, and which are virtual? Equally problematic, what role does she herself play in the fictional scenarios she constructs? Is she in control of her storytelling or, as she increasingly suspects as she finds herself surrendering to the genre of romantic fiction and the uncanny enthralment that the web and her own erotic fantasizing exert, are 'the stories telling her?' (p. 215).

Hollinghurst's *The Swimming-Pool Library*, as well as differing from Winterson's *The Power Book* in concentrating on male homosexuality, focuses, in contrast to the European locations that she introduces, solely on London. And whereas Winterson situates Ali's love affair with Tulip chiefly in virtual reality, Hollinghurst foregrounds the physicality – the 'meatspace' dimension, to cite the term that Ali employs – of his protagonist Will Beckwith's sexual adventures. Both novels, however, share a metafictional element. They both display, in addition, an emphasis on the uncanny and intertextual allusions to Victorian Gothic.

An indication of the role that the uncanny plays in the *The Swimming-Pool Library* occurs in the opening pages. In a passage that has provoked debate,[62] Will refers to the way in which his summer of sexual adventuring – he describes it typically pretentiously as his 'belle époque' – is undermined, while simultaneously rendered more intense, by the sense of 'a faint flicker of calamity, like flames around a photograph, something seen out of the corner of one eye'.[63] Whether we read the passage as an indirect reference to the advent of the AIDS pandemic or as reflecting Will's half-registered perception that his hedonistic lifestyle will leave him with a sense of wasted potential and self-disgust, the recognition of its connection – in referring to a perception that, though important, is fleeting and partially glimpsed – to the uncanny and its operations illuminates the novel's distinctive perspective. Cixous describes the uncanny as appearing 'only on the fringe of something else',[64] while Rosemary Jackson represents it 'as tangential, to one side', in a way that 'subverts any re-presentation of a unified reality'.[65] Royle depicts it 'as concerned with the strange, weird and mysterious, with a flickering sense of (but not conviction) of something supernatural'.[66] The resemblance of Hollinghurst's passage to the theorists' accounts signals the way in which ideas relating to the uncanny pervade the novel, causing its multifaceted perspectives, to cite Jackson, to 'subvert any re-presentation of a unified reality'.

Brookes has already noted some of the most salient of the novel's links with Victorian Gothic. He compares Will's predatory sexual behaviour, aristocratic lineage and preoccupation with secrecy with the representation of the vampire in Bram Stoker's *Dracula*. He also connects the novel with Stevenson's *Jekyll and Hyde* and Wilde's *Dorian Gray*, comparing their different accounts – Hollinghurst's explicit and the two earlier writers' covert – of society's punitive treatment of the homosexual and the panic it reflects.[67] However, the novel also introduces other motifs with Gothic associations that merit attention. These include the representation of the city as an abject space, alternatively alluring or threatening, that entices while morally bewildering the protagonist; the difficulty Will experiences in distinguishing between benevolent and oppressive paternal figures; and the representation of the family as a site of transgressive secrets that, though society would prefer them to remain hidden, nonetheless insist on coming to light. Hollinghurst's treatment of the latter is particularly relevant to queer existence since it relates to the topic, discussed by Sedgwick, of the difference between the 'open' secret and the 'closed'. These motifs are underpinned by concepts with uncanny resonance, including doubling and spectrality.

Like Dickens and Stevenson, Hollinghurst constructs the image of 1980s London where Will pursues his sexual liaisons around the contrast between rich and poor, upper-class and working-class, and the different locations that the members of the groups frequent. As well as creating a social geography of the 1980s metropolis recalling those constructed by the nineteenth-century Henry Mayhew and William Booth, he portrays Will, like the two Victorian commentators, regarding the areas the poor inhabit as a labyrinthine site, ambiguously fascinating and abject. Though this labyrinth is constructed by the concrete paths and walkways traversing modern council estates and high-rise flats rather than the alleys intersecting the tenements and slum dwellings of Victorian London, it resembles, from Will's upper-class viewpoint, 'the intricate maze of narrow streets and courts',[68] with its Gothic associations of mystery and lurking danger, that

Dickens describes. Booth's *In Darkest England and the Way Out*, its title echoing Stanley's exploration of 'the dark continent' of Africa, illustrates as Kelly Hurley observes the tendency of the Victorian middle class to view London's East End as a backwater of empire and typecast its residents as 'exotic natives'.[69] Will's perspective, when he visits the region in search of his black boyfriend Arthur who has mysteriously disappeared, is notably similar. He regards 'the housing estates, the distant gasometers, the mysterious empty fenced-in tracts of waste land, grass and gravelly pools' (p. 168) that he glimpses from the train with the curiosity of a tourist travelling through a foreign land – which, in terms of his upper-class status and public school education, he is. And, like the nineteenth-century colonial traveller, he sometimes badly misreads the signs. He fails to perceive that the gang of National Front skinheads whom he encounters in the 'charm-less passage' (p. 171) separating the blocks of flats where Arthur lives are not there to entertain him with stories about their tattoos or engage in a debate about the term 'poof', as he sarcastically encourages them to do when they taunt him with it. Recognizing that his accent 'must have sounded a parody voice, pickled in culture and money' (p. 172), he wishes he had kept his mouth shut. His regrets, however, come too late. Accusing him of being 'a nigger-fucker' (p. 173), they threaten him with a broken bottle and, when they have him on the ground, kick him in the face and steal his watch.

Another connection that the novel displays with Victorian Gothic and the uncanny motifs informing it is Hollinghurst's utilization of the strategy of doubling, frequently relating to buildings. As in Stevenson's *Jekyll and Hyde*, in which the nondescript back door through which the interloper Hyde enters Jekyll's house doubles with its imposing front entrance, Hollinghurst constructs his narrative around houses and public buildings that double with one another. Lord Nantwich's residence, situated near St Paul's Cathedral in the heart of the capital, doubles with Lord Beckwith's affluent mansion in Surrey, while the public toilet near the Serpentine where Will first makes Nantwich's acquaintance doubles with another, the one where in the 1950s Nantwich had been arrested for cottaging while enjoying what he humorously terms as one of his 'picaresque "Lyric" evenings' (p. 250) cruising in Hammersmith and Soho. Hollinghurst's references to gay sex in public toilets, as in Leavitt's *While England*

Sleeps, are integral to the history of male homosexuality that he constructs. They also relate integrally to the interplay between private and public spheres that typifies metropolitan male gay life.

Other gay venues, including pubs, clubs, public baths and hotels, also feature in the novel, with their locations and clientele frequently described in detail. The Volunteer and Colherne pubs that Will's friend James visits before being arrested for soliciting furnish examples. The emphasis that Hollinghurst places on doubling and repetition emerges not just as a neat device for structuring the narrative. It also illustrates the uncanny tendency of history to repeat itself, bringing about the return of outbreaks of sexual prejudice and homosexual panic. James's arrest is pertinent here since it duplicates and echoes the arrest of Lord Nantwich. It also serves to open Will's eyes to the fact that our recently won gay freedoms are fragile and easily revoked.

Hollinghurst describes one of the buildings that features prominently in the novel as explicitly uncanny. This is Nantwich's *heimlich/unheimlich* house in the city that emerges as central to both Will's personal history and the history of homosexuality in Britain. On visiting it for the first time, Will pauses before entering, 'surprisingly taken aback, by its air of secrecy and seclusion, to the invalidish world of Edwardian ghost stories' (p. 70). He humorously describes Nantwich, when the latter leads him down the stairs to the 'cool mildewy darkness' of the cellar to show him the fragments of the Roman bath and the erotic mosaics that it contains, as having 'the air of a horror-film villain, muttering gleeful asides while leading his victim into the trap' (p. 79). His description, though he is unaware of it, is ironically apt since Nantwich is in fact leading him into a trap, not a physical one but one that history is about to spring. It is after Will's visit to Nantwich's house that he accepts the invitation to write his biography and, on subsequently perusing Nantwich's diary, makes the disturbing discovery that it was his own grandfather who as Director of Public Prosecutions instituted the homophobic purge that led to Nantwich's arrest. Interpreted in the context of these events, the house, representing Nantwich himself and his aristocratic lineage, certainly does have spectral connections. It is haunted metaphorically by the shameful secret of his arrest and imprisonment in Wormwood Scrubs. The traumatic effect that these events have on him is illustrated by his compulsion painfully to repeat the event of his arrest in his dream work, with the details, as he describes in his diary, altering eerily from night to night.

The decision on the part of Will's family and friends to conceal from him the role that his grandfather played in Lord Nantwich's arrest introduces another motif with uncanny connotations. This is the concept of homosexuality and topics relating to it as signifying an unspeakable secret that, as we have seen, is pivotal to the fiction of Donoghue, Hensher, Tóibín and Waters, discussed in chapter 2. By postponing both Will's and the reader's discovery of Nantwich's arrest until the concluding chapters and positioning it to coincide with two other events relating to secrecy that depress Will, namely the arrest of his friend James for cottaging and his discovery that his lover Phil and his friend Bill have been surreptitiously engaging in an affair, Hollinghurst also creates a parodic version of 'the problem of transmission',[70] a motif common in nineteenth-century fiction. This portrays the protagonist being prevented, accidentally or by design, from learning a piece of information of importance to himself that frequently relates to his personal history. Conan Doyle's 'The Musgrave Ritual', centring on a ritual text that each male Musgrave is required ceremonially to recite when he achieves maturity although the clue it gives to the whereabouts of the family treasure is lost, represents a classic example. The problem of transmission in the story, as Peter Brooks illustrates, stems from the failure on the part of the father to pass on a piece of information to his son. However Hollinghurst's treatment of the motif gives an ugly twist to Conan Doyle's since the secret that Will's family fails to pass on to him, namely the role that his grandfather played in the homosexual purge and the imprisonment of Nantwich in which it resulted, has nothing to do with wisdom but is, on the contrary, shameful. Nantwich, disturbed and embarrassed by it, avoids disclosing it to Will directly but leaves him to discover it by reading his diary account. Like the indirect transmission of information in Donoghue's *Stir-Fry*, where Maria's flatmates decide to ambiguously conceal/reveal their lesbian partnership by employing verbal innuendos and double entendres, and Tóibín's *The Blackwater Lightship* where the news of Declan's homosexuality and his contraction of AIDS reaches the older members of the family by indirect transmission with one member nervously passing it on to another, the secret on which Hollinghurst's novel hinges, likewise centring on homosexuality, is regarded as too disturbing to disclose to Will directly. Yet, although its disclosure can be postponed, the secret is bound to emerge. As Salotto remarks, commenting on the role that the device of blocked narration plays in Victorian Gothic and the sensation novel, it inevitably returns 'to haunt the narrative'.[71] Hollinghurst follows this convention, while ingeniously giving it a new and topical slant.

The key difference between the secret that haunts Hollinghurst's novel and those haunting Victorian narratives is that, illustrating the hypocrisies of the 1980s British establishment and its ambivalent view of homosexuality as unmentionable though legal, it is an open one. As Will discovers to his embarrassment, he is about the only person in the upper-class circles that his family and friends frequent who does not know about the role that his grandfather played in Nantwich's arrest. As well as feeling humiliated by the discovery that they have concealed from him facts that are common knowledge, he is forced to re-evaluate his grandfather's character and his own relationship with him. He sees him no longer as a wise 'elder statesman' but, on the contrary, as 'a kind of bureaucratic sadist, a man who has built his career on oppression' (p. 264). He has to confront the unpalatable truth that the success that heterosexual members of the establishment achieve by oppressing their homosexual colleagues, as Richard Dellamora observes, 'in turn, permits self-appointed moral commissars like Will's grandfather to protect and indulge attractive young homosexuals [like Will himself] with the right credentials'.[72]

The Swimming-Pool Library describes London as a treacherous social milieu where matters of any significance take place primarily between men. It is unsurprising, then, to find at its centre the Oedipal motif of the difference between benevolent and oppressive father figures that Grimsley's *Dream Boy*, similarly focusing on male relationships, treats. Hollinghurst however complicates the motif and subverts its moral clarity by illustrating that in the morally shady world of British upper-class society, both of Will's surrogate father figures, Nantwich as well as his grandfather, are morally flawed. By the end of the novel Will regards both men ambivalently. He feels unable totally to reject his bond with his grandfather since, as he himself admits, influenced by happy childhood memories, he continues to love him. His biological connections with him also make rejection problematic since, on looking at his reflection in the mirror while shaving, he recognizes in a moment of uncanny doubling that his face reveals the imprint of his grandfather's features. The episode recalls the mirror scenes in Stevenson's *Jekyll and Hyde* where Jekyll is alarmed to see his face revealing the lineaments of Hyde's.

However, Will's feelings for Nantwich are also ambivalent. While continuing to treat him as a friend, he resents the way Nantwich has manipulated him by concealing his connections with Will's family history and leaving him to discover them for himself. There are also indications that, in perceiving in Nantwich his own moral flaws such as an excessive concern with self-gratification and a readiness sexually to exploit social inferiors including working-class men and blacks, he recognizes him as his double. The one firm decision that Will does make is to resign from the post of Nantwich's biographer. Recapitulating the paradoxes of blocked narration that inform the novel, he wryly tells Nantwich: 'All I could write now . . . would be a book about why I couldn't write the book' (p. 281).

Ritual and ceremony

Ceremonies and rituals, often centring on a particular space or do-mestic or geographical location, conventionally appear in literary and cinematic texts treating the uncanny. They include black masses performed to invoke the devil, as in Roman Polanski's film *Rosemary's Baby*, and ceremonies carried out with the contrary intent of keeping him at bay as in Dennis Wheatley's *The Devil Rides Out*. They may be performed with the aim (frequently unsuccessful as the text, being uncanny, prefers to portray ghosts) of laying the dead to rest, as exemplified by the funeral of Cathy in Emily Brontë's *Wuthering Heights*, or with the intent of impiously resurrecting them, as in King's depiction of the ghoulish activities that occur in the ancient MicMac burial ground in *Pet Sematary*. Alternatively, they may cele-brate acts of somatic transformation as is the case in H. P. Lovecraft's *The Shadow Over Innsmouth* that describes the residents of an isolated New England town assuming amphibious form to emigrate to the sea.

Punter describes Gothic as representing 'a panoply of ceremonies',[73] funereal, erotic, spectral and vampiric. He depicts ceremony as 'a mediating force' (p. 39) linking the material world to the irrational and numinous. The ceremonies and rituals that feature in Gothic, as well as being mysterious or eerie in the general sense, frequently reflect ideas and motifs that Freud and subsequent theorists associate specifically with the uncanny, such as the transformation of the familiar into the unfamiliar and 'a compulsion to repeat'.[74] The repeated appearances of the ghosts of Quint and Miss Jessel in Henry James's *The Turn of the Screw* and the 'queer affair'[75] the couple signify exemplify this. Ceremonies in Gothic works frequently reflect a superstitious approach to life, illustrating an 'animistic conception of the universe'.[76] They can hinge on secrets, disclosing them to the initiated while protecting them from world at large, or illustrate the importance of liminality, bridging the gulf, as the title of August Derleth's *The Lurker at the Threshold* signals, between the familiar material world and the unfamiliar realm of the supernatural. Their significance is often uncertain for, as Punter argues, the meaning of ceremonial transcends the rational and cannot be precisely defined: indeed, if it could, the ceremony itself would be redundant.[77]

On turning to queer approaches to ceremony and ritual, we find uncertainty again in evidence, though for different reasons. Comments voiced by Halberstam help to explain the queer subject's ambivalent or downright hostile approach to the topic. She points out that the concept of time by which present-day society abides and the ceremonies it employs to mark its flux embody heteropatriarchal perspectives and tend to inscribe 'bourgeois rules of respectability and scheduling for married couples'.[78] They focus on issues of familial inheritance and biological ties that 'connect the family to the historical past of the nation' (p. 5). Although in a number of Western countries lesbian and male gay communities now have access to their own ritual events, such as Pride festivities and partnership ceremonies, these are relatively recent and are minimal in number in comparison with those inscribing heterosexual perspectives and ideology. As a result, they have made little impact on fiction and film. Some of the novels discussed above illustrate the sense of unease that the queer individual experiences at the mismatch and contradiction he feels to exist between public mainstream rituals and ceremonies and his own interests and needs. They portray him feeling excluded, associating these rituals with conflict and hypocrisy or regarding them as sterile. Schulman in *People in Trouble* describes the funerals of AIDS victims in 1980s New York as uneasy, discordant occasions, with the biological relatives of the deceased and his gay partner and friends eyeing each other distrustfully and avoiding conversing. The funeral with which Hensher opens *Kitchen Venom* is described as tense and emotionally frigid, with John going through the motions of mourning a wife he habitually deceived.

Other novels move beyond this. They portray the queer individual, alienated by the rituals constructed by heteronormative society to mark events in the life of the patrilineal family and its members, inventing her own rites or subversively reworking existing ones. Clare, the sister of the spectral narrator Sara in Smith's *Hotel World*, angered by the way the guests at her funeral persist in 'saying her name wrong & looking embarrassed' (p. 198), creates her own commemorative rite. Her action of throwing a clock down the lift shaft where Sara fell to her death symbolically re-enacts and commemorates the event. Mala Ramchandin, the traumatized protagonist of Mootoo's *Cereus Blooms at Night*, performs what Otoh, looking on, describes as the 'strange ritual' (p. 119) of placing snail shells along the perimeter of the fence arround her home. The line, 'white as chalk' (p. 119), furnishes a magic barrier to protect her from the hostility of the villagers who stigmatize her as a witch.

Other novels discussed above portray the queer subject subversively reworking traditional hetero-patriarchal rites. The ambulance worker Kay in Waters's *The Night Watch*, discussed in chapter 2, utilizes the gold ring, symbol of the marriage between man and woman, in this manner. On taking Viv to the hospital when she is bleeding from a botched abortion, she surreptitiously removes the ring from her own finger and places it on Viv's to indicate she is married and protect her from a police inquiry. The undershirt stained with his blood that Justin in Purdy's *Mourners Below*, reviewed in chapter 3, instructs his half-brother Duane to take his girlfriend Estelle as a token of his love also receives queer recasting. Duane, having unwillingly performed Justin's bidding and conveyed the gruesome gift to Estelle, is delighted when she returns the box containing it to him, telling him 'to keep this for the both of us' (p. 137). The episode concludes with Duane touching the 'stained undergarment' reverentially, while pondering his conversation with Justin. It moves here from being a token of heterosexual romance to a signifier of his homoerotic attachment to his half-brother. His reverential treatment of the bloodstained shirt also introduces a religious note, relating it perhaps to Christ's shroud.

Whereas the ceremonies and ritual acts described above play a relatively minor role in the texts in which they appear, those that feature in H. Nigel Thomas's *Spirits in the Dark* and Donna Tartt's *The Secret History*, the two novels discussed here, assume centrality. Punter argues that ceremony creates an imaginative or a religious space in which different dimensions interconnect, and the rites that Thomas and Tartt depict operate to similar effect. Associated with particular locations, they construct an uncanny space that gives the participants access to a dimension transcending the material, enabling him to enter the spiritual world or a fantasy realm.

The rituals the two writers describe, though sharing common features, differ significantly in form and cultural context. The spiritual journey on which Thomas's protagonist Jerome Quashee, a native of the Caribbean Isabella Island, embarks in the concluding chapters of *Spirits in the Dark* connects racial with sexual interests. Jerome undertakes it in a desperate, last-ditch attempt both to understand his African history and culture and achieve acceptance of his homosexuality. Its performance is intensely solitary. Taking place in a darkened chamber, it enables Jerome to converse with figures from his past and communicate with the spirits of his ancestors.

The rite of the bacchanal that Tartt portrays a group of college students, inspired by their charismatic Classics tutor, perform in *The Secret History*, set in North America, is, on the contrary, communal in nature. Re-enacting practices associated with Dionysus, celebrated in ancient Greek culture as 'a god of epiphany',[79] it enables the participants to achieve enhanced states of mind and enjoy experiences of sexual jouissance, along with different forms of doubling and somatic transformation, real or imagined. The transgressive nature of the rite and its connection with non-normative forms of sexuality are represented as reflecting the students' own sexualities and the energies they embody, destructive as well as creative. Both novels focus on queer interests for, while Thomas explores the intersection between homosexuality and race, Tartt constructs her narrative around different unorthodox sexualities.

Thomas's *Spirits in the Dark*, in exposing the oppressive effects of the encoding of homosexuality as taboo in Caribbean culture, displays thematic connections with Mootoo's *Cereus Blooms at Night*. However unlike Mootoo who creates a multi-stranded narrative interweaving realist with fantasy episodes, Thomas constructs a single, predominantly realist storyline. His writing, unlike hers, is sparse and unadorned, reflecting the bleakness of his protagonist Jerome Quashee's trajectory and the numerous obstacles and setbacks he encounters.

Like the male nurse Tyler whom Mootoo portrays, Jerome, though aware from an early age that he is sexually attracted to men, experiences difficulty in locating an identification to adopt and accepting his sexuality on account of the treatment of homosexuality as unmentionable in the region. Butler's perception that sexual identification is dependent on the availability of social and cultural norms that enable the subject to achieve the 'exercise of self-determination ... and lay claim to what is one's own'[80] is as pertinent to Jerome's situation as it is to Tyler's. However, unlike Tyler whom Mootoo describes as having the good fortune to meet the supportive Mala Ramchandin and form a partnership with the transgender Otoh, Jerome enjoys few such positive encounters. Thomas, in fact, goes out of his way to subvert the reader's expectations in this respect. Though he leads us to assume from his *Bildungsroman*-style portrayal of Jerome's adolescence and entry into manhood that he is writing a coming-out novel, in order to foreground the frustrations and disappointments typifying homosexual existence in the Caribbean he omits reference to or downplays the positive events that the genre conventionally introduces. These include the protagonist's encounter with a supportive queer social group, his disclosure of his sexuality to family and friends, and – usually positioned as the key point of the narrative – his forming of a gay partnership. In omitting these events or qualifying their significance, *Spirits in the Dark* gives the impression of being constructed around a cluster of absences and gaps. Its interest depends as much on the events that are not directly described but shadow and haunt it in terms of genre as on those that it does depict. Although Thomas does in fact portray Jerome disclosing his homosexuality in the final chapter in the context of the religious rite he performs, he renders the event ambiguous by raising doubts about whether, in the homophobic environment of

Isabella Island, this will enable him to find a partner. In addition, by delaying his coming out until this late point in the narrative, he frustrates the reader's desire to discover whether or not Jerome will achieve this goal, leaving him in a state of uncertainty similar to the character's own.

The frustration and isolation that Jerome suffers on account of the homophobic attitudes prevalent in the region are exacerbated by his sense of injustice at the racist nature of the colonial system. This, as well as concealing his native African culture from him, prevents him from obtaining a professional post suited to his abilities. In representing him longing to achieve sexual and professional fulfilment but suffering repeated disappointment, Thomas treats particularly poignantly the topic that Freud, discussing the phenomenon of doubling and its uncanny connotations, describes as 'all the unfulfilled but possible futures to which we still like to cling in phantasy, all the strivings of the ego which adverse external circumstances have crushed'.[81]

Thomas explores Jerome's 'unfulfilled but possible futures' and the disappointments they breed against the background of Caribbean hybridity. The archipelago was shaped by slavery and colonialism and, as Shalini Puri observes, it has had to 'negotiate its identities in relation to Africa and Asia, from where most of its surviving inhabitants come; to Europe, from where its colonizing settlers came; and to the United States of America, its imperial neighbor'.[82] Jerome, growing up in the region in the 1950s, also has to negotiate these identities. Hybridity, while carrying positive associations of racial inclusiveness and a productive interplay of difference, can alternatively promote tension and conflict. Sinfield describes it representing 'both an imposition and an opportunity', adding: 'Which of these will win out depends on the forces against us, and on our resourcefulness.'[83] Jerome, though resourceful, is confronted by a set of adverse forces that strike the reader as almost insurmountable.

A focus on hybridity is particularly prominent in the novel's opening chapters describing Jerome's boyhood. Despite the moves afoot by the white planters on the island to limit school enrolment on the grounds that if the members of the native population achieve an education they will refuse to work on the land, he succeeds, through intelligence and motivation, in gaining entrance to secondary school. As a boy he takes racial discrimination for granted, uncritically accepting the colonial equation of 'civilization' with white Western culture. It takes Yaw, a citizen of the newly independent Ghana who visits the school on a government initiative in order, as the headmaster describes, 'to develop an understanding between the Africans and Negroes in other parts of the world',[84] to challenge his views. Yaw warns Jerome that if he and his fellow countrymen continue 'imitating the culture of a people that despises you . . . you become a shadow society. You become shadow people' (p. 65). He recommends him to familiarize himself with his native culture, particularly its 'ceremonies' and 'dance' (p. 66) on account of the social unity they promote. Yaw's anxiety that Caribbean society will diminish into the role of 'mimic man',[85] the phantom double of white cultural attitudes, strikes a chord with Jerome. Sensing that his friend's words have 'unburied a part of his African self' (p. 69), he thinks elatedly, 'Yaw must know a lot about shadows. Africans could teach Jung a thing or two about that!' (p. 65).

Another figure who raises Jerome's political awareness is Peter, a British boy who as a result of his father being posted to Isabella Island attends the same school. Unlike the other white pupils who, recognizing that the system works to their advantage, accept the status quo, Peter is fiercely critical of colonial rule, particularly as reflected in the inadequacies of the education system. He spearheads a student revolt against the faulty instruction in grammar that a poorly educated teacher, herself trapped in the inequalities of colonial domination, is giving the class. Jerome regards the revolt with mixed feelings for although he endorses his friend's protest, he fears that if he overtly supports it he will risk expulsion. He keeps a low profile, remembering his grandmother's saying that 'White people always leave the naiggers fo' to put out the fire what them done set together' (p. 26). This is one of a number of native aphorisms punctuating the text that illustrate Caribbean society's distrust of white authority. Peter, unaware of Jerome's insecurities, accuses him of timidity, angrily observing that 'If I were a Negro I'd hate every White son of a bitch!' (p. 74). Apologizing for the colour of his own skin, he takes Jerome's hand and expresses the kindly meant but, in the circumstances, utopian wish that they can relate as 'two human beings and forget the rest – our race, our parents, *everything!*' (p. 77).

Jerome's friendship with Peter is complicated by his growing feelings of sexual attraction towards him. His awareness of the Caribbean prejudice against homosexuality combined with the fact that Peter is white prevent him, however, from broaching them; recognizing that 'is them what hold the handle and we that hold the blade' (p. 77), he regretfully keeps silent. The friendship between the two boys is abruptly severed when Peter is forced by his parents to return to Britain to attend public school. Recognizing the lack of professional prospects available to Jerome in the Caribbean, he promises to contact him when he gets home in order to help him to emigrate. However he fails to do so, thus relegating to fantasy another of the 'possible futures' that Jerome contemplates.

While working for the Isabellan Inland Mail, the only post available to him on leaving school, Jerome finds himself sexually attracted to certain of his male colleagues. However, on noting society's brutal treatment of an effeminate homosexual nicknamed 'Boy-Boy', he rejects any thought of approaching them. Boy-Boy is the target of crude humour and, illustrating the 'homophobic violence'[86] prevalent in Caribbean society, physical abuse. The local population treats him not merely as subhuman but, to cite Butler, 'humanly unthinkable', relegating him to those 'excluded sites that bound "the human" as its constitutive outside'.[87] Watching him tremble at the bullying he receives, Jerome nervously wonders if anyone has deciphered the secret of his own sexuality. He is terrified when a good-looking labourer whom he has observed looking at him on the way to work approaches him with a view to sex and, though he longs to accept, rejects him for fear of gossip. He has by now reached breaking point and the crisis occurs when, in an effort to conform to convention, he forms an attachment with a white female colleague who has indicated that she finds him attractive. After accompanying her to the cinema, he takes her back to his flat. However, while in bed with her, he experiences a temporary blackout and, on regaining consciousness, is appalled to find himself with his hands round her neck about to choke her. 'Yo' is weird!' (p. 159) the terrified woman exclaims and, recommending him to see a psychiatrist, flees the building.

Jerome perceives with distress that the physical assault he attempted to perpetrate on her was motivated by the fact that she is white. His anger at the racial discrimination he has experienced, repressed for years, has eventually erupted, transforming him ironically into the stereotype of the physically violent black man constructed by white racist culture. It is after suffering a breakdown and being released from hospital that, prompted by his father's observations that they 'see God different from the way other people see him' (p. 167) and 'have a lot of things 'bout Africa' in their form of worship, he starts attending the services held by the Spirituals, a religious fellowship in the region. Though worried that his concealment of his homosexuality will block him from achieving enlightenment, he volunteers to participate in the ritual integral to the Spirituals' worship. Though he has previously dismissed such ancestral practices as mere superstition, he turns to them now in desperation.

On entering the dark, cavernous cellar where the rite takes place Jerome attempts to calm his fears by envisaging the descent as an uncanny return to the womb. He recognizes that, from a Christian point of view, he needs 'to generate his own light and energy from within' in order to 'enlighten his own darkness' (p. 190). Having prepared for the event by fasting, he experiences a series of disturbing visions. These include being entrapped in a coffin, representing perhaps the live burial that his closeted existence signifies, and standing trial in a court of law where he hears figures from his past, including his former teachers, accuse him of being a homosexual and demand that he suffer the death penalty. On subsequently describing the experience to Pointer Francis, the priest who acts as his mentor, Jerome is surprised to hear him express the view that sex, homosexual relations included, is in no way sinful. Though sympathetic to his predicament, Pointer Francis nonethless criticizes him. He rebukes him for the fact that 'Yo' put the sex part o' yo' life 'pon a trash heap just fo' please society' (p. 198) and advises him, on returning home, to make an effort to find a male partner.

Reference to his racial and cultural heritage also features in Jerome's spiritual journey, since it concludes with him encountering the spirit of his grandmother. She escorts him on a fantasy journey to a city where the residents, dressed in brightly coloured African robes, are dancing and feasting. Describing the community as a collective where goods are held in common, she jubilantly announces: 'What yo' seeing here is the life o' the ancestors' (p. 209).

Jerome's immediate response to the experience he has undergone is to feel 'ecstatic, glad for all that had happened' (p. 219). However on returning home and recognizing that Pointer Francis is no longer available to support him, he senses his optimism diminish and, as Thomas describes, 'he felt the beginnings of fear' (p. 219). Though relieved by his mentor's non-judgemental attitude towards his homosexuality and his positive advice, he wonders if, in the context of the sexual prejudice rife on the island, he will find the courage to act upon it.

By concluding the narrative here, Thomas leaves Jerome's trajectory tantalizingly open-ended, with the reader ignorant as to whether he will find a partner or if this 'possible future', like the others for which he has fruitlessly yearned, will remain unfulfilled. Thomas's decision to relegate Jerome's conversation with Pointer Francis to the location of the underground cellar, with its associations of spectrality and fantasy encounters, perhaps intimates the latter. It is possible that, as in Leavitt's portrayal of his protagonist Brian's spectral reunion with his lover Edward on Hampstead Heath that concludes *While England Sleeps*, reference to the uncanny furnishes Thomas with a strategy to foreground his protagonist's longing for companionship and love while implying that in the context of the homophobic prejudice operating on the island it represents a compensatory dream unachievable in the material world.

The most vividly described location in Thomas's *Spirits in the Dark* is the womb-like cavity of the cellar where Jerome's descent into his past life and his meeting with the spirits of his ancestors occurs. In Tartt's *The Secret History*, in contrast, it is the landscape surrounding Hampden College where the narrator Richard Papen enrols as a student in the 1960s. Having been raised in Plano, a dreary environment characterized as he scornfully observes by 'drive-ins, tract homes, and waves of heat',[88] he is astonished by the beauty of the Vermont countryside. His description of 'the sun rising over mountains, and birches, and impossibly green meadows' (p. 12) connects the landscape to the idyllic world of American pastoral, while his reference to it resembling 'a country from a dream' (p. 12) looks forward to the sense of enchantment he feels on first meeting the fellow members of the class in classical Greek for which he enrolls.

The class comprises a select group of five students, four men and a woman, all remarkable in Richard's view for their attractiveness and cultural interests, as well as (he subsequently discovers) their affluent backgrounds. He is fascinated by their self-engrossed air and the sense of antiquity they evoke – what he describes as their 'cruel, mannered charm which was not modern in the least but had a strange, cold breath of the ancient world' (p. 34). His interest in them stems partly from the impression they give of uncannily crossing the border between inanimate and animate, culture and nature. When he enters the classroom and they turn to greet him, he thinks: 'It was as if the characters in a favourite painting, absorbed in their own concerns, had looked up out of the canvas and spoken to me' (p. 23).

Richard's fellow students also reveal other connections with the uncanny. The twins Charles and Camilla who, in the intimate bond they share, strike him as representing 'an enigma' and 'mystery' (p. 265), take him to visit a graveyard in the vicinity of the College. It dates from the eighteenth century, and in the gathering dusk he thinks: 'There was something not quite real about any of it, something like a dream' (p. 71). Francis, who appears to be the leader of the group, has connotations of spectrality. Striding along the corridor in 'a swish of blue cashmere and cigarette smoke', he strikes Richard as less 'a creature of flesh and blood' than 'a figment of the imagination stalking down the hallway as heedless of me as ghosts, in their shadowy rounds, are said to be heedless of the living' (p. 23). The tutor Julian Morrow who teaches the class exudes a 'strange mixture of chill and warmth' (p. 354). His allegedly exotic past includes serving as tutor to a Middle Eastern princess. His surname, while evoking the sense of hope associated with a new day, rhymes ominously with 'sorrow'.

The air of uncanny Otherness that Richard senses emanating from his classmates, though at this early stage of his acquaintance with them he is ignorant of the fact, reflects another form of transgressive excess they share. This is their queer sexuality. Henry, who plays the role of surrogate father, is emotionally devoted to Julian, describing him idealistically as 'a divinity' (p. 372). Francis is overtly gay, while the close bond between Camilla and her twin brother Charles reflects, as Richard later discovers, an incestuous relationship. The four students form, on account of their close-knit connections, a kind of queer family. The fifth member of the class, who strikes Richard and the reader as something of a misfit, is the maverick Bunny. In addition to being an inveterate gossip and incapable of keeping confidences, he either is, or mischievously pretends to be, homophobic. He appears to gain a sadistic enjoyment from needling Francis and Camilla about their unorthodox sexualities and relationships, annoying the former by calling him a faggot.

Richard, as a newcomer, exists on the perimeter of the group and is excluded from its more intimate conversations. He occupies as a result, in the novel's structure, the role of naive narrator. His ignorance of his classmates' secrets is illustrated by the fact that he is initially unaware of Camilla's sexual involvement with her brother and, since he is attracted to her himself, he is disappointed when she makes it clear that she does not reciprocate his interest but regards him merely as a friend. While feeling privileged to be accepted into what he esoterically terms the group's 'cyclical, byzantine existence' (p. 97), he feels incapable of deciphering its secrets and understanding its codes. Catching sight of Henry and Julian engrossed in a conversation that concludes with the former kissing the latter on the cheek, he is at a loss to understand what their behaviour signifies. He admits to being puzzled by 'the wildly alien character of the place in which I found myself: a strange land with strange customs and peoples' (p. 82). The geographical metaphor, as well as recalling Kristeva's description of the psyche as 'a strange land of borders and otherness',[89] looks forward to the transformation of the pastoral Vermont countryside into the craggy landscape of ancient Greece that occurs, whether in fact or fantasy Tartt leaves intriguingly ambiguous, in the performance of the bacchanal that his classmates re-enact.

Richard also fails to perceive the significance of the discussion of Greek drama and its relation to religious ritual that occurs in a particularly memorable class that he attends. Argument initially centres on the paradoxical pleasure that Klytemnestra's speech in Aeschylus' *Agamemnon*, describing the murder of her husband Aegisthus, gives the audience despite the brutality of its topic. Henry cites in explanation Aristotle's dictum that 'Objects such as corpses, painful to view in themselves can be delightful to contemplate in a work of art' (p. 43). The discussion turns to Euripides' play *The Bacchae* and its reference to the rite of the bacchanal celebrating the cult of Dionysus, with the students commenting on the frenzy that its performance generated in ancient Greece and the fantastic transformation of celebrants and landscape it allegedly involved. Julian's observation that, in keeping with the Greek love of paradox, 'bloody, terrible things, are sometimes the most beautiful' (p. 46) chimes with Royle's observation that the uncanny 'can be a matter of something gruesome or terrible' or, alternatively, 'a matter of something strangely beautiful, bordering on ecstasy'.[90] Julian associates the Bacchic mystery with the channelling of 'primitive impulses' and, referring to the Maenads who played a role in it, describes them as 'more like deer than human beings' (p. 44). Thinking about the class with hindsight, Richard recognizes that it was no doubt then that the idea of re-enacting the rite first occurred to his fellow students.

Punter describes the paradigmatic ceremony as permitting 'the flow of what is forbidden' and enabling the participant to cross the boundary between 'the mundane and the magical'.[91] This epitomizes what, according to Henry who describes the event to Richard shortly after its performance, he and his companions achieve in re-enacting the bacchanalian rite. Their immersion in Greek culture, combined with their non-normative sexualities and relationships, enable them imaginatively to open themselves to its queer dimension, social and sexual. The god Dionysus, according to Greek tradition, has attributes relating him to 'queer' since, as well as having connotations of transvestism, with incidents of cross-dressing featuring in the rituals he inspired, he exemplifies boundary-transgression in general. He is renowned for his somatic mobility and the epiphanies and different forms of embodiment he assumed, reflected in his ability to traverse the border between god, man and nature. He reputedly travelled to Greece from the Orient, and his foreign origins also relate him to concepts of difference and Otherness.[92]

Henry describes to Richard how, having researched the cultural details of the bacchanal, he and his companions prepared for its re-enactment by fasting and drinking a mind-enhancing brew of herbs as close to the Greek original as they could find in the Vermont countryside. A note of humour is introduced in his reference to the blunders and false starts they initially made. Irony too is apparent in the fact that he and his fellows, though ridiculed by the other students at the College as a group of egg-head pedants who waste their time obsessing over a dead literature instead of getting high on recreational drugs and booze, are in fact taking the risky step of trying to summon up a god whose manifestation, if in fact it occurs, may be notably dangerous.

Ceremonial, Punter argues, 'always points past and beyond, behind itself'.[93] In keeping with this, the bacchanal can be interpreted as a form of 'heterochrony', a space that furnishes imaginative access to traces of a vanished past and its culture.[94] According to the account of the rite that Henry gives Richard, the re-enactment he and his friends perform achieves this goal. He describes himself and his three companions creating, whether in fantasy or fact, the transformation of place and identity, with the element of emotional and sexual excess that characterized its performance in ancient Greece. Descriptions of geographical location in Gothic fiction are frequently structured on 'opposed spaces',[95] the sublimely rugged heath and mountain contrasting with the picturesque valley. Tartt's description of the rite reflects a similar juxtaposition of opposites, with the Vermont country-side temporarily transformed from gentle pastoral to the harsher landscape of the Peloponnese. As occurs in Euripides' *Bacchae*, snakes twine themselves round the trees and the countryside echoes with the bellowing of bulls and the howling of wolves. Day describes the process of uncanny enthralment that the Gothic protagonist experiences as generating 'the metamorphosis of the self into its own hidden double'.[96] The four students likewise acquire uncanny doppelgängers, metamorphosing into Dionysiac revellers. Henry describes how, assuming hyper-normal physical powers, they traverse vast tracts of land in pursuit of a deer – Camilla in animal form, he implies. The rite concludes with an encounter with the god Dionysus. Tartt leaves it uncertain whether the figure is the divinity himself or a fantasy manifestation of their tutor Julian in 'divine' form.

The sensation of 'a film in fast motion ... so the universe expands to fill the boundaries of the self' (p. 196) that Henry describes the rite involving terminates as abruptly as it commenced. The contrast between 'something strangely beautiful, bordering on ecstasy' and 'something gruesome or terrible, above all death or corpses'[97] that the uncanny can evoke becomes frighteningly evident when the four companions, on waking from their trance, find their garments stained not only with leaves but also, ominously, with soil and blood. At their feet lies the corpse of a local farmer whom in their frenzy they have unwittingly killed. Parkin-Gounelas describes the double as a 'figure of jouissance that enjoys at our expense, committing acts that we would not otherwise dream of' and 'forcing us into a position of servitude to our appetites'.[98] Her observation is pertinent here.

The remaining chapters of the novel – the weakest, in my view, on account of their predictable content – describe the final stage of the process of Gothic enthralment when the protagonist, having experienced heightened pleasure and ego enhancement by transgressing convention and moral limits, recoils in horror and disgust at the perverse and violent acts he has committed. Tartt describes Francis and his three companions struggling to cope with the repercussions, both practical and psychological, of their trespass into the world of Dionysiac ritual and excess. They become caught up in the police inquiry into the death of the local farmer and also have to deal with effects of the second act of bloodshed, this time deliberate, that they commit. This is the murder of Bunny who, having deduced from their secretive behaviour that they are concealing an illicit secret, pesters them with questions and appears to be on the verge of discovering their role in the farmer's death.

As a result of these stresses, the students' subjectivities and mental stability begin to disintegrate and, with them, their relationships. They feel that the malevolent spirit of Bunny, his body lying unburied, is exerting a malevolent influence, with Richard admitting to dreaming about him and Charles claiming to have seen his ghost. The sexual relationship between Charles and Camilla ceases to be consensual but becomes dominated by the former's possessive and violent outbursts. Camilla eventually leaves him to live with Henry who collapses, in turn, into a state of drug dependency.

Though advocates of 'queer' who regard the concept and its agenda uncritically may disagree, in my view one can perhaps read Tartt's account of the disintegration of the students' subjectivities and lives into chaos as signifying an indirect critique of 'queer' and its negative features. As Jagose illustrates, its critics complain of its lack of moral discrimination and protest at its totalizing inclusion of a variety of non-normative sexualities, some of them oppressive.[99]

As a result of their irrational behaviour Richard ceases to regard his classmates as attractive but starts to regard their company as a burden. He recognizes, however, that on account of being privy to their guilty secrets he cannot free himself from them. His words echoing those of the protagonists of other Gothic novels who find themselves trapped with companions whom they increasingly dislike and resent,[100] he despondently admits, 'There was no way out. I was stuck with them, all of them, for good.' (p. 544)

The novels discussed in this chapter illustrate the varied approaches that contemporary writers adopt towards images of place and space and their uncanny dimension, and the different strategies they employ to represent them. Grimsley's predominantly psychological and social treatment of the haunted house and the *unheimlich/heimlich* home contrasts with the postmodern representations of Mootoo and Winterson and their excursions into fantasy and magic realism.

The concept of border-crossing, its uncanny aspect signified by the ghost's ability to traverse boundaries and penetrate walls, is to the fore in several novels. Grimsley in *Dream Boy* portrays Nathan's father, in an attempt to make sexual contact with his son, trying to enter his bedroom, and Nathan and Roy leaving the confines of their homes to pursue their relationship in the heterotopic site of the cemetery. It also furnishes an image for transvestism and trans-gender, as is illustrated by Mootoo's focus on the pleasure that Tyler takes in cross-dressing and Otoh's transition from female to male in *Cereus Blooms at Night*. Ali, the protagonist of Winterson's *The Power Book*, likewise fantasizes experiencing a sex change in her love affair with Tulip.

Border-crossing receives reference, in addition, in relation to race in Thomas's representation of the friendship that the Caribbean Jerome forms with the white Peter in *Spirits in the Dark*, and in Hollinghurst's delineation of Will Beckwith's sexually exploitative liaison with the black Arthur in *The Swimming-Pool Library*. It features again in the novels discussed in the following chapter that focuses on the topic of 'Monstrous Others'. Writers investigate the stigmatization

of the queer individual as a freak and unnatural hybrid, while challenging his relegation to the abject and the prejudices it reflects.

5

Monstrous Others

Those deemed illegible, unrecognizable, or impossible nevertheless speak in the terms of 'the human', opening the term to a history not fully constrained by the existing differentials of power.[1]

Hybridity and border-crossing

Discussions of monstrosity and the ambivalent response of horror and fascination that it tends to provoke frequently hinge on hybridity and ambiguity, concepts traditionally carrying connotations of the grotesque and the perverse. Elizabeth Grosz describes the monster as 'an ambiguous being whose existence imperils categories and oppositions dominant in social life'.[2] Discussing its hybrid construction, she refers to its destabilizing of the binary oppositions male/female, human/animal, man/demon and cultural definitions of them. The association of the monster with hybridity and the border-crossing that it implies, along with its connections with concepts of taboo, relate it to the uncanny for, as Bronfen observes: 'The uncanny always entails anxieties about fragmentation, about the disruption or destruction of any narcissistically informed sense of personal stability, body integrity, immortal individuality.'[3] These ideas and definitions are not neutral but carry sociopolitical implications. Since power entails the authority to determine codes of inclusion and exclusion,

definitions of monstrosity are employed in establishing the boundaries of the human; they help to determine, as Punter writes, 'what
is and is not acceptable, what is to be allowed to come to the warm
hearth of society and what is to be consigned to the outer wilder-
ness'.[4]

The homosexual and lesbian, as constructed in homophobic discourse, reveal connections with the monstrous. Lesbian and male
gay partnerships, in challenging the binary male/female, are accused
of 'disturbing identity, system, order' and failing 'to respect borders,
positions, rules'.[5] They are stigmatized as unnatural and unspeakable[6]
and described as posing a threat to family stability. Although lesbian
and male gay sexuality is generally invisible, this, instead of necessarily
protecting the queer individual, can exacerbate the hostility that his
sexuality provokes if discovered. The fact that, as the universalizing
model of homosexuality defined by Sedgwick indicates, the border
between homosexuality and heterosexuality is permeable and unfixed
problematizes the notion of a stable sexual identity, arousing in the
heterosexual fears about his own sexual orientation.

The transsexual, on account of his gender ambiguity and his recourse
to reconstructive surgery, is vilified on occasion as erasing the division
between nature and culture, and scarily heralding the emergence of
a world of 'indifferent creatures, androgynous and hermaphrodite'.[7]
Asking the question 'What sort of anxiety is prompted by the public
appearance of someone who is openly gay, or presumed to be gay,
or whose gender does not conform to norms?'[8] Butler concludes
that it stems from encountering an individual whose sexuality or
gender resists categorization according to the binary gender system.

The association of queer sexuality and transgender with the monstrous is reflected in fiction and film. Halberstam discusses the homosexual's connection with the monster in Victorian Gothic,[9] while
Harry M. Benshoff, referring to contemporary cinema, argues that
'The (homo)sexual implications of the monster movie still continue
to lurk just barely beneath the surface of social awareness'.[10] He
cites in illustration the films *Dressed to Kill* and *Basic Instinct*.

The novels by Randall Kenan, Jeanette Winterson, Ellen Galford
and Paul Magrs discussed in this chapter create inventive variations
on the queer subject's association with the monstrous. While exposing
the prejudiced stereotypes that different cultures assign to him, they

simultaneously interrogate and challenge them, portraying their protagonists confronting the monstrous in an encounter with a fantasy doppelgänger or a character mirroring his difference. Kenan and Winterson centre their novels on the demon and cyborg, investigating the hybrid interplay of supernatural/human and technological/organic the figures represent. They employ different forms of fantasy narrative, Kenan's darkly Gothic and Winterson's dystopian, to explore the responses of fear or unease they generate.

Galford and Magrs employ an alternative strategy. Foregrounding queer difference, they concentrate, as Halberstam recommends, on 'recognising and celebrating our own monstrosities'.[11] For although reference to the monstrous is often utilized to stigmatize the queer subject, the writer, by employing strategies of inversion and parodic recasting, can challenge this. Renegotiating exclusionary constructs of the human, he can create a fictional counter-discourse, achieving, as Butler recommends, the 'reworking of abjection into political agency'.[12] The two writers, substantiating Royle's thesis that 'the uncanny is never far from something comic',[13] treat queer monstrosity and its grotesque connotations in the context of the Bakhtinian carnivalesque, exploiting the humorous reversals and transformations associated with the mode. Interrelating fantasy and realism, they employ ludic strategies to investigate serious issues. Galford, interrogating the interaction between lesbian and Jewish identifications, portrays her lesbian protagonist encountering a dybbuk, a form of Jewish demon embodying the cultural heritage she sees as oppressive and seeks to reject. Magrs, focusing on working-class constructs of male homosexuality and transgender, structures his storyline on the excess that queer sexuality and gender signify in heteronormative culture and investigates different forms of cultural hybridity. He also refers to the topic of AIDS. As Tóibín's and Schulman's AIDS narratives discussed in chapter 2 illustrate, reference to the monstrous is often employed to stigmatize the AIDS sufferer and pathologize homosexuality.

All four writers prioritize reference to the body in their novels. As well as exploring the limitations, excesses and absurdities of the human body, they introduce representations of fantastic, demonic or cyborg bodies and, as exemplified in Magrs's novel, bodies interrelating the human and animal. This agrees with the recommendations voiced by Teresa de Lauretis. She advises the lesbian writer, in 'her struggle with language, to rewrite the female body beyond its pre-coded, conventional, domestic representation' and, rejecting realism, 're-create the body otherwise: to see it perhaps as monstrous, or grotesque or mortal or violent, and certainly also sexual'.[14] The four novels discussed below indicate that her advice is pertinent on occasion for male gay writers as well as lesbian.

Relevant to the representational practices the writers utilize is the distinction that Hurley makes between the Kristevan represen-tation of the body as 'abject-grotesque', generating in the spectator emotions of 'fear tempered with fascination', and Bakhtin's contrary portrayal of it as 'richly comic'[15] evoking carnivalesque festivity and misrule. Kenan and Winterson employ a perspective corresponding to the Kristevan, whereas Galford and Magrs adopt a Bakhtinian approach. Ideas and motifs relating to the uncanny that the four writers recast include the double, the compulsion to repeat and ideas of taboo. In addition, like Donoghue and Hensher, whose fiction is analysed in chapter 2, they introduce the motif of secrets that, though society would prefer them to remain hidden, nonetheless emerge.

Demons and robots

Russo describes the representation of the grotesque and the monstrous in fiction and film as characterized by reference to 'horrific dis-memberments, distortions, hybridities, apparitions . . . and, of course, uncanny doubles'.[16] Kenan's *A Visitation of Spirits* and Winterson's *The Stone Gods*, while both introduce such motifs and images and illustrate the horror or disquiet they arouse, treat them very differently. Kenan utilizes them to depict the hallucinatory apparitions that erupt from the disturbed psyche of his African American protagonist Horace Cross. Raised in the settlement of Tims Creek, North Carolina, in the post-slavery period of the 1970s, Horace is obsessed with guilt on account of his homosexuality and his inability to achieve the model of heterosexual masculinity that the local black community expects of him. Winterson, in contrast, constructing a dystopian narra-tive, employs these images to interrogate the intersection between the human and technological that the cyborg represents and interrogate its contradictions. She also investigates the ambivalent response of her lesbian protagonist Billie Crusoe to what she initially regards as the grotesque construction of *Robo Sapiens* Spike and the hybrid combination of organic and technological that Spike exemplifies.

While both writers utilize reference to the monstrous to interrogate the border between human and nonhuman and the exclusions it generates, they structure their narratives on different literary traditions. Kenan, writing in the context of African American fiction, develops themes pioneered by his precursor James Baldwin. These include a critique of the puritanical attitude of the Christian Fundamentalist Church and an analysis of the difficulty that the African American homosexual on occasion experiences, particularly in the period immediately following the abolition of slavery, in reconciling sexual with racial identification.[17] In exploring Horace's traumatized state and the imaginary visitation of destructive spirits intent, like the Furies, on pursuing him that it provokes, Kenan interweaves fantasy and realism, the unfamiliar and the familiar, moving from one to another with disconcerting rapidity. The momentary disorientation that this triggers enables the reader to identify with Horace's fractured psyche and the conflict he experiences between material reality and the world of his tormented imagination.

Winterson, in contrast, creates a dystopian narrative that queers the Todorovian genre of the fantastic marvellous and builds on the feminist versions of the dystopia exemplified by Margaret Atwood's *The Handmaid's Tale* and Marge Piercy's *He, She And It*. Her novel, though differing from Kenan's in content and form, is, like his, structurally fragmented. It comprises a series of thematically linked narratives that, illustrating her interest in themes of repetition and return and the role they play in history, explore in different social contexts the political and ecological dangers that humanity confronts as a result of the ravages of war and the destruction of the planet's resources.

Kenan portrays the conflict that Horace Cross, the protagonist of *A Visitation of Spirits*, suffers in struggling to reconcile his homosexuality and his sexual liaisons with whites with his racial identification, reflecting familial as well as Christian Fundamentalist pressures. While the black community of Tims Creek in general disapproves of Horace mixing with white men, his grandfather Zeke, who is old enough to remember the humiliations that the black population endured in the era of slavery, finds it especially disturbing. In expressing his indignation, he refers to the slave market, a red brick structure inappropriately ornamented, as he describes, with 'fancy arches' and 'flowers'[18] that still stands in the neighbouring town of Fayetteville. The building serves as a symbol of black oppression, illuminating both Zeke's objections to interracial socialization and the guilt that Horace himself feels about the liaisons with whites in which he engaged while working at a community theatre in the area.

Horace is connected with concepts of metamorphosis and doubling, both psychological and physical, from the start of the narrative. In an effort to solve his sexual conflict and liberate himself from his role as 'a tortured human' and 'the human laws and human rules that he had constantly tripped over' (p. 12), he turns in desperation to magic. Like the arch-transgressor Faustus, the protagonist of Christopher Marlowe's play, he attempts to escape the human condition and its taboos by descending the chain of being and transforming himself into 'a creature wanting soul'.[19] He gives careful thought to his choice of embodiment. Dismissing rabbits and squirrels because they were too vulnerable and mice and rats because, though they 'had a magical smallness, in the end they were much smaller than he wished to be' (p. 11), he eventually selects the form of a bird. He chooses it on account of the freedom it enjoys, manifested in its ability, as he graphically describes, to 'swoop and dive, to dip and swerve over the cornfields and tobacco patches' (p. 12).

Kenan's account of the efforts that Horace, employing the books on magic he has accumulated, makes to locate the talismanic components of the spell that he hopes will effect the transformation, mingles pathos with the grotesque. Searching the North Carolina countryside, Horace admits to being baffled. 'What kind of cake', he wonders, 'could be baked from a cat's urine and the whole head of a humming bird? . . . How do you capture the stale breath of a hag, threescore and ten?' (p. 19). He wavers uncertainly between creating the spell in strict accord with the recipe and compassion for its victims. Appalled by the thought of destroying a human life, he decides to substitute a kitten for the baby that it cites, though he is afraid that it may ruin the spell and render it ineffectual.

When, despite the fact that he performs the magic rite, the meta-morphosis into a bird that he hoped to achieve fails to occur, he finds himself standing naked in the settlement of Tims Creek. Impelled by disappointment, he enters his grandfather's house and steals his gun with the aim of killing himself. However a manifestation of the uncanny grotesque, representing as Russo describes the 'cultural projection of an inner state',[20] unexpectedly intervenes and prevents him from pulling the trigger. Rejected by the black community as a foreign body on account of his homosexuality, Horace responds with uncanny logic by creating what Royle describes as 'a foreign body within oneself'.[21] The monstrous figure of a black demon, a phantom created from the images in the sci-fi magazines and posters that Horace collects, combined with the biblical lore he has imbibed in church, materializes before him in the form of a Masai warrior wielding a spear. The excess that the demon, since it represents Horace's uncanny double, signifies is reflected in the description of 'his eyes glowing a neon orange, his teeth a luminous white against skin the very color of the night air' (p. 67). He orders Horace to kill the dragon that is speeding towards him along the road. In actual fact it is a lorry carrying crates of chickens but it takes the reader, disoriented by his entry into Horace's fantasy world, a moment to perceive this. Convinced of its monstrous appearance, Horace fires at it but misses his target.

In the Gothic novels of Matthew Lewis and James Hogg, as Day explains, 'The devils have no real power over their victims, except in so far as their victims give them power'[22] since they represent not supernatural beings but projections of the human characters' troubled psyches. That this is the case in Kenan's novel is indicated by the fact that the guises that the monstrous spirits pursuing Horace adopt reflect his own cultural interests. The hooded figure with a silver scimitar that haunts him replicates an image from the sci-fi magazines littering his room, while the cluster of reptilian creatures swarming beneath an emaciated body hanging on a cross reflects Christian icon-ography. Resembling the paintings of Hieronymous Bosch, the image gives physical embodiment to his sexual frustrations and guilt-ridden thoughts. The representatives of the monstrous flooding Horace's imagination encompass in their ranks key figures from Gothic fiction and film that contribute to the construction of the queer uncanny in the novels discussed above. They include 'witches and Frankenstein and vampires' (pp. 248–9).

The journey into his past life on which the demon proceeds to escort Horace sheds light on his disturbed mental state and the circumstances contributing to it. Compelled to re-enact the events from which his trauma stems in an effort to master the anxiety they generate, he experiences, to cite Freud, the uncanny 'recurrence of the same thing' and 'the repetition of the same ... vicissitudes'[23] that he has experienced in the past. The mocking cries of 'abomination', 'man lover' and 'filthy knob polisher' (pp. 86–7) that he imagines the swarm of 'unholy elves and imps' who accompany the demon, resembling the grotesque creatures in Christina Rossetti's *Goblin Market*, hurling at him echo the taunt of 'faggot' that his fellow pupils had shouted at his friend Gideon in a raucous queer-baiting session at school. Horace had at first refused to join in the abusive chorus but, cowed by his classmates' bullying, eventually muttered the vituperative word. Gideon, displaying a confidence in his sexuality that Horace lacks, subsequently forgave him his act of betrayal, and the two boys briefly became lovers. However when Horace, intimidated by the ridicule of his classmates, suddenly terminated the relationship, unconvincingly maintaining that he had no desire for queer sex, he found the word 'faggot' addressed to himself. This time it was Gideon who uttered it. Resignifying its meaning, he employed it not as a term of abuse but a statement of fact. Disbelieving Horace's protestations of heterosexuality, he insisted, 'You're a faggot, Horace ... You can run, you can hide, but when the shit comes down ... you suck cock, you don't eat pussy.' (p. 164)

'The horror of not knowing the boundaries distinguishing "me" from "not-me"'[24] that the Kristevan abject denotes and Horace experiences in his encounter with the demon is repeated in his meeting with another uncanny doppelgänger. The figure represents a race-inflected image of carnivalesque misrule. On entering the dressing room at the community theatre where he had worked one summer, Horace is appalled to see a black apparition representing a 'reflection of himself' (p. 220) dressed as a clown sitting at the mirror smearing white makeup on his face. As Kenan describes, 'the double stood up' (p. 220) and, placing the tube in Horace's hand, 'forced him to make a mark on his face' (p. 221). It brands him a traitor to his racial identity, reflecting the notion prevalent in the black community in the 1970s and 1980s that homosexuality is a practice acquired from contact with whites. In consequence it prevents the black man from identifying with his African cultural roots.[25]

Whereas Horace, as illustrated by his inability to perceive the illusory nature of both the demon and the actor at the theatre, mistakes fantasy for fact, his cousin Jimmy Greene, the pastor at the local Baptist church and the only member of his family to whom Horace discloses his homosexuality, ironically does the reverse. He mistakes fact for fantasy. Refusing to accept that any of his relatives could be gay, he disbelieves Horace's disclosure, attributing it to his disturbed state of mind. Like Maria in Donoghue's *Stir-Fry* on being confronted with the evidence of her flatmates' lesbian relationship, and the Caribbean community in Mootoo's *Cereus Blooms at Night* in their uncomprehending response to the nurse Tyler's homosexuality, he dismisses Horace's confession as inconceivable. It is, in fact, only when Horace insists that his gay affairs were no mere instances of youthful experimentation and it is men alone who attract him that Jimmy credits his words. His attitude hardens and, taking refuge in Christian platitudes, he instructs Horace to pray in order to avoid temptation (p. 114). The episode is informed by irony since, as Robert McRuer demonstrates,[26] Kenan hints that Jimmy himself may have engaged in homosexual affairs in his youth prior to marrying and entering the Christian ministry.

After Horace, feeling impelled to do so by the spirits he fantasizes pursuing him, shoots himself, Jimmy is portrayed regretting his rigid stance. He refers to Horace's homosexuality not as a sin but 'a simple, normal deviation', though one 'that this community would never accept' (p. 188). His change of heart, as well as indicating the multiple perspectives on homosexuality operating in North American society in the era, renders Horace's suicide doubly tragic.

A striking passage towards the end of the novel portrays Horace, on the point of death, thinking back to his sexual encounters with men. In interweaving vividly physical references to sexual pleasure with expressions of guilt and remorse, it poignantly evokes his fraught situation:

I remember finally touching a man, finally kissing him. I remember the surprise and shock of someone else's tongue in my mouth. I remember actually feeling someone's else's flesh, warm, smooth . . . I remember the gamy smell of pubic hair. I remember being happy that I was taking a chance with my immortal soul . . . I remember then regretting that it was such a sin. I remember the feelings I got after we climaxed, feeling hollow and undone, wishing I were some kind of animal, a wolf or a bird or a dolphin, so I would not have to worry about wanting to do it again . . . (p. 250)

The references to animal transformation in Horace's soliloquy bring the narrative full circle, recalling Kenan's earlier portrayal of him frantically searching the North Carolina countryside for the components of the spell that he futilely hoped would transform him into a bird. Uncanny motifs of ambivalence, repetition, taboo, and the interplay between the familiar and unfamiliar inform the passage, as they do the narrative as a whole, illuminating the conflict he experiences and the role it plays in his death.

Unlike Kenan who employs motifs and images evoking the monstrous to represent the guilt-ridden fantasies of his protagonist Horace, Winterson utilizes them in *The Stone Gods* in several different contexts. Reference to somatic fragmentation and dismemberment occurs in relation to the reconstruction of the human body by means of gene therapy and surgery that typifies life in the futuristic society of Planet Orbus (the earth) that furnishes the setting for this narrative. It is also to the fore in Winterson's portrayal of the hybrid construction of *Robo Sapiens* Spike and the ontological questions that it raises.

Spike, in being technologically constructed, displays connections with the automaton, described by Freud as uncannily combining the contraries of animate/inanimate.[27] As Castle points out, automata of this kind, initially exhibited in England in the mid-eighteenth century at fairs and exhibitions, evoke in the viewer a response of pleasurable yet uneasy fascination.[28] Spike's construction, however, appears particularly uncanny since unlike the automaton she is programmed to evolve. As the narrative unfolds, she develops human organs and abilities, including growing a heart and learning to experience emotions such as love. Her gender too is uncertain for, while assuming a female form and persona, she refuses to define her sex, dismissing the topic as too boring and passé to merit discussion.

In depicting the futuristic society of Planet Orbus, Winterson describes how, with advances in science making cosmetic surgery and gene therapy generally available, the majority of the population have been technologically reconstructed along similarly youthful and fashionably attractive lines. However people speedily tire of physical perfection, and in the search for somatic variety that ensues images relating to the grotesque body, instead of being denigrated as ugly, are unexpectedly in demand. As Billie, Winterson's lesbian protagonist who opposes the fashion for physical reconstruction and campaigns against the practice of 'Genetic Fixing'[29] (p. 58), ironically observes, 'Sexy sex is now about freaks and children. If you want to work in the sex industry, you get yourself cosmetically altered in shape and size. Giantesses are back in business. Grotesques earn good money' (p. 19). Relevant here is Bronfen's reference to the uncanny grotesque as involving 'anxieties about fragmentation, about the disruption or destruction of any sense of personal stability, bodily integrity'.[30] Winterson plays on the reader's anxieties in this respect, describing a society in which physical fragmentation and hybridity have become the norm. On entering the gym, Billie grotesquely describes how 'my way is barred by an enormous woman with one leg, hopping along on a diamond-studded crutch'. The woman displays, Billie notes, 'impressive breasts – more so because where I would normally expect to find a nipple I find a mouth' (pp. 19–20). However instead of portraying Billie forming a relationship with a character who shares her critique of genetic and technological engineering, Winterson springs a surprise on the reader. She portrays her becoming sexually involved with a figure who is, on the contrary, a product of it: *Robo Sapiens* Spike.

Spike has been programmed as an astronaut, and Billie first encounters her in a television studio where she interviews her about the expedition to the newly discovered Planet Blue from which she has just returned. Spike, having secretly learnt that the authorities, deciding she has served her purpose, are planning to dismantle her, turns to Billie for help. Billie, herself in trouble with the establishment for her opposition to genetic engineering, has her own reasons to wish to emigrate – and she agrees to join Spike on the second voyage scheduled to take place to Planet Blue. At this stage she regards Spike ambivalently, responding to her with a mixture of fascination and disquiet similar to the way she views the exotic 'monsters' (p. 30), with their vivid colours and strange behaviours, that (or so travellers report) inhabit Planet Blue. Though describing her as 'absurdly beautiful' (p. 27) and feeling intensely attracted to her, she is perturbed by her refusal to define her sex. When she enquires her gender, Spike casually replies, 'Does it matter?' She adds as an afterthought: 'Gender is a human concept . . . and not interesting' (p. 63).

As well as featuring as the object of Billie's uneasy fascination, Spike also operates in the narrative as her uncanny double. In the interplay of the organic and technological she exemplifies, she mirrors the role of eccentric hybrid that Billie occupies in having worked for the political establishment as a TV interviewer while being opposed to genetic reconstruction and preferring to write in a notebook rather than employ electronic methods. In addition, in escaping with Billie to Planet Blue in defiance of state control, she shares her dissident status.

In the argument about the discrepancies and connections between robot and human in which the two engage during the flight, Billie insists on their difference while Spike contests her view, criticizing it as narrow and exclusionary. In reply to Billie's observation that she is built not born, Spike points out that in this scientifically advanced age many humans are too since they are cloned or produced outside the womb. Refuting Billie's accusation that she is incapable of emotion, she movingly describes the first occasion she experienced 'feeling'. Referring to the human capacity to dissimulate, she also reminds Billie that 'Humans often display emotion they do not feel. And they often feel emotion they do not display' (p. 62).

As the relationship between human and robot develops and, disregarding the fact that inter-species sex is punishable by death, the two become lovers, Billie partially revises her view of Spike. Though recognizing that she is incapable of giving birth and does not eat or drink, she nonetheless admits: 'She was alive, reinterpreting the meaning of what life is, which is, I suppose, what we have done since life began' (p. 82). Acknowledging her acceptance of Spike's 'otherness', she observes, 'She is the stranger. She is the strange that I am

163

becoming to love' (p. 88). She nonetheless continues to find certain aspects of her embodiment and behaviour disturbing. When sleeping with her, she thinks, 'How strange it was to lie beside a living thing that did not breathe. There was no rise and fall, no small sighs, no intake of air, no movement of the lips or slight flex of the nostrils' (p. 82).

Whereas the interplay of animate/inanimate that Spike exemplifies connects her with the automaton, her classification as *Robo Sapiens*, with the organic component and ability to evolve that it implies, relates her to its more sophisticated relative, the cyborg.[31] Unlike the automaton, the cyborg enjoys agency and is programmed to interact with humans rather than merely mimic them. Haraway in fact portrays it furnishing a blueprint for the postmodern feminist.[32] Armitt however disputes her view, alerting attention to the masculinist bias that, as is often the case with the postmodern reinterpretations of feminist ideas, her representation of the cyborg displays. As well as criticizing Haraway for ignoring the female capacity to give birth and woman's nurturing abilities, Armitt argues that, in foregrounding the smoothness and perfection of the cyborg's construction, she makes it appear closer to the Bakhtinian classical body traditionally associated with the male than to the grotesque body connnected with the female.[33] Winterson's representation of Spike intervenes in the debate between the two theorists since, while foregrounding her gender ambiguity, it reinserts in her construction the feminine element that Haraway ignores. Though portraying Spike as incapable of giving birth, Winterson emphazises her caring abilities and her willingness to nurture. When an asteroid falls on Planet Blue blotting out the sun, Spike self-sacrificially abandons the team of human space-travellers on the grounds that her reliance on their precious store of solar cells will deplete their reserve. In a comment evoking the medieval myth of the pelican that feeds her young with blood from its breast, she tells Billie, who has also left the team in order to accompany her, that she regrets the fact that she is constructed of metal and not flesh and blood since, when she dies, she will be unable to nourish her: 'I'm sorry you can't eat me. I would like to be able to keep you alive' (p. 89).

Another attribute that relates Spike to the feminine is the fact that her body, in its hybrid interplay of the organic and the technological, resembles more closely the Bakhtinian grotesque body than the classical body associated with the male. Winterson playfully advertises Spike's hybridity and grotesque construction in her wittily parodic recasting of the Petrarchist lover's celebration of his mistress's physical perfections. Playfully juxtaposing references to culture and nature and replacing images of cherry lips and marble skin with terms from engineering discourse, Billie playfully proclaims, 'My lover is made of meta-material, a polymer tough as metal, but pliable and flexible and capable of heating and cooling, just like human skin. She has an articulated titanium skeleton and a fibre-optic neural highway' (p. 68).

Cixous associates the contraries of animate/inanimate that the automaton Olympia exemplifies with death and the corpse[34] – and Spike, when on the verge of death, refers to the role these contraries play in her own construction. Juxtaposing the familiar with the unfamiliar, she asks Billie to pass her the screwdriver. When Billie, puzzled by the request, enquires why she needs it, she replies in a matter-of-fact tone, 'Take off my leg. I need to conserve energy' (p. 88). In a line updating Shakespeare's reference to Cleopatra's removal of the armour from her dying lover Antony's body[35] to Spike's dismantling of her technologically constructed limbs, Billie observes: 'Her body is a piece of armour she has taken off' (p. 91).

The final words that Spike utters, 'Nothing is solid. Nothing is fixed' (p. 92) portray her contemplating death and the dissolution and transformation of the body that it brings about. She claims to welcome it on the grounds that, in relating her to mutability and mortality, it gives her, paradoxically, 'the chance to be human' (p. 90). Her comment epitomizes the uncanny interrelation of the organic and technological, the mundane and the strange, that she represents. Her hybrid construction, as Winterson illustrates, fascinates Billie and wins her love, while simultaneously perplexing and disturbing her.

Carnivalesque fantasies

The relation of the grotesque and the monstrous and their uncanny associations with humour and laughter, though perhaps less familiar to the reader than their scary, horrific aspect, receives discussion from critics working in Gothic and postmodern literary studies. Mishra describes certain eighteenth- and nineteenth-century Gothic texts as reflecting 'a discourse of instability' that 'like "laughter" and the "carnivalesque" is always on the verge of madness, the state of complete dissolution of logic',[36] while Jesse Bier describes 'grim laughter' as therapeutically providing 'a protection against total disintegration'.[37] Comments voiced by Gordon E. Slethaug are also pertinent. Discussing postmodern narrative, he demonstrates that fiction of this kind gives a new slant to the uncanny motifs of the double and monstrous Other, transforming them, by means of play and parodic humour, into vehicles for the liberating power of fantasy.[38] Royle too acknowledges that laughter, either 'diabolical or affirmative', can be uncanny.[39]

Humour of different styles, such as the absurd and the subversively satirical, is also employed effectively in contemporary queer culture and narrative.[40] Novels exemplifying it include Anna Livia's *Relatively Norma*, Winterson's *Oranges Are Not the Only Fruit* and Armistead Maupin's *Tales of the City*, along with other titles. While utilizing humour to expose and ridicule the contradictions and exclusionary effects of heteronormative conventions, writers also employ it to comment on the comic anomalies and changing fashions that lesbian and gay culture manifests. Texts contributing to this tradition, such as Anna Livia's *Minimax*[41] that playfully queers the motif of the vampire, and Benjamin L. Perez's *The Evil Queen*, structured on the camp recasting of a weird assortment of vampires, witches and demons, inscribe Gothic conventions, playfully reworking themes and motifs associated with them.

Galford's *The Dyke and the Dybbuk* and Magrs's *Could It Be Magic*, the two novels discussed here, develop this tradition, prioritizing like Livia and Perez motifs with Gothic and uncanny resonance. They exploit the 'discourse of instability' that Mishra sees as inherent in Gothic and the scope for parodic humour and play that Slethaug identifies as typifying postmodern narrative. Features associated with the Bakhtinian carnivalesque also appear in the two novels. Galford and Magrs depict the fantastic and bizarre transformations, psychological and physical, that their characters undergo in the context of carnivalesque mirth and misrule, celebrating the instances of queer jouissance they generate. The spirit of play informing their texts does not mean that reference to the darker aspects of the uncanny are entirely absent. The disturbance that they threaten to provoke is however controlled by the reassurance the comic dimension provides.

As well as utilizing humour to expose the rigidities of hetero-normative culture and the exclusions it promotes, Galford and Magrs alert attention to the comic aspects of queer identification and culture. A topic they exploit particularly effectively is that of the absurdities and ironies to which identifying as homosexual and leading a lesbian or male gay lifestyle can give rise in heteronormative society. They foreground the contradictions and farcical situations in which the lesbian or gay subject can find himself as a result of being at odds with or, as Ahmed writes, 'out of place' (p. 9) with heterosexual conventions and the so-called 'family values' they inscribe. The un-expected role-reversals and emotional transformations in which the imperative of desire can unexpectedly land him is another topic that they amusingly exploit.

The two writers, while utilizing similar styles of humour, employ them in different sociopolitical contexts. Galford, locating her nar-rative in 1980s London, employs reference to the monstrous and grotesque to explore the conflict that her lesbian protagonist experi-ences between her Jewish heritage and her lesbian–feminist identifi-cation and way of life. Magrs, writing slightly later in the 1990s, introduces them to represent the problems that his male protagonist encounters in coming to terms with his homosexuality, and to articulate the transgressive excess that queer sexuality signifies. Both writers foreground the liberating power of fantasy, psycho-logical and literary, employing reference to the carnivalesque to interrogate behavioural conventions and norms. Bakhtin describes the carnivalesque not as a genre but 'a flexible form of artistic vision'.[42] Strategies the two writers utilize to promote this vision include the humorous interrogation of the characters' (and the reader's) preconceptions of 'normality' and a focus on the everyday life of 'the carnival square' (p. 106) exemplified by the marginalized or lower-class segments of society. They also foreground, in typically carnivalesque fashion, the disintegration of outdated hierarchical social structures, followed by their replacement by the formation of new, incongruous alliances and relationships. Galford represents these as sexual and social, whereas Magrs also introduces an intriguing element of the animal.

The Dyke and the Dybbuk, as the title Galford selects for her novel signals, centres on the incongruous relationship that develops between the lesbian protagonist Rainbow Rosenblum and the female dybbuk Kokos, the Jewish demon whom Mephistico Industries dispatches to haunt her. Both characters merit the designation 'monstrous' in different ways. Kokos, in her role of dybbuk and the shape-changing abilities it permits, represents the monster in the traditional supernatural sense. Rainbow merits the term in its popular sense, from the perspective of her numerous Jewish relatives who are shocked to learn of her rejection of her Jewish heritage and her adoption of a lesbian identification.

Advertising the fictionality of her narrative, Galford premises its plot on that antiquated cliché of Gothic fiction and film, the family curse. This particular curse, as the dybbuk Kokos explains in the opening chapter, originated in the Middle Ages in a humble Eastern European dorf when an orphan girl of mixed parentage, contemptuously known by the Jewish residents as Anya the Apostate, decided to take revenge on her Jewish lover Gittel for betraying the vow of sisterhood that she had previously sworn by getting married. Angrily watching the wedding procession wind through the narrow streets of the dorf, Anya directs the curse not only at this particular Gittel but also at all her future female descendants until the thirty-third generation. She vows that, as well as disappointing their husbands by giving birth only to daughters, they will be possessed by a dybbuk, a demon that enters the psyche of the human subject and drives her insane. The unfortunate ninth-generation recipient of the curse turns out to be the twentieth-century Rainbow Rosenblum. Kokos is dispatched post-haste by her infernal superiors to haunt and mentally unhinge Rainbow – or 'Gittel-plus-nine',[43] as Kokos disparagingly calls her.

'Rainbow' is not, of course, the name that her Jewish parents gave to Galford's strong-willed lesbian feminist protagonist. She rebelliously appropriated it after the LGBT Rainbow Alliance in an effort to free herself from her Jewish heritage and celebrate her lesbian identification. While earning a living as a taxi driver, she spends her leisure time gorging herself on what Galford, reflexively advertising her own contribution to lesbian genre fiction, irreverently describes as 'the mind candy' of 'dyke detective thrillers, biographies of self-destructing rock-stars and science fiction tales of intergalactic sex wars' (p. 40). Rainbow enjoys both the popular appeal and generic hybridity of these texts, as well as the grotesque aspect of the characters and scenarios they portray. On locating her whereabouts, Kokos finds her cosily ensconced in a flat comprising 'three rooms above a Cypriot bakery in North London' (p. 40).

Reference to the monstrous and its uncanny associations are apparent in Galford's parodic description of the supernatural guises that Kokos adopts with the aim of terrifying Rainbow and driving her mad by, as she eerily puts it, 'searching out the secret places where her ghosts hide' (p. 65). However the image of the Brocken Spectre she conjures up and the appearance of a giant squid with tentacles 'slipping across Rainbow's body like ribbons of seaweed' (p. 69) that she assumes in the pool at the local bathhouse prove a total failure in this respect. As Rainbow, drawing on her extensive knowledge of horror film, breezily remarks, they 'cut little ice with someone who's seen every celluloid shocker from Nosferatu to middle-period Ridley Scott' (p. 118). Illustrating Rainbow's cinematic interests, Galford litters the texts with intertextual references to Hammer Horror productions introducing 'bats, secret chambers and Vincent Price' (p. 75) and films with a lesbian content such as Garbo's *Queer Christina* and 'that old lezzie boarding-school classic, *Mädchen in Uniform*' (p. 101). These references to Gothic fantasy and films treating minority sexualities reflect the marginalized social role that, as a Jewish lesbian feminist, Rainbow occupies in British culture. They also relate Galford to the cultural interests of her lesbian readership.

As well as enjoying watching films at the local arts picture house, Rainbow also writes about them, producing reviews for a film magazine appropriately entitled *The Outsider*. The collective that edits the magazine is represented having its office in 'two rooms above an Indian takeaway in the Holloway Road' (p. 43). It is here that, as Galford describes, commenting humorously on the democratization of lesbian and gay culture in the 1970s and 1980s, 'the spiritual heirs and heiresses of Marlowe, Wilde, Sappho and Stein operate' (p. 43).

169

In order to carry out the act of demonic possession that Mephistico Industries has assigned her to perform Kokos needs, as her infernal mentor instructs her, 'to take control of the subject . . . and transform her into something other than she was before' (p. 39). Here, however, she encounters difficulties. As she sarcastically observes on meeting Rainbow: 'By any conventional standards, this rather eccentric individual is pretty Other to begin with' (p. 39). Instead of behaving demurely as a nice Jewish girl should, Rainbow is assertive and outspoken. She has 'a mouth that always wants to have the last word – and often gets it' (p. 39). And, instead of dressing in a feminine style to attract a prospective husband, she wears 'a faded purple T-shirt with a clenched fist and a washed out political slogan' (p. 40) and forms intimate relationships with women. Her lesbian identification, as Kokos anxiously perceives, augurs badly for the creation of future Gittels. How, she wonders, can she make the contract of infernal possession last until the thirty-third generation 'unless I can actually persuade the dear girl to succumb to a broody fit and procreate?' (p. 41). Rainbow, unfortunately for Kokos, shows not the slightest interest in procreating. She is not, as Kokos regretfully observes, 'one of your self-propagating Amazonian Earth Mothers, who does it all with a test-tube and a turkey-baster' (p. 41).

In sharing Rainbow's cultural heritage Kokos is positioned in the narrative as her uncanny double. She hopes, by haunting her, to arouse in her repressed memories of her Jewish past. However, with Rainbow having rejected all interest in it, Kokos is at a loss. Her situation is further complicated by the fact that as her relationship with Rainbow develops she discovers, against her better judgement, that she rather likes her and enjoys her alternative lifestyle. Quickly accommodating to Rainbow's taste for art cinema and Chinese food, she admits with surprise that she has eventually found a human she finds interesting and whose company she enjoys. Infernal dybbuk and lesbian dyke spend much of their time together in playful argument. The good-humoured sparring in which they engage recalls Bakhtin's concept of carnivalesque mirth and the raillery typifying it. It is during these playfully argumentative sessions that Kokos perceives with alarm that her friendly feelings toward Rainbow are transmuting into love. Feeling sexually attracted to a client, let alone falling in love with her, is against the rules of Mephistico Industries.

It is regarded as unprofessional, and Kokos fears that it may lose her her job.

Rainbow too experiences an unexpected transformation – though not the kind that Kokos initially intended. Unconsciously following the example of the medieval Anya the Apostate, she unexpectedly falls in love with Riva, an attractive young Jewish matron celebrated by the local Jewish community as the 'Flower of Stamford Hill' (p. 120). She first encounters her when visiting one of her numerous aunts. Riva, though an acclaimed beauty 'with eyes like blue-black plums and hair even blacker' (p. 60), is, as Kokos points out, by no means an appropriate object of desire for the lesbian feminist Rainbow. She is married to a renowned Orthodox Jewish scholar and has fulfilled her wifely duty by bearing him six children. The infatuated Rainbow, however, is undeterred by these obstacles and, with Riva's husband absent in New York, makes a determined effort to win her love. To achieve this, she gives up visiting the cinema and instead spends her time boning up on Jewish history and theology. As a result of these events, Galford's dyke protagonist and her demonic dybbuk double unexpectedly reverse roles. Lesbian feminist Rainbow, albeit motivated by self-interest, re-embraces her Jewish culture while Kokos experiences pangs of unrequited lesbian desire. This role reversal agrees with carnivalesque perspectives that are characterized, as Bakhtin observes, by 'sharp contrasts and oxymoronic combinations . . . *mésalliances* of all sorts' (p. 97). They effectively deconstruct the oppositional roles of infernal dybbuk/lesbian victim of her attempted diabolic possession that the two characters occupied at the start of the novel.

In keeping with the spirit of carnival that, as Bakhtin describes, creates 'in a half real, half play-acted form, a new modus of inter-relationship' (p. 101), Kokos proceeds to playfully demonstrate the affinities existing between Jewish identification and culture, on the one hand, and lesbian on the other. Both Jews and lesbian feminists, she points out, exemplify marginalized groups, the members of which frequently encounter prejudice and discrimination. Both, in addition, display positive attributes, including a capacity for survival, a strong sense of community, and literary and artistic inventiveness. However, in the case of both, these positive features are often undermined by negative ones. The latter include moral smugness, ideological narrowness, a masochistic obsession with the role of victim and a propensity to form cliques. Both, in addition, tend to be obsessed with dress codes and ritual festivities. They are strongly territorial and prefer to congregate in separatist venues. Whereas Rainbow's territory and sphere of knowledge is, as Kokos describes, 'every dyke bar and women-only disco between here and Brixton', her own Jewish one is the 'Chasidic wedding hall' (p. 131). She concludes her provocative spiel by sarcastically pointing out to Rainbow that, since in Orthodox Jewish society the sexes tend to lead separate lives and 'hardly talk to each other', her beloved Riva 'is more like a classic right-on radical separatist than you'll ever be!' (p. 98).

Kokos's irreverent demonstration of the attributes that the lesbian separatist and the respectable Jewish matron share illustrates Galford's ability to critique, while simultaneously celebrating, cultural and ethnic differences. She treats both Jewish and lesbian identifications ambivalently and, while acknowledging their respective strengths, astutely pinpoints their negative features. As well as exposing the oppressive nature of Orthodox Jewish culture reflected in its relegation of women to the home and its encoding of homosexuality as taboo, she playfully criticizes the political rigidities of 1980s lesbian feminism. Her novel, being structured, as is usual in the fiction of the early 1990s, on the concept of lesbian identification, operates primarily in terms of identity categories. However, in problematizing the differences between Jewish and lesbian identifications and culture and portraying Rainbow and Kokos reversing roles, it moves playfully towards a queer viewpoint.

Though published eleven years later than *The Dyke and the Dybbuk* and inscribing an explicitly queer perspective, Magrs's *Could It Be Magic?* displays features in common with Galford's novel. Like Galford, Magrs structures his narrative on motifs relating to the carnivalesque and treats images with associations of the monstrous and grotesque in the context of carnivalesque humour and play. He also resembles Galford in situating his narrative in an urban setting inhabited by several close-knit, vividly described social groups, the members of which display a strong sense of communal allegiance and a proprietorial approach to territory.

In addition, despite the fact that Galford prioritizes the identity category 'lesbian feminist' whereas Magrs adopts an overtly queer viewpoint and introduces a range of different sexualities including male gay, bisexual, transgender and heterosexual, the facets of sexuality that they prioritize are notably similar. Both writers emphasize, in typically comedic manner, the mobility and unpredictability of desire. Whereas Galford portrays the dybbuk Kokos unexpectedly becoming attracted to the lesbian Rainbow and Rainbow fancying the Orthodox Jewish Riva, Magrs represents his characters moving from heterosexual attachments to homosexual. In addition, the intertextual references to sci-fi films that he introduces comment reflexively on the experimental interplay of fantasy and realism that he creates in the novel in much the same way as Galford's references to Gothic fantasy and lesbian cinema comment on her own literary and cultural interests.

The two novels nonetheless reveal significant differences. Important here is their disparate treatment of monstrosity. In contrast to *The Dyke and the Dybbuk* that establishes Kokos's role as dybbuk from the start, the focus on the monstrous in Magrs's novel emerges gradually. Originating in a scary encounter with the animal world that the protagonist experienced as a child and continues to haunt his adult dreams, it proceeds, triggered by a sexual encounter in which he engages, to assume material form. The transformations it effects, unlike those that Galford describes, are physical as well as psychological. In representing them, Magrs employs imagery of the grotesque body and foregrounds the uncanny responses they trigger.

Magrs locates his narrative on the Phoenix Court estate in the town of Newton Aycliffe in north-east England. The majority of the residents have lived there since childhood and the ties they form with one another verge in their physical intimacy on the incestuous. As the alcoholic Elsie, sentimentally reminiscing about life at the local factory where she worked in her youth and introducing the reference to the body and the animal world that comes to dominate the novel, recalls:

> It was a joke at the Sugar Factory in those years that everyone had had everyone else. So what if they had? …They'd grown up together in the same small town. In a way it was no wonder they'd all *had* each

other, if that was the way you'd wanted to put it. They were part of the same litter. Like animals, pulling and nuzzling at each other in unguarded moments.[44]

Magrs describes life on the housing estate as stressfully though excitingly unpredictable. It combines incidents of sexual intimacy, of the kind that Elsie describes, with eruptions of macho violence exemplified by the fights between rival youth gangs and their pit bull dogs. Contradictions relating to sex and gender abound, with homosexual attachments coexisting with brutal incidents of homophobia and hate-crime. The insecurity of the gay members of the community is aggravated by the fear of AIDS, haunting them as an ever-present threat.

References to the monstrous, its hybrid construction and the grotesque body associated with it scatter the text, reflecting the physicality of the characters' lives and the exuberant fertility of their imaginations, enhanced on occasion by alcohol and drugs. Middle-aged Elsie, her looks raddled by drink, is described by a neighbour as resembling 'a bloody witch' (p. 55), while references to other Gothic motifs including the vampire (pp. 13, 55) and spectrality (p. 91) recur. Hybrid curiosities of a sexual kind furnish food for gossip. A rumour circulates on the estate that the fashion-conscious Liz, who always dresses in the smartest feminine fashion, is both the mother and the father of her daughter Penny. This uncanny riddle is solved when we discover that Liz is gender-ambiguous since, after marrying and siring a daughter, she underwent a sex change.

It is, however, Penny's nineteen-year-old flat mate Andy, known in the neighbourhood as 'an obvious queer' (p. 147), whose encounter with the monstrous is the focus in the narrative. Andy first makes an appearance, very appropriately considering the emphasis that Magrs places on carnivalesque mirth and transformation, masquerading in a cowboy costume at a fancy-dress party celebrating the New Year. The guests' attention, however, is focused not on the varied costumes in evidence at the event but on the tattooed limbs of Mark Kelly[45] and their bizarrely hybrid, eye-catching images of 'horned and feathered beasts, fragments of clockwork and cartography, of texts and petals and microscopic creatures' (p. 38). This is the first in the series of 'strange sights, unveilings, revelations'[46] that, though the more conservative residents of the estate disapprove and would prefer them to remain hidden, emerge and come to light.

When Mark engages him in conversation, Andy, aware that Mark was once married, assumes him to be a well-meaning heterosexual 'doing the sensitive straight man act' (p. 59) and taking pity on his isolation. That is until, having accepted his invitation to coffee in his room, Mark leans forward and starts to undress him. The sexual encounter to which this forms the prelude, though Andy certainly enjoys it, concludes disastrously. While dressing, Mark casually informs him that the condom he was wearing when he penetrated him split. Andy panics, terrified that he may have contracted AIDS. His mind befuddled by sex and drink, he thinks confusedly, 'I got fucked dangerously by an older man. An older tattooed-all-over man! And maybe now I'll die!' (p. 92). Recalling 'the moment of penetration, the snug and gagging seconds that Mark spent inside him' (p. 83), he remembers, or thinks he does, the 'exact second' when the condom split. He also dazedly wonders if he really did see 'seahorses and centaurs ... great, splashy butterflies ... cherubs and turtles malformed with age' (p. 98) inscribed on Mark's body? Or 'was he making it all up and giving Mark's body more credit than it deserved?' (p. 98).

Mark's tattooed body, the focus of the party guests' curiosity and Andy's fascinated gaze, is particularly rich in cultural and sexual significance. In exemplifying the transformation of nature into art, it unites the traditional image of the carnivalesque body with the poststructuralist concept of the gay aesthetic[47] and the artifice and performativity typifying it. The tattooed images, like the translucently colourful appearance of the ghosts of Duane's half-brothers in Purdy's *Mourners Below*, create a potent image of queer excess. As well as symbolically representing the anti-normative and, from a hetero-sexual viewpoint, 'monstrous' nature of gay sexuality, they can be read as representing a parodic version of the gay body regarded by straight society as a text to be suspiciously scrutinized and deciphered for telltale signs of sexual deviance.[48] Mark's body subsequently emerges, in addition, as a source of sexual potency. As Magrs mysteri-ously writes, hinting at the excursion into magic realism that awaits the reader when the product of the two men's surreptitious sexual encounter comes to light: 'Whatever was in Mark was in Andy now' (p. 85).

An indication of the hybrid and, from a conventional viewpoint, 'monstrous' nature of this product is furnished by the heterosexual Elsie. On catching sight of Mark and Andy kissing at the New Year party, she is momentarily startled by what, unaccustomed to seeing two men engaging in sexual contact, she regards as the *mésalliance* between the two male bodies. Employing imagery interrelating the animal with the fantastic, she bemusedly thinks, 'There was moment of doubt, as if she had seen something entirely fabulous, a made-up animal. And then, with a bit more thought, it seemed all too obvious and real' (p. 85). Her surprise at seeing two same-sex bodies embracing, where she expected to see a male and female, reflects the heterosexual view of homosexual relations as inconceivable and 'impossible', a topic that, as we have seen, features in the novels discussed above.

Bakhtin describes the carnivalesque text as characterized by dreams that reveal to the dreamer 'the *possibility* of a completely different life, organised according to different laws than normal life' (p. 122). In the weeks following his sexual encounter with Mark, Andy experiences dreams of precisely this kind. They are haunted by the image of a leopard that, though frightening, is enticingly beautiful. Andy recognizes it as originating in a scary encounter with the creature that he had experienced as a child in the local safari park. He also experiences curious physical symptoms, including a stabbing pain in his stomach resembling, as he puts it, 'a stitch, trapped wind, a claw in my gut' (p. 117) and a purplish blue mark on his skin. He interprets the latter as an AIDS lesion until, on inspecting it closely, he sees with astonishment 'a single leopard's spot staring back at him' (p. 148).

Instead of portraying Andy metamorphosing into a leopard, as the reader familiar with films such as *The Cat Woman* that specialize in uncanny animal transformations expects, Magrs avoids this predictable outcome and portrays him, in a fantastic instance of 'the doubling and dividing of the self',[49] giving birth to one – or rather to a hybrid creature that is part leopard, part boy. In a magic realist episode that interweaves the familiar with the bizarrely unfamiliar, Magrs describes the birth taking place in a toilet in the Carpenters, the pub frequented by the local gay community. With the help of Andy's current date Cameron, who is commandeered into acting as midwife, the cub emerges from Andy's thigh in a manner resembling the emergence of Dionysus from Zeus' thigh in classical myth. The reference to the leopard likewise associates Andy with Dionysus. As illustrated in Tartt's *The Secret History* discussed in chapter 4, the god has connections with festive excess, secret epiphanies and the dissolution of the boundaries between god, man and animal.

Andy, in keeping with the carnivalesque approach to life that pervades the novel, is delighted by the birth and proudly names his 'bright, leopard printed' (p. 328) boy-cub 'Jep'. No longer is he typecast by the locals as 'dress-you-up Andy', 'go out all week-end Andy' and 'be-off-your-tits Andy' (p. 228), as he unexpectedly transmutes into a caring father. With the assistance of Mark, who acknowledges the role that he and his tattooed body played in siring him, he successfully raises Jep to adulthood.

Magrs's representation of Jep's conception and birth has multiple connotations. As well as evoking the much debated topic of male pregnancy, it symbolically challenges the association of homosexuality with sterility and death that has grimly haunted gay male existence, especially during the AIDS crisis of the 1980s and 1990s. Magrs portrays Andy and Mark creating from their sexual encounter and the pleasure it generates not death but an exotic and uniquely beautiful form of life.

A focus on queer excess and the anti-normative 'monstrosity' of queer existence features not only in relation to the involvement between the homosexual Andy and the bisexual Mark, but also with reference to Liz, the transsexual father/mother of Penny. Discussing the 'contradictory site' that the transsexual body signifies, Halberstam observes that, while it can be celebrated as 'a kind of heroic fulfilment of postmodern promises of gender flexibility', it is alternatively open to criticism as reflecting an egocentric politics of the self and promoting, in its associations with expensive surgery, the commodification of the body.[50] Liz's sex change reflects elements of both. While possibly motivated by an egocentric desire for novelty and glamour, it challenges in positive terms the narrowly essentialist attitudes to gender prevalent on the estate.

Magrs utilizes Liz's gender-ambiguous body in a disturbing episode to illustrate the violence that can occur if a queer phenomenon that society prefers to remain concealed unexpectedly comes to light. Having previously left Newton Aycliffe in order to make a new life,

Liz returns unannounced to the estate, like the ghost of New Year's Eves past, on the night of Penny's party. Dressed in a glamorous ensemble of fur coat and high heels, with her hair 'shaken out, wavy and golden white' (p. 63), she steps out of the taxi and starts to make her way across the snow-covered square to the flat where the party is in full swing. Her flashy feminine gear alerts the attention of a gang of youths who have gathered there, making her an obvious target for baiting and abuse. Magrs describes how, as is typical of the abject, 'Her glamour attracts and repels them. They think her ridiculous and long to drag her down' (p. 64). Her screams make them panic and, with the first blow they deliver, her wig falls off. Her grotesquely gender-ambiguous appearance provokes them to attack further – and she collapses in a rumpled heap in the snow.

Liz nevertheless survives the youths' assault and, on being taken to the local hospital, lies speechless in a coma. Here Magrs portrays her undergoing another transformation, one even more striking than her previous sex change. Her state of suspension between life and death, the animate and inanimate, relates her to the spectral and its capacity for border-crossing. Her daughter Penny, sitting by her bedside, in fact fantasizes her 'floating up to a high luminous white point on the ceiling' and 'coming back from the brink of the next world and telling us all about it' (p. 91). Her phantomic metamorphosis recalls Cixous's comparison of the automaton Olympia to the ghost in being 'neither alive nor dead' but 'erasing the limit between the two states'.[51] The episode represents yet another uncanny event that enriches Magrs's fantastic and inventively queer narrative.

Galford's *The Dyke and the Dybbuk* and Magrs's *Could It Be Magic?* are appropriate novels with which to conclude this study. Their utilization of humour and emphasis on carnivalesque play remind us that although many of the novels discussed in this study focus on the bleaker aspects of queer existence, such as confrontations with prejudice and the problems involved in negotiating heteronormative conventions, they nonetheless frequently introduce comic elements. Donoghue's *Stir-Fry*, Leavitt's *While England Sleeps* and Purdy's *Mourners Below*, to mention only three such texts, employ, either consistently or in particular episodes, humour of different kinds – verbal, social or situational and, as suits the narrative's queer perspective, subversive.

However, Galford's and Magrs's novels, intellectually rich though they are, represent only a small proportion of those reviewed, and others too merit attention. The selection of fictional texts that I discuss is notably diverse. It comprises a variety of genres and fictional forms, including examples of Gothic fantasy, historiographic metafiction, AIDS narratives, dystopian fiction, the comic novel and the lesbian thriller. It furnishes an insight into the roles that reference to the uncanny plays in contemporary queer fiction, providing an opportunity to consider the different uses to which writers put it.

The novels reviewed above indicate that references to the uncanny, rather than being incidental and merely contributing to the novel's atmospheric effect (though in some cases they do do this) tend to be employed instrumentally to investigate and represent key aspects of queer existence. Indicative of this is the position that perceptions and events with uncanny import occupy in the narrative. Reference to them frequently occurs at crucial or climactic moments, suggesting that the writer finds realism inadequate effectively to evoke, to cite Ahmed, the 'slantwise' and 'oblique'[52] relationship that the queer subject has to heteronormative culture. Representing it necessitates a move into the uncanny and the 'tangential, to one side' dimension that it epitomizes,[53] involving perceptions and sensations relating to spectrality, the return of repressed fears and desires, different forms of doubling, secrets and their disclosure and other motifs with uncanny connotations. Episodes illustrating this include Donoghue's description in *Stir-Fry* of the dreams of witchy metamorphosis and flight that Maria experiences while in the process of recognizing her lesbian sexuality; Leavitt's reference to his protagonist Brian unexpectedly glimpsing the face of his deceased lover in spectral form in the concluding pages of *While England Sleeps*; Hensher's reference in *Kitchen Venom* to John's dark meditation, after killing his lover Giacomo, on the uncanny city characterized in his overwrought imagination by 'queer acts after nightfall, and violence in silence' (p. 240); and Waters's portrayal in *Fingersmith* of Sue momentarily thinking that she sees the ghost of Marianne Lilly at Briar, signalling the repressed maternal genealogy that underpins her and her lover Maud's narrative and Briar's significance as an *heimlich/unheimlich* house.

Some of the writers discussed above, while keeping one foot, as it were, firmly in the world of the material and sociopolitical, move increasingly in the later stages of the narrative into the world of uncanny fantasy. Mootoo in *Cereus Blooms at Night* portrays her traumatized protagonist Mala in an episode of magic realism addressing her childhood double Pohpoh, encouraging her to escape and watching her fly away over the trees. Magrs in *Could It Be Magic?* moves from a social realist description of life on the Phoenix Court estate and Andy's sexual encounter with Mark at the New Year party in the opening chapters to focus increasingly on events of a fantastic kind, including Andy giving birth to his boy-cub Jep at the Carpenters pub and Penny sitting in the hospital envisaging her transsexual father/mother Liz floating up to the realm of death and back to the world of the living.

In employing perceptions and motifs with uncanny associations, writers frequently introduce intertextual allusions to Gothic or texts with Gothic affiliations. Mary Shelley's *Frankenstein*, Gilman's *The Yellow Wallpaper*, Stevenson's *Jekyll and Hyde*, the tales of Poe and novels by Dickens and Collins feature significantly in this respect. They are accompanied by the recasting, with reference to the present day, of motifs appropriated from Gothic such as the family secret or curse, the haunted house, different forms of ritual and ceremony, the uncanny city and the breakdown of the family unit on account of paternal incest. Gothic motifs also inform the narrative structure of the novels discussed above. Hollinghurst constructs *The Swimming-Pool Library* around 'the problem of transmission' associated with the nineteenth-century Gothic, while the movement of the narrative in Tóibín's *The Blackwater Lightship* is impeded, as likewise occurs in earlier Gothic texts, by the introduction of topics encoded as socially taboo and unspeakable, in this case homosexuality and AIDS.

With reference to the motifs and perceptions relating to the uncanny that writers prioritize, spectrality and different kinds of haunting acquire particular prominence. As Freud's treatment of spectrality in 'The Uncanny' leads us to expect, writers employ them to represent the return of the characters' fears, as illustrated by Tartt's portrayal of Charles in *The Secret History* when convinced that he sees the ghost of the murdered Bunny. They also utilize them to depict their desires, as exemplified by Purdy's account in *Mourners Below* of the re-emergence of Duane's feelings of erotic attraction to his half-brother Justin, stirred into life by the news of his death.

Spectrality, in accord with Castle's analysis of the spectralization of the figure of the lesbian in nineteenth- and twentieth-century novels, also furnishes writers of lesbian fiction with a strategy to represent hetero-patriarchal culture's tendency to render the lesbian invisible, while also illustrating the ability of her desire to survive attempts at suppression and 'return'. Smith employs as narrator in *Hotel World* the ghost of a young girl who has recently recognized her lesbian sexuality. Waters moves in *The Night Watch* from portraying the lesbian ambulance worker Kay remarking on the spectral appearance of London during the bombing raids to portraying the spectralization of Kay herself when, with the ending of the war rendering her unemployed and aimless, she 'haunts the attic floor like a ghost' (p. 4).

Writers employ spectrality in notably innovative ways, assigning it new and topical meanings. Winterson in *The Power Book* contrasts the phantomic dimension of virtual reality and its technology with the haunting of the present by the inhabitants and culture of the past, exemplified by the ghostly foosteps audible in Ali's house in Spitalfields and the Dracula tour, with its echoes of Victorian Gothic, taking place in the street outside. Hollinghurst in *The Swimming-Pool Library* employs spectral references as a vehicle to explore the uncanny repetitions and returns that history itself enacts, threatening to erode, through the re-emergence of incidents of homophobia and homosexual panic, the sexual freedoms and gay rights achieved post-1967.

Caribbean and African American writers also employ spectrality powerfully to explore homophobic prejudice and its destructive effect on their protagonists' lives and psyches. Thomas portrays Jerome Quashee in *Spirits in the Dark* confronting, in addition to the spirits of his African ancestors, ghostly figures from his past who accuse him of homosexuality, while Kenan in *A Visitation of Spirits* represents Horace Cross, guilt-ridden about his same-sex desires, pursued by a retinue of spirits and demons, their grotesquely monstrous appearance indicating their origins in Gothic and sci-fi fiction and film.

Relating to spectrality are the key motifs, with their implications of uncanny domestic disturbance, of the haunted house and the *heimlich/unheimlich* home. Grimsley in *Dream Boy* and Mootoo in *Cereus Blooms at Night* employ them to represent the home destablized by secrets relating to homosexuality and, in consonance with Parkin-Gounelas's psychoanalytic interpretation,[54] the disruptive effects of paternal incest. Waters in *The Night Watch* and Leavitt in *While England Sleeps* utilize the motifs to contrary effect to represent the home life of the lesbian or gay couple rendered insecure and tense by the infiltration of homophobic influences from the public world. Houses employed by other writers as fictional settings also reveal an *unheimlich* aspect. They include the attic flat in Donoghue's *Stir-Fry*, troubled by the lesbian secrets it harbours, and John's affluent home in Hensher's *Kitchen Venom* emotionally disturbed by his closeted existence and the damaging effect that it has on the lives of his wife and daughters.

The motif of secrets and their disclosure – to recall Schelling, 'Everything that ought to have remained secret and hidden . . . but has come to light'[55] – also informs the AIDS narratives of Tóibín and Schulman. Both writers, while treating the genre very differently, introduce reference to silence and the unspeakable to represent the uncaring response of the general public to the pandemic and to explore the secrets and confidences of a personal nature that surface in its wake.

Royle, commenting on secrets and their inappropriate disclosure, describes how 'Uncanny feelings can be generated by strange sights, unveilings, revelations, by what should have remained out of sight'.[56] The motif furnishes writers with a vehicle to explore the effect that the unexpected perception of the physicality of lesbian or male gay sex can have on the heterosexual spectator or the spectator who assumes himself to be heterosexual. In Donoghue's *Stir-Fry* it prompts the protagonist to reassess her own sexuality, leading her eventually to form a lesbian relationship, while in Grimsley's *Dream Boy* it provokes, in contrast, an attack of homosexual panic triggering an act of assault. The disclosure of the secret of Liz's transsexuality in Magrs's *Could It Be Magic?* likewise precipitates an act of violence.

In addition to spectrality, and secrets and their disclosure, a number of other motifs and ideas with uncanny resonance infiltrate the novels reviewed above. They include doubling, a compulsion to repeat, the interplay between the familiar and unfamiliar, the corpse, reference to place and space, and a superstitious return to what Freud terms an 'animistic conception of the universe'[57] involving the presence of spirits and demons. Freud's reference to the psychological phenomenon of 'doubling and dividing of the self'[58] is especially relevant, as Duffy's *Beneath the Blonde* and McGrath's *Dr Haggard's Disease* illustrate, to the gender ambiguity and sense of self-division experienced by the the transsexual or transgender person.

Another feature of contemporary queer fiction that this study illuminates is the difference between lesbian and male gay fiction and their treatment of the uncanny. Novels with a lesbian focus, as well as foregrounding the topic of lesbian invisibility, frequently reflect the influence of Female Gothic. The motifs of the witch and 'the madwoman in the attic',[59] along with themes and storylines appropriated from fairy tale, inform the fiction of Donoghue, Mootoo, Waters and Winterson. The interest that the latter two writers display in the topic of lesbian sexual representation, and the contradictions it involves stemming from the writer's desire to represent and celebrate lesbian sexuality while avoiding appealing to male heterosexual voyeurism, give *Fingersmith* and *The Power Book* an intriguingly reflexive, metafictional dimension. Lesbian fiction also reflects, as the reader might expect, the influence of lesbian/feminist theoretical discourses. Themes of female commonality, sisterhood, mother-daughter relations, Rich's theory of lesbian continuum and Irigarayan concepts of masquerade and *déréliction* are to the fore in this respect. They are accompanied on occasion by the movement of the narrative from the sphere of the personal and domestic into the political and public, recalling the structure of the feminist fiction produced in the 1970s and 1980s. Fears are sometimes voiced by critics that feminist concepts and narrative strategies of this kind are losing their currency. They are, I am pleased to report, alive and well in the lesbian fiction produced today.

Writers who focus on male gay sexuality and existence, such as Hollinghurst, Leavitt and Hensher, foreground the motif of the city, exploring the opportunities for anonymous sexual liaisons, cross-class relationships and public sex that an urban environment can offer the queer subject, the gay man in particular. The American

Grimsley and the African American Kenan, locating their novels in the American South, underpin their focus on male gay oppression with reference to the haunting of the country by memories of slavery and the massacre of the indigenous peoples. Tóibín and Magrs explore the threat that AIDS exerts. With reference to Gothic themes, intertextual allusions to 'paranoid Gothic'[60] inform Hensher's portrayal of the relationship between John and Giacomo in *Kitchen Venom*, while echoes of the homoerotic bond between Frankenstein and his creature add tension to Bram's portrayal of the involvement between James Whale and his yardman Boone in *Father of Frankenstein*. These novels reflect, among other theoretical influences, Weeks's and Bray's analysis of the role that the metropolis plays in the development of modern homosexuality, discussions of AIDS in the work of Sinfield and Bersani, and Sedgwick's analysis of the closet and the binary opposition inside/out informing it.

As well as furnishing an insight into the utilization of motifs and concepts relating to the uncanny in contemporary queer fiction and their differing lesbian and male gay representations, this study sheds light on the political and ideological perspectives that operate in it, especially regarding the interplay between 'queer' and 'identity categories', the two key theoretical approaches available to us at the present time. Written at a moment when queer theory and its agenda, though to the fore in academia in gender studies and literary courses, is receiving criticism on a number of counts, this study is particularly pertinent in this respect. As I indicated in the introductory chapter, the criticisms directed at 'queer' are many and various. Accusations of vagueness, excessive utopianism, and a lack of political vigour and moral discrimination are among those commonly voiced. Another frequently articulated complaint is that 'queer', while claiming to be gender-neutral, tends increasingly to be associated with male gay interests, marginalizing and occluding as a result other sexualities and genders that seek to achieve visibility and their distinctive interests, cultures and histories. This helps to explain why, in contrast to academia, non-academic, town-based organizations often prefer to organize around the identification 'LGBT' associated with identity politics and gay liberation. This, however, does not prevent representatives of different sexualities and genders from working together in running joint projects and events.

On turning to contemporary fiction, we find that the situation, as illustrated by the novels analysed in the chapters above, is similarly complex. Resisting being bound by a single identification or ideology, writers often bring together and interweave elements from different sources. Certain novels, such as Winterson's *The Power Book*, Mootoo's *Cereus Blooms at Night*, Magrs's *Could It Be Magic?* and Purdy's *Mourners Below*, employ a predominantly queer approach; they introduce a range of different sexualities, represent desire as to a degree fluid, and depict gender as discursively constructed, created through the performative effect of reiterated acts. Others, in contrast, such as Leavitt's *While England Sleeps* and Galford's *The Dyke and the Dybbuk*, reflect an approach that is more in tune with 'identity categories'; they select as protagonists characters who adopt a clearly defined male gay or lesbian identification and represent coming out as the key route to sexual liberation. However, on investigating these novels and their narrative structure closely, we perceive significant ambiguities and ideological cross-currents in evidence. Leavitt, though focusing chiefly on male gay sexuality, foregrounds the resistance that acts of public sex signify to heteronormative conventions and regimes in a manner that looks forward to 'queer'. Mootoo interrelates a range of different sexualities and genders, a feature connecting her novel with 'queer', with the portrayal of the silvery-haired Mala Ramchandin whose associations with the witch and wise woman recall the affirmative portrayals of older women in the lesbian feminist fiction of the 1970s and 1980s. She further enriches her narrative with intertextual references to Rhys's *Wide Sargasso Sea*. Galford too interweaves different cultural and ideological elements. Whereas her utilization of the lesbian feminist Rainbow Rosenblum as a protagonist links her writing to the identity politics of the 1970s and 1980s, the playful mix of celebration and critique with which she portrays her, reflected in her humorous description of her dumping her radical politics when the imperative of desire prompts her to fall in love with the Orthodox Jewish Riva, indicates that she recognizes the problems inherent in a strict lesbian feminist identification and politics. Her introduction of the dybbuk Kokos's ingeniously carnivalesque demonstration of the affinities existing between the separatist lesbian feminist and the Orthodox Jewish matron, as well as illustrating the perceptiveness and linguistic exuberance of lesbian feminist writing, anticipates queer perspectives in interrogating the concept of identity.

Donoghue's *Stir-Fry* and Hensher's *Kitchen Venom*, in their re-working of the political themes and narrative structures of the coming-out novel in the very different context of the queer theoretical perspectives pioneered by Butler and Sedgwick, also illustrate the ability of writers to recast in a postmodern light fictional forms and political positions and debates inherited from gay liberation and lesbian feminism.

It is interesting to note that in some cases the dates of production and publication of a novel act as no clear indicator of its approach to sexuality. Purdy's *Mourners Below*, one of the queerest of the novels that I have discussed in its portrayal of the interrelation of homosexual/ heterosexual desires and identifications and anti-normative erotic practices, was first published in 1981 many years before 'queer' achieved common currency.[61]

With reference to the scope of representation, some writers are particularly wide ranging in their deployment of characters with different sexualities and viewpoints, creating, as a result, unusual configurations and contrasts. Waters in *The Night Watch* combines depictions of cross-class lesbian relationships and friendships between lesbian and heterosexual women with the portrayal of the homoerotic Duncan and his sexually ambiguous friendship with Fraser, the conscientious objector whom he encounters in Wormwood Scrubs. Tóibín takes the unusual step of centring *The Blackwater Lightship* on the warm, though prickly, relationship that develops between a trio of young gay men and three heterosexual women of different ages whose lives unexpectedly converge, in the breakdown of social convention triggered by the AIDS pandemic, in an isolated *heimlich/ unheimlich* house on the Irish coast.

The novels discussed in this study are of interest as much for the topics that they fail to treat as for those they do. It is noticeable that contemporary writers, while representing characters moving from heterosexual to homosexual liaisons and partnerships, seldom depict the opposite. Nor do they generally combine detailed portrayals of male gay and lesbian characters or relationships within a single text. As a result, male gay and lesbian narrative traditions, in contradiction to the queer preference for integrating different sexualities and genders, remain on the whole discrete and distinct. This is, of course, under-standable taking into account the major differences existing between the histories and cultures of the two groups, as well as the disparate lifestyles that men and women frequently lead, reflecting their differ-ing economic circumstances and access to public space. It will be interesting to see whether the two traditions of fiction continue to remain distinct or if, as a result of the influence exerted by 'queer', they begin to converge and interrelate. And, if eventually they do converge, what role will the uncanny, and perceptions and sensations relating to it, play in the 'slantwise' fictions they produce?

Notes

Introduction

1 Nicholas Royle, *The Uncanny* (Manchester: Manchester University Press, 2003), p. 43.
2 Randall Kenan, *A Visitation of Spirits* (New York: Vintage Books, 1989), p. 219. Further page references are to this edition and in the text.
3 Sigmund Freud, 'The uncanny', in *The Pelican Freud Library*, ed. Angela Richards and James Strachey, vol. 14 (Harmondsworth: Penguin, 1985), p. 363.
4 Freud, 'The uncanny', p. 371.
5 Hélène Cixous, 'Fiction and its phantoms: a reading of Freud's *Das Unheimliche* ("The uncanny")', *New Literary History*, 7/3 (1973), 528.
6 Rosemary Jackson, *Fantasy: The Literature of Subversion* (London: New Accents, 1981), p. 68.
7 Sarah Ahmed, *Queer Phenomenology: Orientations, Objects, Others* (Durham, NC: Duke University Press, 2006), p. 107. Further page references are to this edition and in the text.
8 Annamarie Jagose, *Queer Theory* (Melbourne: Melbourne University Press, 1996), p. 3.
9 Judith Halberstam, *In a Queer Time and Place: Transgender Bodies, Subcultural Lives* (New York: New York University Press, 2005), p. 50.
10 Eve Kosofsky Sedgwick, *Tendencies* (Durham, NC: Duke University Press, 1993).
11 Jeffrey Weeks, *The World We Have Won: The Remaking of Erotic and Intimate Life* (London: Routledge, 2007), p. 148.

12 See Royle, *The Uncanny*, p. 4; Ken Gelder, *Reading the Vampire* (London: Routledge, 1994), pp. 20–1.

13 Saul Newman, 'Spectres of the uncanny: the return of the repressed', *Telos*, 124 (2002), 117.

14 Andrew Bennett and Nicholas Royle (eds), *An Introduction to Literature, Criticism and Theory: Key Critical Concepts* (London: Longman, 1995), p. 36.

15 Jackson, *Fantasy: The Literature of Subversion*, p. 70.

16 Diana Fuss, 'Inside/Out', in Fuss (ed.), *Inside/Out: Lesbian Theories/Gay Theories* (London: Routledge, 1991), p. 3.

17 James Kincaid, 'Designing gourmet children or KIDS FOR DINNER', in Ruth Robbins and Julian Wolfreys (eds), *Victorian Gothic: Literary and Cultural Manifestations in the Nineteenth Century* (Basingstoke: Macmillan, 2000), p. 8.

18 Lee Edelman, *Homographesis: Essays in Literary and Cultural Theory* (London: Routledge, 1994), p. 197.

19 Fuss, 'Inside/Out', p. 3.

20 Lisabeth During and Terri Fealy, 'Philosophy', in Andy Medhurst and Sally Munt (eds), *Lesbian and Gay Studies: A Critical Introduction* (London: Cassell, 1997), p. 127.

21 Harold Beaver, 'Homosexual signs (in memory of Roland Barthes)', *Critical Inquiry*, 8/1 (1981), 104.

22 Bonnie Zimmerman, 'Lesbians like this and that', in Sally Munt (ed.), *New Lesbian Criticism: Literary and Cultural Readings* (Hemel Hempstead: Harvester Wheatsheaf, 1992), p. 4.

23 Freud, 'The uncanny', pp. 348–51, 369; Jane Marie Todd, 'The veiled woman in Freud's "Das Unheimliche"', *Signs*, 2/3 (1986), 519–28.

24 Judith Butler, 'Imitation and gender insubordination', in Fuss, *Inside/Out*, p. 23.

25 Freud, 'The uncanny', p. 345.

26 Royle, *The Uncanny*, pp. 42–3.

27 Beaver, 'Homosexual signs', 105.

28 Les Brookes, *Gay Male Fiction Since Stonewall: Ideology, Conflict, and Aesthetics* (London: Routledge, 2009), p. 25.

29 Butler, 'Imitation and gender insubordination', p. 14.

30 See Leo Bersani, *Homos* (Cambridge, MA: Harvard University Press, 1995), pp. 5–6; Alan Sinfield, *Gay and After* (London: Serpent's Tail, 1998), p. 21.

31 Iain Morland and Annabelle Wilcox (eds), *Queer Theory* (Basingstoke: Palgrave Macmillan, 2005), p. 187. See also Mandy Merk's 'Afterword' to the collection, pp. 187–93.

---

32 Joseph A. Boone, *Queer Frontiers: Millennial Geographies, Genders and Generations* (Madison: University of Wisconsin Press, 2000), p. 11. Also relevant is Suzanna Danuta Walters's cogently argued essay 'From here to queer: radical feminism, postmodernism and the lesbian menace', in Morland and Wilcox, *Queer Theory*, pp. 14–17.

33 Linda Garber, *Identity Poetics: Race, Class and the Lesbian Feminist Roots of Queer Theory* (New York: Columbia University Press, 2001), pp. 182–95.

34 Adrienne Rich, 'Compulsory heterosexuality and lesbian existence', in Rich, *Blood, Bread and Poetry: Selected Prose* (London: Virago, 1987), p. 38.

35 Elizabeth Meese, 'Theorising lesbian writing: a love letter', in Karla Jay and Joanne Glasgow (eds), *Lesbian Texts and Contexts: Radical Revisions* (New York: New York University Press, 1990), p. 83.

36 Freud, 'The uncanny', p. 356.

37 Jay Prosser, *Second Skins: The Body Narratives of Transsexuality* (New York: Columbia University Press, 1998), pp. 159–86.

38 Royle, *The Uncanny*, p. 2.

39 Julian Wolfreys, *Transgression: Identity, Space, Time* (Basingstoke: Palgrave Macmillan, 2008), p. 97.

40 William Hughes and Andrew Smith (eds), *Queering the Gothic* (Manchester: Manchester University Press, 2009), p. 1.

41 Eve Kosofsky Sedgwick, *Between Men: English Literature and Male Homosexual Desire* (New York: Columbia University Press, 1985), pp. 113–17.

42 William Veeder, 'Children of the night: Stevenson and patriarchy', in William Veeder and Gordon Hirsch (eds), *Dr Jekyll and Mr Hyde after One Hundred Years* (Chicago: University of Chicago Press, 1988), pp. 107–60; Elaine Showalter, *Sexual Anarchy: Gender and Culture at the Fin de Siècle* (London: Virago, 1992), pp. 103–18; George E. Haggerty, *Queer Gothic* (Urbana and Chicago: University of Illinois Press, 2006), pp. 123–8.

43 Haggerty, *Queer Gothic*, pp. 201–3.

44 Terry Castle, *The Apparitional Lesbian: Female Homosexuality and Modern Culture* (New York: Columbia University Press, 1993), pp. 1–65.

45 Lucie Armitt, *Theorising the Fantastic* (London: Arnold, 1996), p. 144.

46 Kelly Hurley, '"The inner chamber of all nameless sin": *The Beetle*, Gothic female sexuality, and Oriental barbarism', in Fred Botting and Dale Townshend (eds), *Gothic Critical Concepts in Literary and Cultural Studies*, vol. 3 (London: Routledge, 2004), pp. 241–55.

47 Andrew Smith, 'Death, art, and bodies: queering the queer Gothic in Will Self's *Dorian*', in Hughes and Smith (eds), *Queer Gothic*, pp. 177–92.

48 Freud, 'The uncanny', p. 345.

49 Eve Kosofsky Sedgwick, *Epistemology of the Closet* (Hemel Hempstead: Harvester Wheatsheaf, 1991), pp. 71–3.

50 Jacques Derrida, *Memoires for Paul de Man* (New York: Columbia University Press, 1986), p. 80.

51 Halberstam, *In a Queer Time and Place*, p. 34.

52 Halberstam, *Skin Shows: Gothic Horror and the Technology of Monsters* (Durham, NC: Duke University Press, 1995), p. 4.

53 See Royle, *The Uncanny*, pp. 2, 205–6.

54 Freud, 'The uncanny', p. 347. The motif has connections, as Freud points out, with the Gothic topos of the haunted house (p. 364).

55 Royle, *The Uncanny*, p. 45.

56 Iris Marion Young, *Justice and the Politics of Difference* (Princeton, NJ: Princeton University Press, 1990), p. 146.

57 Earl Jackson, Jr, 'Explicit instruction: teaching male gay sexuality in literature classes', in George E. Haggerty and Bonnie Zimmerman (eds), *Professions of Desire: Lesbian and Gay Studies in Literature* (New York: MLA, 1995), p. 147.

58 See Luce Irigaray, *Speculum of the Other Woman*, trans. Gillian C. Gill (Ithaca, NY: Cornell University Press, 1985), pp. 47–9.

59 Butler, 'Imitation and gender insubordination', p. 20.

60 Passages of John Rechy's *City of Night* (New York: Grove Press, 1963) illustrate this problem.

61 Luce Irigaray, *This Sex Which Is Not One*, trans. Catherine Porter with Carolyn Burke (Ithaca, NY: Cornell University Press, 1985), pp. 25–6.

62 Judith Roof, 'The match in the crocus: representations of lesbian sexuality', in Marleen S. Barr and Richard Feldstein (eds), *Discontented Discourses: Feminism/Textual Intervention/Psychoanalysis* (Urbana: University of Illinois Press, 1989), p. 110.

63 Jill Dolan, 'Lesbian subjectivity in realism: dragging at the margins of structure and ideology', in Sue-Ellen Case (ed.), *Performing Feminisms* (Baltimore, MD: Johns Hopkins University Press, 1990), p. 41.

64 Philip Hensher, *Kitchen Venom* (London: Harper Collins, 2003), p. 36.

65 For discussion of the witch in lesbian writing see Paulina Palmer, *Lesbian Gothic: Transgressive Fictions* (London: Cassell, 1999), pp. 29–58.

Chapter 2

1 Adrienne Rich, 'Twenty-one love poems', in Rich, *The Dream of a Common Language: Poems 1974–1977* (New York: W. W. Norton, 1978), p. 35.

2   Freud, 'The uncanny', p. 345.

3   Royle, *The Uncanny*, p. 2.

4   Nicolas Abraham, 'Notes on the phantom: a complement to Freud's metapsychology', *Critical Inquiry*, 1/2 (1987), 289–94.

5   Sedgwick, *Epistemology of the Closet*, p. 671.

6   Butler, 'Imitation and gender insubordination', p. 20.

7   Castle, *The Apparitional Lesbian*, p. 4.

8   Sedgwick, *Epistemology of the Closet*, pp. 186, 206–7. See also Sedgwick, *Between Men*, pp. 103–11.

9   Halberstam, *Skin Shows*, p. 71.

10. See Sara Mills, *Michel Foucault* (London: Routledge, 2003), pp. 78–9.

11 For discussion of the coming-out novel see Robert McRuer, *The Queer Renaissance: Contemporary American Literature and the Reinvention of Lesbian and Gay Identities* (New York: New York University Press, 1997), pp. 32–41; and Bonnie Zimmerman, *The Safe Sea of Women: Lesbian Fiction 1969–1989* (London: Onlywomen Press, 1992), pp. 35–8.

12 Judith Roof, *Come As You Are: Sexuality and Narrative* (New York: Columbia University Press, 1996), pp. 103, 105.

13 Angus Gordon, 'Turning back: adolescence, narrative and queer theory', *GLQ: A Journal of Lesbian and Gay Studies*, 5/1 (2001), 20.

14 Sedgwick, *Epistemology of the Closet*, p. 68.

15 Butler, 'Imitation and gender insubordination', p. 25.

16 Sedgwick, *Epistemology of the Closet*, p. 3.

17 During and Fealy, 'Philosophy', p. 127.

18 Affrica Taylor, 'A queer geography', in Medhurst and Munt (eds), *Lesbian and Gay Studies*, pp. 14–15.

19 Margaret Sonser Breen, *Narratives of Queer Desire: Deserts of the Heart* (Basingstoke: Palgrave Macmillan, 2009), p. 39.

20 John D'Emilio, *Making Trouble: Essays in Lesbian and Gay History, Politics and the University* (New York: Routledge, 1992), p. 249.

21 Butler, 'Imitation and gender insubordination', p. 20.

22 Emma Donoghue, *Stir-Fry* (London: Hamish Hamilton, 1994), p. 174. Subsequent references are to this edition and in the text.

23 Taylor, A queer geography, p. 15.

24 Ahmed, *Queer Phenomenology*, p. 88.

25 Royle, *The Uncanny*, p. 45.

26 Butler, 'Imitation and gender insubordination', p. 20.

27 Angela Carter, 'The Courtship of Mr Lyon', in *The Bloody Chamber and Other Stories* (Harmondsworth: Penguin, 1981), p. 51.

28 See Marilyn R. Farwell's theorization of the concept in 'Heterosexual plots and lesbian narratives: towards a theory of lesbian narrative space',

in Karla Jay and Joanne Glasgow (eds), *Lesbian Texts and Heterosexual Contexts: Radical Revisions* (New York: New York University Press, 1990), pp. 91–103.

29 Philip Hensher, *Kitchen Venom* (London: Flamingo, 2003), pp. 46–7. Further references are to this edition and in the text.

30 D. A. Miller, *The Novel and the Police* (Berkeley and Los Angeles: University of California Press, 1988), p. 195.

31 Cixous, 'Fiction and its phantoms', 432–43.

32 Butler, *Bodies That Matter: On the Discursive Limits of Sex* (New York: Routledge, 1993), p. 236.

33 See Gregory Woods, *A History of Gay Literature: The Male Tradition* (New Haven, CT: Yale University Press, 1998), pp. 145–8, 275–82.

34 Elisabeth Bronfen, *Over Her Dead Body: Death, Femininity, and the Aesthetic* (Manchester: Manchester University Press, 1992), pp. 84–5.

35 Nicolas Abraham and Maria Torok, *The Shell and the Kernel*, trans. Nicholas T. Rand (Chicago: University of Chicago Press, 1994), p. 171. See also Royle, *The Uncanny*, p. 280.

36 Section 28 of the Local Government Act was sponsored by a group of Conservative members of the British Parliament and, despite considerable opposition, became law in the United Kingdom on 24 May 1988. It prohibits local authorities from: a) promoting homosexuality or publishing material that promotes homosexuality; b) promoting the teaching in maintained schools of the acceptability of homosexuality as a pretended family relationship; and c) giving financial assistance to any person for either of these purposes. It resulted, among other things, in the closure of homosexual support groups in schools and colleges and, as Duncan Fallowell points out, gave 'official approval to homophobia in the country at large' ('When sex becomes sin – today is World Aids Day. Far from confronting the epidemic, the British are retreating in deceit. Artists should lead the way to realism and honesty', *The Guardian*, 1 December 1989, p. 36). The Section was repealed in Scotland on 21 June 2000 and in the rest of the United Kingdom on 18 November 2003. For discussion of the Section and its significance see Madeleine Colvin with Jane Hawksley, *Section 28: A Practical Guide to the Law and its Implications* (National Council for Civil Liberties, 1989).

37 Emmanuel S. Nelson (ed.), *AIDS: The Literary Response* (New York: Twayne, 1992), p. 1.

38 Woods, *A History of Gay Literature*, p. 359.

39 Alan Sinfield, *Cultural Politics: Queer Readings* (London: Routledge, 1994), p. 78.

40 Brookes, *Gay Male Fiction Since Stonewall*, pp. 158–64.

41 Douglas Crimp, *AIDS: Cultural Analysis / Cultural Activism* (Cambridge, MA: MIT Press, 1988), p. 12.

42 Derrida, *Aporias: Dying – Awaiting (One Another at) the 'Limits of Truth'*, trans. Thomas Dutoit (Stanford, CA: Stanford University Press, 1993), p. 74.

43 Freud, 'The uncanny', p. 336.

44 Lee Edelman, 'The plague of discourse: politics, literary theory and AIDS', *The South Atlantic Quarterly*, 88 (1989), 310.

45 Colm Tóibín, *The Blackwater Lightship* (London: Picador, 1999), p. 3. Further page references are to this edition and in the text.

46 See Sara Salih, *Judith Butler* (London: Routledge, 2002), pp. 102–3.

47 Eve Kosofsky Sedgwick, *The Coherence of Gothic Conventions* (London: Methuen, 1986), p. 13.

48 Freud, 'The uncanny', p. 368.

49 Julia Kristeva, *Powers of Horror: An Essay on Abjection*, trans. Leon S. Roudiez (New York: Columbia University Press, 1982), p. 4.

50 Margaret Whitford (ed.), *The Irigaray Reader* (Oxford: Blackwell, 1991), p. 91.

51 Pamela Thurschwell, *Sigmund Freud* (London: Routledge, 2000), p. 119.

52 Nelson, *AIDS: The Literary Response*, p. 2.

53 See Elizabeth Rosen, *Apocalyptic Transformations: Apocalypse and the Postmodern Imagination* (Lanham, MD: Lexington Books, 2008), xii–xxiv.

54 Sarah Schulman, *People in Trouble* (London: Sheba Feminist Publishers, 1990), p. 1. Further page references are to this edition and in the text.

55 Alan Sinfield, *Culture and Authority* (São Paulo: Universidade de São Paulo Press, 1997), p. 28.

56 Martin Duberman, Martha Vicinus and George Chauncey (eds), *Hidden from History: Reclaiming the Gay and Lesbian Past* (London: Penguin, 1989), p. 5.

57 Laura Gowing, 'History', in Medhurst and Munt (eds), *Lesbian and Gay Studies*, p. 54.

58 Caroline Gonda and Chris Mounsey, *Queer People: Negotiations and Expressions of Homosexuality 1700–1800* (Lewisburg, PA: Bucknell University Press, 2007), p. 9.

59 Valerie Traub, 'The present future of lesbian historiography', in George E. Haggerty and Molly McGarry (eds), *A Companion to Lesbian, Gay, Bisexual and Queer Studies* (Oxford: Blackwell, 2007), pp. 131–2.

60 Heather K. Love, '"Spoiled Identity": Stephen Gordon's loneliness and the difficulties of queer history', *GLQ*, 7/4 (2001), 491, 492.

61 Homi K. Bhabha, *The Location of Culture* (London: Routledge, 1994), p. 103. Further page references are to this edition and in the text.
62 Garber, *Identity Poetics*, p. 205.
63 Sarah Waters, *The Night Watch* (London: Virago, 2006), p. 180. Further page references are to this edition and in the text.
64 Castle, *The Apparitional Lesbian*, p. 5.
65 Butler, 'Imitation and gender insubordination', p. 20.
66 Irigaray, *This Sex Which Is Not One*, p. 133.
67 Michel Foucault, *The Will to Knowledge: The History of Sexuality*, vol. 1, trans. Robert Hurley (London: Penguin, 1998), p. 27.
68 David Leavitt, *While England Sleeps* (London: Abacus, 1998), p. 3. Further page references are to this edition and in the text.
69 Alan Sinfield, *On Sexuality and Power* (New York: Columbia University Press, 2004), p. 140.
70 Freud, 'The uncanny', pp. 361–2; Royle, *The Uncanny*, p. 1.
71 See Sedgwick, *Epistemology of the Closet*, pp. 164–6.
72 Anthony Giddens, *The Transformation of Intimacy: Sexuality, Love and Eroticism in Modern Societies* (Cambridge: Polity Press, 1992), p. 147.
73 Freud, 'The uncanny', p. 345.
74 Sedgwick, *Epistemology of the Closet*, pp. 164–6.

Chapter 3

1 Hélène Cixous, 'Fiction and its phantoms: a reading of Freud's *Das Unheimliche* ("The uncanny")', *New Literary History*, 7/3 (1973), 542.
2. Terry Castle, *The Female Thermometer: Eighteenth-century Culture and the Invention of the Uncanny* (Oxford: Oxford University Press, 1995), p. 7.
3 Cixous, 'Fiction and its phantoms', 543.
4 Neil Cornwell, 'Ghost writers in the sky (and elsewhere): notes towards a spectro-poetics of ghosts and ghostliness', *Gothic Studies*, 1/2 (1999), 157.
5 See Fuss, 'Inside/Out', pp. 3–7; Butler, *Bodies that Matter*, p. 8.
6 Castle, *The Apparitional Lesbian*, p. 62.
7 See Derrida, *Memoires for Paul de Man* (New York: Columbia University Press, 1986), p. 80.
8 Julian Wolfreys, *Victorian Hauntings: Spectrality, Gothic, the Uncanny and Literature* (Basingstoke: Palgrave, 2002), pp. 1–3; Susanne Becker, *Gothic Forms of Feminine Fiction* (Manchester: Manchester University Press, 1999), pp. 66–83.
9 Freud, 'The uncanny', p. 356.

10   Haggerty, *Queer Gothic*, p. 133.
11   Cornwell, 'Ghost writers in the sky (and elsewhere)', 158.
12   James Purdy, *Mourners Below* (London: Arrow Books, 1986), p. 13. Further page references are to this edition and in the text.
13   Kristeva, *Powers of Horror*, p. 4.
14   Alan Sinfield, *On Sexuality and Power* (New York: Columbia University Press, 2004), p. 40.
15   See Jonathan Dollimore, *Death, Desire and Loss in Western Culture* (London: Allen Lane, 1998), pp. 294–311.
16   Rosemary Jackson, *Fantasy: The Literature of Subversion*, p. 68.
17   Angus Wilson, review in Purdy, *Mourners Below*, i.
18   Elisabeth Bronfen, *Over Her Dead Body: Death, Femininity and the Aesthetic* (Manchester: Manchester University Press, 1992), p. 349.
19   Fuss, 'Inside/Out', p. 4.
20   Ali Smith, *Hotel World* (London: Hamish Hamilton, 2001), p. 30. Further page references are to this edition and in the text.
21   See Irigaray, *Speculum of the Other Woman*, p. 141; Bronfen, *Over Her Dead Body*, xi–xiii.
22   Kristeva, *Powers of Horror*, p. 4.
23   Castle, *The Apparitional Lesbian*, p. 34.
24   Freud, 'The uncanny', p. 358.
25   See 'Chronology: Slavoj Žižek', *www.lacan.com/zizekchro.1.htm*.
26   Anthony Vidler, *The Architectural Uncanny: Essays in the Modern Unhomely* (Cambridge, MA: MIT Press, 1999), pp. 17–45.
27   Derrida, 'Sending: on representation', *Social Research*, 49/2 (1982), 308.
28   Derrida, *Memoires for Paul de Man*, p. 80.
29   Wolfreys, *Victorian Hauntings*, pp. 111, 117.
30   Vijay Mishra, *The Gothic Sublime* (New York: State University of New York Press, 1994), p. 71.
31   Jodey Castricano, 'Cryptomimesis: The Gothic and Jacques Derrida's ghost writing', *Gothic Studies*, 2/1 (2000), 11.
32   Teresa de Lauretis, 'Feminist studies/critical studies: issues, terms and contexts', in De Lauretis (ed.), *Feminist Studies/Critical Studies* (London: Macmillan, 1988), p. 10.
33   See Elizabeth Young, *Black Frankenstein: The Making of an American Metaphor* (New York: New York University Press, 2008), p. 181.
34   Christoper Bram, *Father of Frankenstein* (London: Dutton, 1995), p. 70. Further page references are to this edition and in the text.
35   Allan Lloyd Smith, '"This Thing of Darkness": racial discourse in Mary Shelley's *Frankenstein*', *Gothic Studies*, 6/2 (2004), 216.

36 Haggerty, *Queer Gothic*, p. 55.

37 Christa Knellwolf and Jane Goodall (eds), *Frankenstein Science: Experimentation and Discovery in Romantic Culture, 1780–1830* (Aldershot: Ashgate, 2008), p. 12.

38 Michael Eberle-Sinatra, 'Readings of homosexuality in Mary Shelley's *Frankenstein* and four film adaptations', *Gothic Studies*, 7/2 (2005), 188.

39 Haggerty, *Queer Gothic*, p. 54.

40 Eleanor Salotto, *Gothic Returns in Collins, Dickens, Zola and Hitchcock* (Basingstoke: Palgrave Macmillan, 2006), p. 7.

41 'Sarah Waters: Sex and the Victorian city', Interview with Lisa Jardine on BBC2, 4 May 2005.

42 Linda Hutcheon, *The Politics of Postmodernism* (London: Routledge, 1989), p. 137.

43 Sarah Waters, *Fingersmith* (London: Virago, 2002), p. 17. Further page references are to this edition and in the text.

44 Irigaray, *This Sex Which Is Not One*, p. 194.

45 E. T. A. Hoffmann, 'The Sandman', in *Tales of Hoffmann*, trans. and ed. R. J. Hollingdale (Harmondsworth: Penguin, 1982), p. 115.

46 Dianne Chisholm, 'The uncanny', in Elizabeth Wright (ed.), *Feminism and Psychoanalysis: A Feminist Dictionary* (Oxford: Blackwell, 1992), pp. 438–9.

47 Irigaray, *This Sex Which Is Not One*, p. 78.

48 Whitford, *The Irigaray Reader*, p. 91.

49 D. A. Miller, *The Novel and the Police*, pp. 197–9.

50 Mark Llewellyn, 'Breaking the mould? Sarah Waters and the politics of genre', in Ann Heilman and Mark Llewellyn (eds), *Metafiction and Metahistory in Contemporary Women's Writing* (Basingstoke: Palgrave Macmillan, 2007), p. 205.

51 Lillian Faderman, *Surpassing the Love of Men: Romantic Friendship and Love between Women from the Renaissance to the Present* (London: Junction Books, 1981), pp. 38–46.

52 Emma Donoghue, *Passions between Women: British Lesbian Culture 1668–1801* (London: Scarlet Press, 1993).

53 'Sarah Waters: Sex and the Victorian city', interview with Lisa Jardine on BBC2, 4 May 2005.

54 Emma Healey, *Lesbian Sex Wars* (London: Virago, 1996), p. 142.

55 Wolfreys, *Victorian Hauntings*, p. 15.

56 Gordon E. Slethaug, *The Play of the Double in Postmodern American Fiction* (Carbondale: Southern Illinois University Press, 1993), pp. 10–12.

57   Sedgwick, *Between Men*, p. 105.

58   Armitt, *Theorising the Fantastic*, pp. 144–7.

59   Dale Townshend, '"Love in a convent" or, Gothic and the perverse father of queer enjoyment', in Hughes and Smith (eds), *Queering the Gothic*, pp. 11–35; Paulina Palmer, 'Antonia White's *Frost in May*: gothic mansions, ghosts and particular friendships', in Hughes and Smith (eds), *Queering the Gothic*, p. 119.

60   Freud, 'The uncanny', p. 356.

61   Sandy Stone, 'The empire strikes back: a posttranssexual manifesto', in Julia Epstein and Katrina Straub (eds), *Body Guards: The Cultural Politics of Gender Ambiguity* (New York: Routledge, 1991), pp. 296–9.

62   Halberstam, *In a Queer Time and Place*, p. 59.

63   Prosser, *Second Skins*, p. 159.

64   Susan Stryker, 'The transgender issue: an introduction', *GLQ*, 4/2 (1998), 147.

65   See Jeffrey Weeks, *Invented Moralities: Sexual Values in an Age of Uncertainty* (New York: Columbia University Press, 1994), p. 104.

66   Jean Baudrillard, *The Transparency of Evil: Essays on Extreme Phenomena*, trans. James Benedict (London: Verso, 1993), p. 25.

67   Donna Haraway, 'A manifesto for cyborgs: science, technology and socialist feminism in the 1980s', in Linda Nicholson (ed.), *Feminism/Postmodernism* (London: Routledge, 1990), p. 163.

68   Kate Bornstein, *Gender Outlaw: On Men, Women and the Rest of Us* (New York: Routledge, 1994), pp. 51–92.

69   Stella Duffy, *Beneath the Blonde* (London: Serpent's Tail, 1991), p. 206. Further page references are to this edition and in the text.

70   See Prosser's peceptive discussion of 'real' with reference to transsexuality in *Second Skins*, p. 114.

71   Prosser, *Second Skins*, p. 119.

72   Royle, *The Uncanny*, p. 1.

73   Mary Russo, *The Female Grotesque: Risk, Excess and Modernity* (London: Routledge, 1994), pp. 53–4.

74   Bornstein, *Gender Outlaw*, pp. 125–8.

75   Mary Shelley, *Frankenstein or the Modern Prometheus* (Oxford: Oxford University Press, 1969), p. 55.

76   Patrick McGrath, *Dr Haggard's Disease* (London: Penguin, 1994), p. 40. Further page references are to this edition and in the text.

77   Freud, 'Psychoanalytic notes on an autobiographical case of paranoia' (1911), in *The Pelican Freud Library*, vol. 9, p. 147. Further page references are to this edition and in the text.

78 Butler, *The Psychic Life of Power: Theories in Subjection* (Stanford, CA: Stanford University Press, 1997), pp. 131–42.

79 William Patrick Day, *In the Circles of Fear and Desire: A Study of Gothic Fantasy* (Chicago: University of Chicago Press, 1985), p. 51

Chapter 4

1   David Punter, 'Introduction: of apparitions', in Glennis Byron and David Punter (eds), *Spectral Readings: Towards a Gothic Geography* (Basingstoke: Macmillan, 1999), p. 4.

2   See Fred Botting, 'Power in darkness: heterotopias, literature and gothic labyrinths', *Genre*, 26 (1993), 253–81.

3   Day, *In the Circles of Fear*, p. 29.

4   Freud, 'The uncanny', p. 365.

5   Ibid., p. 359.

6   Hélène Cixous, 'Fiction and its phantoms: a reading of Freud's *Das Unheimliche* ("The uncanny")', *New Literary History*, 7/3 (1973), 540.

7   Freud, 'The uncanny', p. 368.

8   Freud, 'Dreams and delusions in Jensen's *Gradiva*' (1907), in *The Pelican Freud Library*, vol. 14 (Harmondsworth: Penguin, 1985), pp. 43–5.

9   Derrida, 'Theses', in *Archive Fever: A Freudian Impression*, trans. Eric Prenowitz (Chicago: University of Chicago Press, 1995), p. 86.

10 See Eve Kosofsky Sedgwick, *The Coherence of Gothic Conventions* (New York: Methuen, 1980), pp. 19–28; and *Epistemology of the Closet*, pp. 67–74.

11 Sedgwick, *Epistemology of the Closet*, p. 68

12 Sedgwick, *The Coherence of Gothic Conventions*, pp. 20–5.

13 Ibid., p. 20.

14 Marilyn R. Farwell, *Heterosexual Plots and Lesbian Narratives* (New York: New York University Press, 1996), pp. 20–1, 147–56.

15 Wolfreys, *Victorian Hauntings*, p. 7.

16 Ibid., p. 133; Mark Wigley, *The Architecture of Deconstruction: Derrida's Haunt* (Cambridge, MA: MIT Press, 1993), p. 110.

17 Ellis Hanson, 'Undead', in Fuss, *Inside/Out*, p. 336.

18 Halberstam, *In a Queer Time and Place*, p. 34.

19 John Fletcher, 'The haunted closet: Henry James's queer spectrality', *Textual Practice*, 14/1 (2000), 53–80.

20 Steven Bruhm, 'Picture this: Stephen King's queer Gothic', in David Punter (ed.), *A Companion to the Gothic* (Oxford: Blackwell, 2000), p. 270.

21   John Corr, 'Queer nostalgia and unnatural disgust in Shani Mootoo's *Cereus Blooms at Night*', *Journal of West Indian Literature*, 14/1–2 (2005), 92.

22   Lizabeth Paravisini-Gebert, 'Colonial and postcolonial Gothic: the Caribbean', in Jerrold Hogle (ed.), *The Cambridge Companion to Gothic Fiction* (Cambridge: Cambridge University Press, 2002), pp. 230–5.

23   Ruth Parkin-Gounelas, *Literature and Psychoanalysis: Intertextual Readings* (Basingstoke: Palgrave, 2001), p. 120.

24   Jim Grimsley, *Dream Boy* (Chapel Hill, NC: Algonquin Books, 1995), p. 33. Further page references are to this edition and in the text.

25   Fred Botting, 'The Gothic production of the unconscious', in Byron and Punter, *Spectral Readings*, p. 28; Ruth Perry, 'Incest as the meaning of the Gothic novel', *The Eighteenth Century*, 39/3 (1998), 260–77.

26   Haggerty, 'Literature and homosexuality in the late eighteenth century: Walpole, Beckford, and Lewis', *Studies in the Novel*, 18/4 (1986), 341–51.

27   Perry, 'Incest as meaning', 268.

28   Laurie Vickroy, *Trauma and Survival in Contemporary Fiction* (Charlottesville: University of Virginia Press, 2002), p. 3.

29   Botting, 'The Gothic production of the unconscious', p. 29.

30   Woods, *The History of Gay Literature*, pp. 108–23; Zimmerman, *The Safe Sea of Women*, pp. 79–86.

31   Leslie A. Fiedler, *Love and Death in the American Novel* (New York: Stein and Day, 1966), p. 414.

32   Sinfield, *Gay and After*, p. 20.

33   Shani Mootoo, *Cereus Blooms at Night* (London: Granta Books, 1996), p. 8. Further page references are to this edition and in the text.

34   Butler, *Undoing Gender*, p. 7.

35.   Isabel Hoving, 'Moving the Caribbean landscape: *Cereus Blooms at Night* as a re-imagination of the Caribbean environment', in Elizabeth M. DeLoughrey, Renée K. Gosson and George B. Handley (eds), *Caribbean Literature and the Environment: Between Nature and Culture* (Charlottesville: University of Virginia Press, 2005), p. 161.

36   Ann Cvetkovich, 'Sexual trauma/queer memory: incest, lesbianism, and therapeutic memory', *GLQ*, 2/4 (1995), 380.

37   Bhabha, *The Location of Culture*, p. 122.

38   Vickroy, *Trauma and Survival in Contemporary Fiction*, pp. 27–8.

39   Jean Rhys, *Wide Sargasso Sea* (Harmondsworth: Penguin, 1980), p. 154.

40   Vidler, *The Architectural Uncanny*, pp. 131, 132.

41   Lois Zamara and Wendy B. Faris, *Magical Realism: Theory, History, Community* (Durham, NC: Duke University Press, 1995), p. 6.

42   Robert Mighall, *A Geography of Victorian Gothic Fiction: Mapping History's Nightmares* (Oxford: Oxford University Press, 1999), pp. 28–45.

43   See Elaine Showalter, *Sexual Anarchy: Gender and Culture at the Fin de Siècle* (London: Virago, 1992), pp. 105–26.

44   See Alan Bray, *Homosexuality in Renaissance England* (London: Gay Men's Press, 1992), pp. 81–114; Jeffrey Weeks, 'Discourse, desire and sexual deviance: some problems in a history of homosexuality', in K. Plummer (ed.), *The Making of the Modern Homosexual* (London: Hutchinson, 1991), pp. 82–6.

45   John D'Emilio, 'Gay politics and community in San Francisco since World War II', in Duberman, Martha and Chauncey, Jr, *Hidden from History*, pp. 456–73.

46   David Higgs (ed.), *Queer Sites: Gay Urban Histories since 1600* (London: Routledge, 1999).

47   Elizabeth Wilson, *Hidden Agendas: Theory, Politics and Experience in the Women's Movement* (London: Tavistock Publications, 1986), p. 169.

48   Tamar Rothenberg, 'And she told two friends: lesbians creating urban space', in David Bell and Gillian Valentine (eds), *Mapping Desire: Geographies of Sexualities* (London: Routledge, 1995), pp. 165–81.

49   Shari Benstock, 'Paris, lesbianism and the politics of reaction, 1900–1940', in Duberman, Vicinus and Chauncey, Jr, *Hidden from History*, pp. 332–46.

50   Judith R. Walkowitz, *City of Dreadful Delight: Narratives of Sexual Danger in Late-Victorian London* (London: Virago, 1992), p. 17.

51   Day, *In the Circles of Fear*, pp. 22–7.

52   Warner (ed.), *Fear of a Queer Planet*, xxvii.

53   See Brookes, *Gay Male Fiction Since Stonewall*, pp. 131–4.

54   Winterson, *The Power Book* (London: Vintage, 2001), p. 3.

55   Charles Dickens, *The Old Curiosity Shop* (Oxford: Oxford University Press, 1999), p. 11.

56   Andrew Pane and Mark Lewis, 'Ghost dance: interview with Jacques Derrida', *Public*, 2 (1989), 61.

57   Derrida, 'Word processing', in Timothy Clark and Nicholas Royle (eds), *Oxford Literary Review: Technologies of the Sign*, 21/1–2 (1999), 14–15.

58   Peter Brooks, *Reading for the Plot: Design and Invention in Narrative* (Cambridge, MA: Harvard University Press, 1984), p. 37.

59   Halberstam, 'F2M: the making of female masculinity', in Laura Doan (ed.), *The Lesbian Postmodern* (New York: Columbia University Press, 1994), p. 226.

60   Jean Baudrillard, *Selected Writings*, ed. Mark Poster (Cambridge: Polity Press, 2001), p. 167.

61   Ana Cecília Acioli Lima, 'Corpos sem corpos em *The Powerbook*, de Jeanette Winterson', in Ermeinda Mara Araujo Ferreira (ed.), *Interseccoes: Ciencia e tecnologia, literatura e arte* (Recife: Editora Universitaria, 2009), pp. 249–66.

62   For discussions of the passage, see Brookes, *Gay Male Fiction Since Stonewall*, pp. 134–5.

63   Alan Hollinghurst, *The Swimming-Pool Library* (London: Vintage, 1998), p. 3. Further page references are to this edition and in the text.

64   Cixous, 'Fiction and its phantoms', 528.

65   Jackson, *Fantasy: The Literature of Subversion*, p. 68.

66   Royle, *The Uncanny*, p. 1.

67   Brookes, *Gay Male Fiction Since Stonewall*, pp. 131–5.

68   Charles Dickens, *Oliver Twist* (Oxford: Oxford University Press, 1982), p. 74.

69   Kelly Hurley, *The Gothic Body* (Cambridge: Cambridge University Press: 1996), p. 161.

70   Brooks, *Reading for the Plot*, p. 26.

71   Salotto, *Gothic Returns*, p. 20.

72   Richard Dellamora, *Apocalyptic Overtures: Sexual Politics and the Sense of an Ending* (New Brunswick, NJ: Rutgers University Press, 1994), p. 187.

73   David Punter, 'Ceremonial gothic', in Byron and Punter (eds), *Spectral Readings*, p. 37.

74   Freud, 'The uncanny', p. 360.

75   Henry James, *The Turn of the Screw and the Aspern Papers*, ed. Kenneth B. Murdock (London: Everyman, 1967), p. 34.

76   Freud, 'The uncanny', p. 362.

77   Punter, 'Ceremonial gothic', p. 39.

78   Halberstam, *In a Queer Time and Place*, p. 5.

79   Paul Woodruff, *Euripides' Bacchae* (Indianapolis: Hackett Publishing Company, 1998), xiii.

80   Butler, *Undoing Gender*, p. 7.

81   Freud, 'The uncanny', p. 358.

82   Shalini Puri, *The Caribbean Postcolonial: Social Equality, Post-Nationalism, and Cultural Hybridity* (Basingstoke: Palgrave Macmillan, 2004), p. 2.

83   Sinfield, *Gay and After*, p. 34.

84   H. Nigel Thomas, *Spirits in the Dark* (Portsmouth, NH: Heinemann, 1994), p. 27. Further page references are to this edition and in the text.

85   Bhabha, *The Location of Culture*, p. 82.

86 Paige Schilt, 'Queering Lord Clarke: diasporic formations and travelling homophobia in Isaac Julien's *The Darker Side of Black*', in John C. Hawley (ed.), *Post-colonial, Queer: Theoretical Intersections* (New York: State University of New York Press, 2001), p. 170.

87 Butler, *Bodies That Matter*, p. 8.

88 Donna Tartt, *The Secret History* (London: Penguin, 1993), p. 5. Further references are to this edition and in the text.

89 Kristeva, *Strangers to Ourselves*, p. 191.

90 Royle, *The Uncanny*, p. 2.

91 Punter, 'Ceremonial gothic', p. 45.

92 Richard Seaford, *Introducing Dionysos* (London: Routledge, 2006), pp. 3–25.

93 Punter, 'Ceremonial gothic', p. 38.

94 Botting, 'Power in darkness', 257–9.

95 Ibid., 255.

96 Day, *In the Circles of Fear*, p. 21.

97 Royle, *The Uncanny*, p. 2.

98 Parkin-Gounelas, *Literature and Psychoanalysis*, p. 110.

99 See Jagose, *Queer Theory*, pp. 106–14.

100 Richard's situation resembles that of the vampire Louis in Anne Rice's *Interview with the Vampire* who, though he longs to leave Lestat, cannot do so.

Chapter 5

1 Butler, *Undoing Gender*, pp. 13–14.

2 Grosz, 'Intolerable ambiguity: freaks as/at the limit', in Rosemary Garland Thomson (ed.), *Freakery: Cultural Spectacles of the Extraordinary Body* (New York: New York University Press, 1996), p. 57.

3 Bronfen, *Over Her Dead Body*, p. 113.

4 David Punter, *Postcolonial Imaginings: Fictions of a New World Order* (Edinburgh: Edinburgh University Press, 2000), p. 111.

5 Kristeva, *Powers of Horror*, p. 4.

6 Sedgwick, *Epistemology of the Closet*, p. 202.

7 Baudrillard, *The Transparency of Evil*, p. 25.

8 Butler, *Undoing Gender*, p. 34.

9 Halberstam, *Skin Shows*, p. 17.

10 Harry M. Benshoff, *Monsters in the Closet: Homosexuality and the Horror Film* (Manchester: Manchester University Press, 1997), pp. 230–75.

11 Halberstam, *Skin Shows*, p. 27.

12   Butler, *Bodies That Matter*, p. 21.

13   Royle, *The Uncanny*, p. 2.

14   Teresa de Lauretis, 'Sexual indifference and lesbian representation', *Theatre Journal*, 40/2 (1988), 167.

15   Kelly Hurley, 'Abject and grotesque', in Catherine Spooner and Emma McEvoy (eds), *The Routledge Companion to Gothic* (London: Routledge, 2007), p. 138.

16   Russo, *The Female Grotesque*, p. 9.

17   For reference to Kenan's development of Baldwin's treatment of these themes, see David Bergman, *Gaiety Transfigured: Gay Self-Representation in American Literature* (Madison: University of Wisconsin Press, 1991), pp. 163–87; and Robert McRuer, *The Queer Renaissance: Contemporary American Literature and the Reinvention of Lesbian and Gay Identities* (New York: New York University Press, 1997), pp. 79–83.

18   Randall Kenan, *A Visitation of Spirits* (New York: Vintage, 2000), p. 64. Further references are to this edition and in the text.

19   Christopher Marlowe, *The Tragedy of Dr Faustus*, V/ii, 182, in *The Complete Plays* (Harmondsworth: Penguin, 1969), p. 337.

20   Russo, *The Female Grotesque*, p. 9.

21   Royle, *The Uncanny*, p. 2.

22   Day, *In the Circles of Fear*, p. 39.

23   Freud, 'The uncanny', p. 356.

24   Chisholm, 'The uncanny', in Wright, *Feminism and Psychoanalysis*, p. 439.

25   Bergman, *Gaiety Transfigured*, p. 175.

26   McRuer, *The Queer Renaissance*, pp. 100–5.

27   Freud, 'The uncanny', p. 347.

28   Castle, *The Female Thermometer: Eighteenth-century Culture and the Invention of the Uncanny* (Oxford: Oxford University Press, 1995), pp. 11–15.

29   Jeanette Winterson, *The Stone Gods* (London: Hamish Hamilton, 2007), p. 58. Further references are to this edition and in the text.

30   Bronfen, *Over Her Dead Body*, p. 113.

31   Hurley refers to the grotesqe hybridity of the cyborg in 'Abject and grotesque', p. 139.

32   Donna Haraway, 'The cyborg manifesto: science, technology and socialist feminism in the late twentieth century', in Haraway, *Simians, Cyborgs and Women: The Reinvention of Nature* (London: Free Association Books, 1991), p. 17.

33   Armitt, *Theorising the Fantastic*, pp. 78–81.

34   Cixous, 'Fiction and its phantoms', 542–4.

35 William Shakespeare, *Antony and Cleopatra*, IV/xv, 37–52, in Stephen Greenblatt (ed.), *The Norton Shakespeare* (New York: W. W. Norton, 1997), p. 1004.

36 Mishra, *The Gothic Sublime*, p. 55.

37 Jesse Bier, *The Rise and Fall of American Humor* (New York: Holt, Rinehart and Winston, 1968), p. 307.

38 Slethaug, *The Play of the Double*, pp. 28–9.

39 Royle, *The Uncanny*, p. 50, n. 26.

40 See the discussion of lesbian humour and novels exemplifying it in Paulina Palmer, *Contemporary Lesbian Writing: Dreams, Desire, Difference* (Buckingham: Open University Press, 1993), pp. 78–97; and Palmer, *Lesbian Gothic: Transgressive Fictions*, pp. 105–12.

41 See the discussion of the novel in Palmer, *Lesbian Gothic*, pp. 108–12.

42 Mikhail Bakhtin, *Problems of Dostoevsky's Poetics*, trans. R. W. Rotsel (Ann Arbor, MI: Ardis, 1973), p. 27. Further references are to this edition and in the text.

43 Ellen Galford, *The Dyke and the Dybbuk* (London: Virago, 1993), p. 27. Further references are to this edition and in the text.

44 Paul Magrs, *Could It Be Magic?* (London: Chatto and Windus, 1997), p. 4. Further references are to this edition and in the text.

45 Magrs's description of Mark's tattooed body recalls Ray Bradbury's *The Illustrated Man*, a collection in which each story is based on a tattooed image on the body of a vagrant.

46 Royle, *The Uncanny*, p. 45.

47 The concept of 'the gay aesthetic' and the cultural perspectives associated with it develop in a poststructuralist context the aesthetic of style and wit associated with the writing of Marcel Proust and Wilde, illuminating the counter codes of masquerade and parody that inform male gay and lesbian cultural traditions. See During and Fealy, 'Philosophy', pp. 113–32.

48 See Lee Edelman, *Homographesis: Essays in Gay Literary and Cultural Theory* (New York: Routledge, 1994), pp. 8–11.

49 Freud, 'The uncanny', p. 536.

50 Halberstam, *In a Queer Time and Place*, p. 18.

51 Cixous, 'Fiction and its phantoms', 543.

52 Ahmed, *Queer Phenomenology*, p. 106.

53 Jackson, *Fantasy and the Literature of Subversion*, p. 68.

54 Parkin-Gounelas, *Literature and Psychoanalysis: Intertextual Readings*, p. 120.

55 Freud, 'The uncanny', p. 345.

56 Royle, *The Uncanny*, p. 45.

57 'Freud, 'The uncanny', p. 362.
58 Ibid., p.346.
59 Gilbert and Gubar, *The Madwoman in the Attic*.
60 See Sedgwick, *Between Men*, p. 116.
61 Jagose suggests that 'queer' was 'popularly adopted' in the early 1990s (*Queer Theory*, p. 76).

Bibliography

༄

Fiction

Note: dates of the first publication appear in square brackets after the title.

Bram, Christopher, *Father of Frankenstein* (London: Dutton, 1995).
Brontë, Emily, *Wuthering Heights* [1847] (London: Penguin Classics, 2010).
Carter, Angela, *The Bloody Chamber and Other Stories* (London: Gollancz, 1979).
Collins, Wilkie, *The Woman in White* [1860] (Oxford: Oxford University Press, 1999).
Dickens, Charles, *The Adventures of Oliver Twist* [1839] (Oxford: Oxford University Press, 1982).
——, *The Old Curiosity Shop* [1841] (Oxford: Oxford University Press, 1999).
——, *Bleak House* [1853] (Oxford: Oxford University Press, 1996).
Donoghue, Emma, *Stir-Fry* (London: Hamish Hamilton, 1994).
Duffy, Stella, *Beneath the Blonde* (London: Serpent's Tail, 1997).
Du Maurier, Daphne, *Rebecca* (London: Gollancz, 1938).
French, Marilyn, *The Women's Room* (New York: Summit Books, 1977).
Galford, Ellen, *The Dyke and the Dybbuk* (London: Virago, 1993).
Gilman, Charlotte Perkins, *The Yellow Wallpaper* (London: Virago, 1981).
Grimsley, Jim, *Dream Boy* (Chapel Hill, NC: Algonquin Books, 1995).

Hensher, Philip, *Kitchen Venom* [1996] (London: Harper Collins, 2003).

Hoffmann, E. T. A., 'The Sandman', in *Tales of Hoffmann*, trans. R. J. Hollingdale (Harmondsworth: Penguin, 1982).

Hogg, James, *The Private Memoirs and Confessions of a Justified Sinner* [1824] (Oxford: Oxford University Press, 2010).

Hollinghurst, Alan, *The Swimming-Pool Library* [1988] (London: Vintage, 1998).

Jackson, Shirley, *The Haunting of Hill House* [1959] (London: Robinson Publishing, 1987).

James, Henry, *The Turn of the Screw and the Aspern Papers* [1898] (London: Dent, 1967).

James, M. R., 'Casting the Runes', in *Casting the Runes and Other Ghost Stories* (Oxford: Oxford University Press, 1987).

Kenan, Randall, *A Visitation of Spirits* [1989] (London: Vintage, 2000).

King, Stephen, *The Shining* (New York: Doubleday, 1977).

——, *Pet Sematary* (London: Hodder and Stoughton, 1983).

Leavitt, David, *While England Sleeps* [1998] (London: Flamingo, 2003).

Livia, Anna, *Minimax* (Portland, OR: Eighth Mountain Press, 1991).

Lovecraft, H. P., 'The Shadow Over Innsmouth' [1936], in *The Lurking Fear and Other Stories* (London: Panther, 1964).

Magrs, Paul, *Could It Be Magic?* (London: Chatto and Windus, 1997).

Marsh, Richard, *The Beetle: A Mystery* [1897] (London: Wordsworth Editions, 2007).

Maturin, Charles Robert, *Melmoth the Wanderer: A Tale* [1820] (London: Penguin, 2000).

McGrath, Patrick, *Dr Haggard's Disease* [1993] (London: Penguin, 1994).

Mootoo, Shani, *Cereus Blooms at Night* [1996] (London: Granta Books, 1998).

Perez, Benjamin L., *The Evil Queen: A Pornolexicology* (New York: Spuyten Duyvil, 2005).

Piercy, Marge, *Braided Lives* (New York: Summit Books, 1982).

Poe, Edgar Allan, 'The Fall of the House of Usher' [1839], in *The Complete Tales and Poems* (Harmondsworth: Penguin, 1982), pp. 231–45.

Purdy, James, *Mourners Below* [1981] (London: Arrow Books, 1986).

Rechy, John, *City of Night* (New York: Grove Press, 1963).

Rhys, Jean, *Wide Sargasso Sea* [1966] (Harmondsworth: Penguin, 1980).

Rice, Anne, *Interview with the Vampire* (New York: Alfred A. Knopf, 1976).

Rich, Adrienne, *The Dream of a Common Language: Poems 1974–1977* (New York: W. W. Norton, 1978).

Schulman, Sarah, *People in Trouble* (London: Sheba Feminist Publishers, 1990).

Self, Will, *Dorian: An Imitation* (London: Penguin, 2002).

Shelley, Mary, *Frankenstein or the Modern Prometheus* [1818] (Oxford: Oxford University Press, 1969).

Smith, Ali, *Hotel World* (London: Hamish Hamilton, 2001).

Stevenson, Robert Louis, *The Strange Case of Dr Jekyll and Mr Hyde* [1886] (Oxford: Oxford University Press, 2008).

Tartt, Donna, *The Secret History* [1992] (London: Penguin, 1993).

Thomas, H. Nigel, *Spirits in the Dark* [1993] (Portsmouth, NH: Heinemann, 1994).

Tóibín, Colm, *The Blackwater Lightship* [1999] (London: Picador, 2000).

Waters, Sarah, *Fingersmith* (London: Virago, 2002).

——, *The Night Watch* (London: Virago, 2006).

Wilde, Oscar, *The Picture of Dorian Gray* [1891] (Oxford: Oxford University Press, 2006).

Winterson, Jeanette, *Oranges Are Not the Only Fruit* (London: Pandora, 1985).

——, *The Power Book* [2000] (London: Vintage, 2001).

——, *The Stone Gods* (London: Hamish Hamilton, 2007).

Zimmer Bradley, Marion, *The Mists of Avalon* (New York: Ballantine, 1982).

Theoretical and critical works

Abraham, Nicolas, 'Notes on the phantom: a complement to Freud's meta-psychology', *Critical Inquiry*, 1/2 (1987), 289–94.

—— and Maria Torok, *The Shell and the Kernel*, trans. Nicholas T. Rand (Chicago: University of Chicago Press, 1994).

Acioli, Ana Cecília Lima, 'Corpos sem corpos em *The Powerbook*, de Jeanette Winterson', in Ermeinda Mara Araujo Ferreira (ed.), *Interseccoes: Ciencia e tecnologia, literatura e arte* (Recife: Editora Universitaria, 2009).

Ahmed, Sara, *Queer Phenomenology: Orientations, Objects, Others* (Durham, NC: Duke University Press, 2006).

Armitt, Lucie, *Theorising the Fantastic* (London: Arnold, 1996).

Bakhtin, Mikhail, *Problems of Dostoevsky's Poetics*, trans. R. W. Rotsel (Ann Arbor, MI: Ardis, 1973).

Baudrillard, Jean, *The Transparency of Evil: Essays on Extreme Phenomena*, trans. James Benedict (London: Verso, 1993).

Beaver, Harold, 'Homosexual signs (in memory of Roland Barthes)', *Critical Inquiry*, 8/1 (1981).

Becker, Susanne, *Gothic Forms of Feminine Fiction* (Manchester: Manchester University Press, 1999).

Bennett, Andrew and Nicholas Royle (eds), *An Introduction to Literature, Criticism and Theory: Key Critical Concepts* (London: Longman, 1995).

Benshoff, Harry M., *Monsters in the Closet: Homosexuality and the Horror Film* (Manchester: Manchester University Press, 1997).

Benstock, Shari, 'Paris, lesbianism and the politics of reaction, 1900–1940', in Martin Duberman, Martha Vicinus and George Chauncey, Jr (eds), *Hidden from History: Reclaiming the Gay and Lesbian Past* (London: Penguin, 1989).

Bergman, David, *Gaiety Transfigured: Gay Self-Representation in American Literature* (Madison: University of Wisconsin Press, 1991).

Bersani, Leo, *Homos* (Cambridge, MA: Harvard University Press, 1995).

Bhabha, Homi K., *The Location of Culture* (London: Routledge, 1994).

Bier, Jesse, *The Rise and Fall of American Humor* (New York: Holt, Rinehart and Winston, 1968).

Boone, Joseph A., *Queer Frontiers: Millennial Geographies, Genders and Generations* (Madison: University of Wisconsin Press, 2000).

Bornstein, Kate, *Gender Outlaw: On Men, Women and the Rest of Us* (New York: Routledge, 1994).

Botting, Fred, 'Power in darkness: heterotopias, literature and gothic labyrinths', *Genre*, 26 (1993).

——, 'The gothic production of the unconscious', in Glennis Byron and David Punter (eds), *Spectral Readings: Towards a Gothic Geography* (Basingstoke: Macmillan, 1999).

Bray, Alan, *Homosexuality in Renaissance England* (London: Gay Men's Press, 1992).

Breen, Margaret Sonser, *Narratives of Queer Desire: Deserts of the Heart* (Basingstoke: Palgrave Macmillan, 2009).

Bronfen, Elisabeth, *Over Her Dead Body: Death, Femininity, and the Aesthetic* (Manchester: Manchester University Press, 1992).

Brookes, Les, *Gay Male Fiction Since Stonewall: Ideology, Conflict, and Aesthetics* (London: Routledge, 2009).

Brooks, Peter, *Reading for the Plot: Design and Invention in Narrative* (Cambridge, MA: Harvard University Press, 1984).

Bruhm, Steven, 'Picture this: Stephen King's queer Gothic', in David Punter (ed.), *A Companion to the Gothic* (Oxford: Blackwell, 2000).

Butler, Judith, 'Imitation and gender insubordination', in Diana Fuss (ed.), *Inside/Out: Lesbian Theories/Gay Theories* (New York: Routledge, 1991).

——, *Bodies That Matter: On the Discursive Limits of Sex* (New York: Routledge, 1993).

——, *The Psychic Life of Power: Theories in Subjection* (Stanford, CA: Stanford University Press, 1997).

——, *Undoing Gender* (New York: Routledge, 2004).

Castle, Terry, *The Apparitional Lesbian: Female Homosexuality and Modern Culture* (New York: Columbia University Press, 1993).

——, *The Female Thermometer: Eighteenth-century Culture and the Invention of the Uncanny* (Oxford: Oxford University Press, 1995).

Castricano, Jodey, 'Cryptomimesis: The Gothic and Jacques Derrida's ghost writing', *Gothic Studies*, 2/1 (2000).

Chisholm, Dianne, 'The uncanny', in Elizabeth Wright (ed.), *Feminism and Psychoanalysis: A Feminist Dictionary* (Oxford: Blackwell, 1992).

Cixous, Hélène, 'Fiction and its phantoms: a reading of Freud's *Das Unheimliche* ("The uncanny")', *New Literary History*, 7/3 (1973), 525–48.

Colvin, Madeleine with Jane Hawksley, *Section 28: A Practical Guide to the Law and its Implications* (National Council for Civil Liberties, 1989).

Cornwell, Neil, 'Ghost writers in the sky (and elsewhere): notes towards a spectropoetics of ghosts and ghostliness', *Gothic Studies*, 1/2 (1999).

Corr, John, 'Queer nostalgia and unnatural disgust in Shani Mootoo's *Cereus Blooms at Night*', *Journal of West Indian Literature*, 14/1–2 (2005).

Crimp, Douglas, *AIDS: Cultural Analysis/Cultural Activism* (Cambridge, MA: MIT Press, 1988).

Cvetkovich, Ann, 'Sexual trauma/queer memory: incest, lesbianism, and therapeutic memory', *GLQ*, 2/4 (1995).

Day, William Patrick, *In the Circles of Fear and Desire: A Study of Gothic Fantasy* (Chicago: University of Chicago Press, 1985).

de Lauretis, Teresa, 'Feminist studies/critical studies: issues, terms and contexts', in de Lauretis (ed.), *Feminist Studies/Critical Studies* (London: Macmillan, 1988).

——, 'Sexual indifference and lesbian representation', *Theatre Journal*, 40/2 (1988).

Dellamora, Richard, *Apocalyptic Overtures: Sexual Politics and the Sense of an Ending* (New Brunswick, NJ: Rutgers University Press, 1994).

D'Emilio, John, 'Gay politics and community in San Francisco since World War II', in Martin Duberman, Martha Vicinus and George Chauncey, Jr (eds), *Hidden from History: Reclaiming the Gay and Lesbian Past* (London: Penguin, 1989).

——, *Making Trouble: Essays in Lesbian and Gay History, Politics and the University* (New York: Routledge, 1992).

Derrida, Jacques, 'Sending: on representation', *Social Research*, 49/2 (1982).

——, *Memoires for Paul de Man* (New York: Columbia University Press, 1986).

——, *Aporias: Dying – Awaiting (One Another at) the 'Limits of Truth'*, trans. Thomas Dutoit (Stanford, CA: Stanford University Press, 1993).

——, 'Theses', in *Archive Fever: A Freudian Impression*, trans. Eric Prenowitz (Chicago: University of Chicago Press, 1995).

——, 'Word processing', in Timothy Clark and Nicholas Royle (eds), *Oxford Literary Review: Technologies of the Sign*, 21/1–2 (1999).

Doan, Laura, *The Lesbian Postmodern* (New York: Columbia University Press, 1994).

Dolan, Jill, 'Lesbian subjectivity in realism: dragging at the margins of structure and ideology', in Sue-Ellen Case (ed.), *Performing Feminisms* (Baltimore, MD: Johns Hopkins University Press, 1990).

Dollimore, Jonathan, *Death, Desire and Loss in Western Culture* (London: Allen Lane, 1998).

Donoghue, Emma, *Passions between Women: British Lesbian Culture 1668–1801* (London: Scarlet Press, 1993).

During, Lisabeth and Terri Fealy, 'Philosophy', in Andy Medhurst and Sally Munt (eds), *Lesbian and Gay Studies: A Critical Introduction* (London: Cassell, 1997).

Eberle-Sinatra, Michael, 'Readings of homosexuality in Mary Shelley's *Frankenstein* and four film adaptations', *Gothic Studies*, 7/2 (2005).

Edelman, Lee, 'The plague of discourse: politics, literary theory and AIDS', *The South Atlantic Quarterly*, 88/1 (1989).

——, *Homographesis: Essays in Literary and Cultural Theory* (London: Routledge, 1994).

Faderman, Lillian, *Surpassing the Love of Men: Romantic Friendship and Love between Women from the Renaissance to the Present* (London: Junction Books, 1981).

Farwell, Marilyn R., *Heterosexual Plots and Lesbian Narratives* (New York: New York University Press, 1996).

Fiedler, Leslie A., *Love and Death in the American Novel* (New York: Stein and Day, 1966).

Fletcher, John, 'The haunted closet: Henry James's queer spectrality', *Textual Practice*, 14/1 (2000).

Foucault, Michel, *The History of Sexuality, vol. 1: The Will to Knowledge*, trans. Robert Hurley (London: Penguin, 1998).

Freud, Sigmund, *The Pelican Freud Library*, ed. Angela Richards and James Strachey (Harmondsworth: Penguin, 1973–86).

Fuss, Diana, 'Inside/Out', in Fuss, *Inside/Out: Lesbian Theories/Gay Theories* (London: Routledge, 1991).

Garber, Linda, *Identity Poetics: Race, Class and the Lesbian Feminist Roots of Queer Theory* (New York: Columbia University Press, 2001).

Gelder, Ken, *Reading the Vampire* (London: Routledge, 1994).

Giddens, Anthony, *The Transformation of Intimacy: Sexuality, Love and Eroticism in Modern Societies* (Cambridge: Polity Press, 1992).

Gilbert, Sandra M. and Susan Gubar, *The Madwoman in the Attic: The Woman Writer and the Nineteenth-century Literary Imagination* (New Haven, CT: Yale University Press, 1979).

Gonda, Caroline and Chris Mounsey, *Queer People: Negotiations and Expressions of Homosexuality 1700–1800* (Lewisburg, PA: Bucknell University Press, 2007).

Gordon, Angus, 'Turning back: adolescence, narrative and queer theory', *GLQ*, 5/1 (2001).

Gowing, Laura, 'History', in Andy Medhurst and Sally Munt (eds), *Lesbian and Gay Studies* (London: Cassell, 1997).

Grosz, Elizabeth, 'Intolerable ambiguity: freaks as/at the limit', in Rosemary Garland Thomson (ed.), *Freakery: Cultural Spectacles of the Extraordinary Body* (New York: New York University Press, 1996).

Haggerty, George E., 'Literature and homosexuality in the late eighteenth century: Walpole, Beckford, and Lewis', *Studies in the Novel*, 18/4 (1986).

——, *Queer Gothic* (Urbana: University of Illinois Press, 2006).

Halberstam, Judith, 'F2M: the making of female masculinity', in Laura Doan (ed.), *The Lesbian Postmodern* (New York: Columbia University Press, 1994).

——, *Skin Shows: Gothic Horror and the Technology of Monsters* (Durham, NC: Duke University Press, 1995).

——, *In a Queer Time and Place: Transgender Bodies, Subcultural Lives* (New York: New York University Press, 2005).

Hanson, Ellis, 'Undead', in Diana Fuss (ed.), *Inside/Out* (London: Routledge, 1991).

Haraway, Donna, 'A manifesto for cyborgs: science, technology and socialist feminism in the 1980s', in Linda Nicholson (ed.), *Feminism/Postmodernism* (London: 1990).

Healey, Emma, *Lesbian Sex Wars* (London: Virago, 1996).

Higgs, David (ed.), *Queer Sites: Gay Urban Histories since 1600* (London: Routledge, 1999).

Hoving, Isabel, 'Moving the Caribbean landscape: *Cereus Blooms at Night* as a re-imagination of the Caribbean environment', in Elizabeth M. DeLoughrey, Renée K. Gosson and George B. Handley (eds), *Caribbean Literature and the Environment: Between Nature and Culture* (Charlottesville: University of Virginia Press, 2005).

Hughes, William and Andrew Smith (eds), *Queering the Gothic* (Manchester: Manchester University Press, 2009).

Hurley, Kelly, *The Gothic Body* (Cambridge: Cambridge University Press: 1996).

——, '"The Inner Chamber of All Nameless Sin": *The Beetle*, Gothic female sexuality, and Oriental barbarism', in Fred Botting and Dale Townshend (eds), *Gothic Critical Concepts in Literary and Cultural Studies* (London: Routledge, 2004).

——, 'Abject and grotesque', in Catherine Spooner and Emma McEvoy (eds), *The Routledge Companion to Gothic* (London: Routledge, 2007), p. 138.

Hutcheon, Linda, *The Politics of Postmodernism* (London: Routledge, 1989).

Irigaray, Luce, *Speculum of the Other Woman*, trans. Gill C. Gill (Ithaca, NY: Cornell University Press, 1985).

——, *This Sex Which Is Not One*, trans. Catherine Porter with Carolyn Burke (Ithaca, NY: Cornell University Press, 1985).

Jackson, Earl Jr, 'Explicit instruction: teaching male gay sexuality in literature classes', in George E. Haggerty and Bonnie Zimmerman (eds), *Professions of Desire: Lesbian and Gay Studies in Literature* (New York: MLA, 1995).

Jackson, Rosemary, *Fantasy: The Literature of Subversion* (London: New Accents, 1981).

Jagose, Annamarie, *Queer Theory* (Melbourne: Melbourne University Press, 1996).

Kincaid, James, 'Designing gourmet children or KIDS FOR DINNER', in Ruth Robins and Julian Wolfreys (eds), *Victorian Gothic: Literary and Cultural Manifestations in the Nineteenth Century* (Basingstoke: Macmillan, 2000).

Knellwolf, Christa and Jane Goodall (eds), *Frankenstein Science: Experimentation and Discovery in Romantic Culture, 1780–1830* (Aldershot: Ashgate, 2008).

Kristeva, Julia, *Powers of Horror: An Essay on Abjection*, trans. Leon S. Roudiez (New York: Columbia University Press, 1982).

——, *Strangers to Ourselves*, trans. Leon S. Roudiez (London: Harvester Wheatsheaf, 1991).

Llewellyn, Mark, 'Breaking the mould? Sarah Waters and the politics of genre', in Ann Heilman and Mark Llewellyn (eds), *Metafiction and Metahistory in Contemporary Women's Writing* (Basingstoke: Palgrave Macmillan, 2007).

Love, Heather K., '"Spoiled identity": Stephen Gordon's loneliness and the difficulties of queer history', *GLQ*, 7/4 (2001).

McRuer, Robert, *The Queer Renaissance: Contemporary American Literature and the Reinvention of Lesbian and Gay Identities* (New York: New York University Press, 1997).

Meese, Elizabeth, 'Theorising lesbian writing: a love letter', in Karla Jay and Joanne Glasgow (eds), *Lesbian Texts and Contexts: Radical Revisions* (New York: New York University Press, 1990).

Mighall, Robert, *A Geography of Victorian Gothic Fiction: Mapping History's Nightmares* (Oxford: Oxford University Press, 1999).

Miller, D.A., *The Novel and the Police* (Berkeley and Los Angeles: University of California Press, 1988).

Mills, Sara, *Michel Foucault* (London: Routledge, 2003).

Mishra, Vijay, *The Gothic Sublime* (New York: State University of New York Press, 1994).

Morland, Iain, and Annabelle Wilcox (eds), *Queer Theory* (Basingstoke: Palgrave Macmillan, 2005).

Nelson, Emmanuel S. (ed.), *AIDS: The Literary Response* (New York: Twayne, 1992).

Newman, Saul, 'Spectres of the uncanny: the return of the repressed', *Telos*, 124, (2002).

Palmer, Paulina, *Contemporary Women's Fiction: Narrative Practice and Feminist Theory* (Hemel Hempstead: Harvester Wheatsheaf, 1989).

——, *Contemporary Lesbian Writing: Dreams, Desire, Difference* (Buckingham: Open University Press, 1993).

——, *Lesbian Gothic: Transgressive Fictions* (London: Cassell, 1999).

——, 'Lesbian Gothic: genre, transformation, transgression', *Gothic Studies*, 6/1 (2004).

——, 'Antonia White's *Frost in May*: Gothic mansions, ghosts and particular friendships', in William Hughes and Andrew Smith (eds), *Queering the Gothic* (Manchester: Manchester University Press, 2009).

Pane, Andrew, and Mark Lewis, 'Ghost dance: interview with Jacques Derrida', *Public*, 2 (1989).

Paravisini-Gebert, Lizabeth, 'Colonial and postcolonial Gothic: the Caribbean', in Jerrold Hogle (ed.), *The Cambridge Companion to Gothic Fiction* (Cambridge: Cambridge University Press, 2002).

Parkin-Gounelas, Ruth, *Literature and Psychoanalysis: Intertextual Readings* (Basingstoke: Palgrave, 2001).

Perry, Ruth, 'Incest as the meaning of the gothic novel', *The Eighteenth Century*, 39/3 (1998).

Poster, Mark (ed.), *Jean Baudrillard: Selected Writings* (Cambridge: Polity Press, 2001).

———

Prosser, Jay, *Second Skins: The Body Narratives of Transsexuality* (New York: Columbia University Press, 1998).

Punter, David, 'Ceremonial Gothic', in Glennis Byron and David Punter (eds), *Spectral Readings: Towards a Gothic Geography* (Basingstoke: Macmillan, 1999).

——, 'Introduction: of apparitions', in Byron and Punter (eds), *Spectral Readings: Towards a Gothic Geography*.

——, *Postcolonial Imaginings: Fictions of a New World Order* (Edinburgh: Edinburgh University Press, 2000).

Puri, Shalini, *The Caribbean Postcolonial: Social Equality, Post-Nationalism, and Cultural Hybridity* (Basingstoke: Palgrave Macmillan, 2004).

Rich, Adrienne, 'Compulsory heterosexuality and lesbian existence', in *Blood, Bread and Poetry: Selected Prose* [1980] (London: Virago, 1987).

Roof, Judith, 'The match in the crocus: representations of lesbian sexuality', in Marleen S. Barr and Richard Feldstein (eds), *Discontented Discourses: Feminism/Textual Intervention/Psychoanalysis* (Urbana: University of Illinois, 1989).

——, *Come As You Are: Sexuality and Narrative* (New York: Columbia University Press, 1996).

Rosen, Elizabeth, *Apocalyptic Transformations: Apocalypse and the Postmodern Imagination* (Lanham, MD: Lexington Books, 2008).

Rothenberg, Tamar, 'And she told two friends: lesbians creating urban space', in David Bell and Gillian Valentine (eds), *Mapping Desire: Geographies of Sexualities* (London: Routledge, 1995).

Royle, Nicholas, *The Uncanny* (Manchester: Manchester University Press, 2003).

Russo, Mary, *The Female Grotesque: Risk, Excess and Modernity* (London: Routledge, 1994).

Salih, Sara, *Judith Butler* (London: Routledge, 2002).

Salotto, Eleanor, *Gothic Returns in Collins, Dickens, Zola and Hitchcock* (Basingstoke: Palgrave Macmillan, 2006).

Schilt, Paige, 'Queering Lord Clarke: diasporic formations and travelling homophobia in Isaac Julien's *The Darker Side of Black*', in John C. Hawley (ed.), *Post-colonial, Queer: Theoretical Intersections* (New York: State University of New York Press, 2001).

Seaford, Richard, *Introducing Dionysos* (London: Routledge, 2006).

Sedgwick, Eve Kosofsky, *Between Men: English Literature and Male Homosexual Desire* (New York: Columbia University Presss, 1985).

——, *The Coherence of Gothic Conventions* (London: Methuen, 1986).

——, *Tendencies* (Durham, NC: Duke University Press, 1993).

Sheba Collective (ed.), *Serious Pleasure: Lesbian Erotic Stories and Poetry* (London: Sheba Feminist Publishers, 1989).

Showalter, Elaine, *Sexual Anarchy: Gender and Culture at the Fin de Siècle* (London: Virago, 1992).

Sinfield, Alan, *Cultural Politics: Queer Readings* (London: Routledge, 1994).

——, *Culture and Authority* (Brazil: Universidade de São Paulo Press, 1997).

——, *Gay and After* (London: Serpent's Tail, 1998).

——, *On Sexuality and Power* (New York: Columbia University Press, 2004).

Slethaug, Gordon E., *The Play of the Double in Postmodern American Fiction* (Urbana: Southern Illinois University Press, 1993).

Smith, Allan Lloyd, '"This thing of darkness": racial discourse in Mary Shelley's *Frankenstein*', *Gothic Studies*, 6/2 (2004).

Smith, Andrew, 'Death, art, and bodies: queering the queer Gothic in Will Self's *Dorian*', in William Hughes and Andrew Smith (eds), *Queering the Gothic* (Manchester: Manchester University Press 2009).

Stone, Sandy, 'The empire strikes back: a posttranssexual manifesto', in Julia Epstein and Katrina Straub (eds), *Body Guards: The Cultural Politics of Gender Ambiguity* (New York: Routledge, 1991).

Stryker, Susan, 'The transgender issue: an introduction', *GLQ*, 4/2 (1998).

Taylor, Affrica, 'A queer geography', in Andy Medhurst and Sally Munt (eds), *Lesbian and Gay Studies: A Critical Introduction* (London: Cassell, 1997).

Thurschwell, Pamela, *Sigmund Freud* (London: Routledge, 2000).

Todd, Jane Marie, 'The veiled woman in Freud's "Das Unheimliche"', *Signs*, 2/3 (1986).

Townshend, Dale, '"Love in a convent" or, Gothic and the perverse father of queer enjoyment', in William Hughes and Andrew Smith (eds), *Queering the Gothic* (Manchester: Manchester University Press, 2009).

Traub, Valerie, 'The present future of lesbian historiography', in George E. Haggerty and Molly McGarry (eds), *A Companion to Lesbian, Gay, Bisexual and Queer Studies* (Oxford: Blackwell, 2007).

Veeder, William, 'Children of the night: Stevenson and patriarchy', in William Veeder and Gordon Hirsch (eds), *Dr Jekyll and Mr Hyde after One Hundred Years* (Chicago: University of Chicago Press, 1988).

Vickroy, Laurie, *Trauma and Survival in Contemporary Fiction* (Charlottesville: University of Virginia Press, 2002).

Vidler, Anthony, *The Architectural Uncanny: Essays in the Modern Unhomely* (Cambridge, MA: MIT Press, 1999).

Walkowitz, Judith R., *City of Dreadful Delight: Narratives of Sexual Danger in Late-Victorian London* (London: Virago, 1992).

Walters, Suzanna Danuta, 'From here to queer: radical feminism, post-modernism and the lesbian menace', in Iain Morland and Annabelle Wilcox (eds), *Queer Theory* (Basingstoke: Palgrave Macmillan, 2005).

Warner, Michael (ed.), *Fear of a Queer Planet: Queer Politics and Social Theory* (Minneapolis: University of Minnesota, 1993).

Weeks, Jeffrey, 'Discourse, desire and sexual deviance: some problems in a history of homosexuality', in K. Plummer (ed.), *The Making of the Modern Homosexual* (London: Hutchinson, 1991).

——, *Invented Moralities: Sexual Values in an Age of Uncertainty* (New York: Columbia University Press, 1994).

——, *The World We Have Won: The Remaking of Erotic and Intimate Life* (London: Routledge, 2007).

Whitford, Margaret (ed.), *The Irigaray Reader* (Oxford: Blackwell, 1991).

Wigley, Mark, *The Architecture of Deconstruction: Derrida's Haunt* (Cambridge, MA: MIT Press, 1993).

Wilson, Elizabeth, *Hidden Agendas: Theory, Politics and Experience in the Women's Movement* (London: Tavistock Publications, 1986).

Wolfreys, Julian, *Victorian Hauntings: Spectrality, Gothic, the Uncanny and Literature* (Basingstoke: Palgrave, 2002).

——, *Transgression: Identity, Space, Time* (Basingstoke: Palgrave Macmillan, 2008).

Woodruff, Paul, *Euripides' Bacchae* (Indianapolis: Hackett Publishing Company, 1998).

Woods, Gregory, *A History of Gay Literature: The Male Tradition* (New Haven, CT: Yale University Press, 1998).

Young, Elizabeth, *Black Frankenstein: The Making of an American Metaphor* (New York: New York University Press, 2008).

Young, Iris Marion, *Justice and the Politics of Difference* (Princeton, NJ: Princeton University Press, 1990).

Zamara, Lois and Wendy B. Faris, *Magical Realism: Theory, History, Community* (Durham, NC: Duke University Press, 1995).

Zimmerman, Bonnie, 'Lesbians like this and that', in Sally Munt (ed.), *New Lesbian Criticism: Literary and Cultural Readings* (Hemel Hempstead: Harvester Wheatsheaf, 1992).

——, *The Safe Sea of Women: Lesbian Fiction 1969–1989* (London: Onlywomen Press, 1992).

Index